# DYNAMICS OF NEW PANCHAYATI RAJ SYSTEM IN INDIA

**Volume IV** : EMPOWERING WOMEN

## *Dynamics of New Panchayati Raj in India Series*

| | | |
|---|---|---|
| Vol. I | : | Select States |
| Vol. II | : | Select States |
| Vol. III | : | Select States |
| Vol. IV | : | Empowering Women |
| Vol. V | : | Panchayati Raj and Multi-level Planning |
| Vol. VI | : | Panchayati Raj and Empowerment of Dalits |
| Vol. VII | : | Finance in Panchayati Raj System |
| Vol. VIII | : | Panchayati Raj and Common Property Resource Management |
| Vol. IX | : | Participatory and Direct Democracy : Gram Sabha |
| Vol. X | : | Capacity Building for Panchayati Raj Leaders and Functionaries |
| Vol. XI | : | State-Local Body Relationship |
| Vol. XII | : | Panchayati Raj and Socio-Political and Economic Transformation |
| Vol. XIII | : | Leadership in Panchayati Raj Institution |
| Vol. XIV | : | Thinkers Framework on Panchayati Raj |
| Vol. XV | : | Theoretical Nuances of Local Bodies |

**About the Editor**

**Prof. Ganapathi Palanithurai,** Coordinator in Rajiv Gandhi Chair, Gandhigram Rural Institute is an academic activist working with the people in rural areas for building the capacity of the leaders and people to reinvent sustainable grass roots democracy. He is heading the Department of Political Science and Development Administration, in Gandhigram Rural University, Tamil Nadu. His policy advocacy role at the governmental level is increasingly felt at present in all the three levels, namely sub-regional, regional and national as he does more field work than theorisation. He has been associating himself with Centre Planning Commission, State Planning Commission of Tamil Nadu, Population Foundation of India, Ford Foundation, UNICEF, Rajiv Gandhi Foundation, CAPART, Ministry of Rural Areas and Employment and DANIDA (Danish-Indo Development Agency) in specific areas of activities in connection with empowerment of people. He is in the network of the Non-Governmental Organisations for Panchayat activities. He involves himself in capacity building exercise for local body leaders. He has to his credit twenty-nine books, seventy-five articles on three major areas, namely, Legislative Behaviour, Ethnicity and Panchayati Raj System. He was a recipient of Fellowship from Sastri Indo-Canadian Institute, New Delhi and World Academy of Art and Science, USA. He is the Chairman of the Tamil Nadu Council for Sustainable Livelihoods. He has visited the US and Canada, on academic assignments. He was a visiting fellow in the MiGill University, Canada in 1989. He is a life member of Indian Institute of Public Administration, Indian Association of Public Administration, Indian Association of Political Science, Indian Association of American Studies and Indian Association of Canadian Studies. He is a member of the expert committee constituted by the Government of Tamil Nadu to monitor the training programme for local body leaders.

# DYNAMICS OF NEW PANCHAYATI RAJ SYSTEM IN INDIA

**Volume IV**

EMPOWERING WOMEN

*Edited by*

**G. PALANITHURAI**

CONCEPT PUBLISHING COMPANY, NEW DELHI-110059

ISBN 81-8069-130-6 (Vol. IV)
ISBN 81-7022-910-3 (Series)

First Published 2004



*Published and Printed by*
Ashok Kumar Mittal
**Concept Publishing Company**
A/15-16, Commercial Block, Mohan Garden
New Delhi-110059 (India)

*Phones:* 25351460, 25351794
*Fax.* 091-11-25357103
*E-mail:* publishing@conceptpub.com

TO

**THE DIVINE MOTHER**

(In India) one should begin with the old panchayat system in the villages and the work upto the top. The panchayat system and the guilds are more representative and they have a living contact with people, they are the parts of the people's ideas.

– *Sri Aurobindo*

The village Republic will be managed by a panchayat which will be living political force and entity. Panchayats will be united in a free and voluntary association by "ever widening circle of village republics". It will not be an "apex sustained by the bottom", but an oceanic circle where centre will be the individual always ready to perish for the village, the latter ready to perish for the circle of villages and so on, sharing the majesty of the oceanic circle which they are parts.

– *Mahatma Gandhi*

We trust the people

We have faith in the people

It is the people who must

determine their own destinies

and the destiny of the Nation

To the people of India, let us

ensure maximum democracy and

maximum devolution. Let the

people be empowered.

– *Rajiv Gandhi*

# PREFACE

Women empowerment is a much debated subject and it has gained a new momentum and impetus after the introduction of one-third reservation of seats for women in grass roots governance. It has been viewed differently by different segments and perspectives have been developed to look at the women empowerment process through women newly brought in as leaders in grass roots governance. In the whole of the country one million women are in position as leaders and representatives of the people. It is no doubt a critical mass and the critical mass is expected to perform a critical role in Panchayati Raj. The marginalized sections have found a space to tackle their problems which continue to persist despite the presence of the leaders emerging from the marginalized sections. The elected women representatives have to face an array of problems to retain their power. Further, to bring the issues of women to the centre stage for decision making, elected women representatives have to play a difficult role as there is stiff resistance from the patriarchical structure. Thus the process of the emergence of women leaders and their handling of power and management of institutions while tackling the issues of women are the major issues to be studied. This volume tries to present a picture of the aspects which have been mentioned above. Experience are drawn from various States though one cannot say that they contribute a picture of the whole of India. However it does present a fair picture of the on going process of empowerment of women in India.

The contributors have played a major part in the compilation of this volume and hence I place on record my deep sense of gratitude to them for their painstaking efforts. Equally I have to register my thanks to my colleagues who are working on different projects on Panchayati Raj for their unremitting support by performing their assigned roles. Our unit is working for decentralization of power and practice decentralization and hence my colleagues have not taken much of my time in carrying out their activities. I profusely thank all my colleagues working in the Rajiv Gandhi Chair and

The Hunger Project for their generous and hard work in performing their roles and responsibilities.

My wife P. Mala, my daughter P. Senthil Vadivu and my son P. Aurobindh deserve my appreciation as they valued my work and helped me in all possible ways to complete this work. I thank them profusely.

The Gandhigram Rural Institute, where I work, has to be remembered as it provides opportunity and enabling conditions to pursue such academic work with a lot of freedom. The Institute was started with the noble idea of women empowerment and integrated rural development. I place on record my deep sense of gratitude to the founders of this Institute and the people of the Gandhigram community for their generous support. Mr. Ashok Mittal of Messrs Concept Publishing Company deserves appreciation as he has always evinced keen interest in Panchayat Administration.

G. PALANITHURAI

# CONTENTS

# LIST OF CONTRIBUTORS

**Abdul Aziz**

Former Professor
Institute of Social and Economic Change
Bangalore - 560 072

**B.S. Bhargava**

Senior Fellow, Institute of Social Sciences
Bangalore

**A. Celine Rani**

Reader in Political Science, Gandhigram Rural Institute
Deemed University
Gandhigram - 624 302

**Devaki Jain**

Activist and Development Expert
Singamma Sreenivasan Foundation
Bangalore

**N. Lalitha**

Reader in Rural Development, Gandhigram Rural Institute
Deemed University
Gandhigram - 624 302

**P. Manikyamba**

Department of Political Science, University of Hyderabad
(Central University) Hyderabad

**P.V. Mary Matilda**

FIP Research Scholar, Department of Political Science
Gandhigram Rural Institute
Gandhigram - 624 302

**B. Mohanan**
Reader in Political Science, Department of Political Science
Gandhigram Rural Institute
Gandhigram - 624 302

**M.S. Swaminathan Research Foundation**
3rd Cross Road, Taramani, Institutional Area
Chennai - 600 113

**S. Nagabhushana Rao**
Asst. Director (CNRM)
National Institute of Rural Development,
Rajendra Nagar
Hyderabad - 500 030

**G. Palanithurai**
Dean, Faculty of Rural Social Sciences
Gandhigram Rural Institute
Deemed University
Gandhigram - 624 302

**K. Pazhani**
Reader in Economics, T. MNS College, T. Kallikulam,
Tamil Nadu - 627 113

**V. Ragupathy**
Reader in Political Science, Gandhigram Rural Institute
Deemed University
Gandhigram - 624 302

**K. Subha**
Regional Coordinator, Institute of Social Sciences
Bangalore

**C. P. Sujaya,** ***IAS***
Visiting Fellow, Tata Institute of Social Sciences
Mumbai

# INTRODUCTION

Studies about women have been gaining momentum in the whole of the world. From Anthropologists to Feminists volumes of literature on women have been generated by innumerable scholars from Anthropologists and Feminists and yet the condition of women has not been improved and sometimes it has become complicated as Globalization and Localization of economy and polity continue to haunt women. UN statistics tell us that women own about only 1 per cent of the property in the world and receive 10 per cent of the income distributed in the world, while they perform 66 per cent of the total work. In terms of women's presence in governance in the last decade of the twentieth century, only 3.5 per cent of the world's cabinet ministers are women. Women hold no ministerial position in 93 countries. In other words, in about half of the world national policies are determined without the participation of the female population. Men occupy 90 per cent of the parliament seats leaving less than 10 per cent for women.

In India the conditions are not very different. The Country Report (India) of the Fourth World Conference on Women, Beijing 1995, on the status of Indian women states that lack of education information, lack of training and low levels of literacy aggravate the situation of deprivation that women in many parts of the country experience in spite of constitutional guarantees on women's equality. In spite of constitutional ratification of the principle of elimination of all forms of discrimination against women, gender inequalities persist in India. It admits that women are thereby excluded not merely from political, social and economic power but knowledge power as well. What makes the condition still worse is a general societal inability to discern the inadequacy and the discrepancy in the developmental process. Women are made to internalize all the discriminatory practices as they are socially ordained and irrevocable.

It is also true that the condition of Indian women has improved a lot since independence in terms of literacy, life expectancy and maternal mortality. Yet the women continue to occupy a subordinate position to Indian men in economic, social and political spheres. It is obvious from the decline in the sex ratio over the last nine decades that the position of Indian women may have worsened at present. Whatever improvements women have achieved are not substantial because only the privileged groups have gained the advantages.

It is true that after the declaration of the UN Decade for Women a large number of women scholars and activists have systematically analysed the issues of women and highlighted the condition of women throughout the world. In India, the benchmark survey under the title "Status of Women in India Report of 1974" provoked the scholars and activists to start their work from this report. This report was an eye opener for many as the role played by social, economic and political forces in reinforcing the subordination was highlighted and, as a result, many understood the reality. The growing awareness of the status of women prompted the emergence of a women's movement to bring to light the plight of women in Indian society and pressure was brought on the government and other political institutions to realize the poor status of women in India. As a result steps were taken to enact a series of legislations and launch a series of development programmes to raise the women from their low status and plight.

The laudable achievements are not the result of random activity and awareness but of a series of activities with the involvement of the women with a sense of commitment and conviction. In this direction the provision of reservation of one-third seats to women in local bodies is a milestone in creating a critical mass as one million women are in position in local bodies in India. It is natural on the part of every one to expect that the critical mass would perform the critical function. Different kinds of approaches have been developed over a period of one decade after the introduction of 73rd and 74th Amendment to the Constitution of India to the reservation of seats in the grass roots institutions for women. It is argued that reservation has been provided in order to bring out the potential of women for governance. There is yet another argument that it is the development of a space wherein the women have to concentrate more on the issues of development and more specifically on the development of women and children. There is another strong view that the representation given to women in local bodies cannot be seen in a narrow perspective. Women are also in position and they have to perform their duties like the men representatives. It is a legitimate space given to women for governance.

Any accurate analysis will reveal that one cannot find effectiveness in the performance of women leaders in the Panchayat Raj System because of the lack of commitment on the part of the State and the Central government. Further there is resistance to women representatives in grass roots institutions taking up power in their hands to manage the public affairs through Panchayati Raj Institutions. On the one hand being women, they have to face a volley of problems in Panchayati institutions and equally they have to swim against the current while taking up the cause of women in Tamil Nadu. Womenfolk in India have been sensitized to think as men want them to as they like in a patriarchical system. At the same time the elected women representatives who are sensitized properly by the training institutions take a different course in managing the Panchayats and the issues of women. The elected women representatives have to cross several barriers and obstacles to emerge as leaders.

Devaki Jain and C.P. Sujaya, in their article entitled "Development Planning for and by Women: Over Five Decades of the Indian Experience", have traced the contours of the government sponsored "Planning for Women" as it has evolved over the post-Independence era and examined the extent to which the women themselves have been involved in the planning exercise to decide the process of development of women. While tracing the contours the authors have critically examined the planning process. Illustrations have been made from a case study of Kerala to validate their arguments. All the positive and negative aspects of the new experiment made in Kerala have been illustrated in their case study. The main issues arising from the experiences have been brought to light in this article.

C.P. Sujaya and Devaki Jain, in their article, "Role of Women in Decentralization" argue that women's experience of local government cannot and should not be used merely in a limited gender focused manner to enhance the participation of women and to improve women's contribution to the Panchayat's achievement. Further this article explains the riddles in women's participation in politics and brings out the positive trends in women's activities in grass roots institutions.

P. Manikyamba, in her paper, "Women in Local Governance Experience in Andhra Pradesh", focuses on the pattern of recruitment and performance of elected women representatives in Panchayati Raj Institutions in Andhra Pradesh. It is a sharing of experience of the author in awareness creation, information dissemination and training of women in general and elected women representatives in particular. She has identified the future trends of women empowerment and suggested strategies to be adopted for political empowerment of rural women.

In "Political Empowerment of Women at the Grass Roots: The Case of Karnataka" K. Subha and B.S. Bhargava have analysed the process of empowerment of women at grass roots in Karnataka against the backdrop of a feminist perspective. They have touched upon the problems of the elected women representatives and contextually placed them against the backdrop of the Indian social setting. They have indicated the trend and the processes of political empowerment of women in Karnataka.

"Women in Local Governance: Field Experience from Karnataka" by Abdul Aziz brings out the plethora of problems faced by the elected women representatives while managing the Panchayats. It is an indepth analysis of the issues of the elected women representatives. Aziz brings out all the issues from his case studies carried out in specific locations. He has indicated the needs of the elected women representatives to perform their role and function on their own. He has suggested ways and means of improving the condition of the elected women representatives.

B. Mohanan and P.V. Mary Matilda have taken up the innovative women component plan for analysis in the backdrop of the status and position of Kerala women in the society. In their analysis they brought out the major implications of the women component plan and at the same time all the negative factors which were in the whole process had also been highlighted. It brought out the contradictory and paradoxical position of women empowerment in Kerala.

"Political Empowerment of Women through Decentralized Institutions in Karnataka" by K. Subha and B.S. Bhargava made a significant attempt in this article to analyse the political empowerment activities which are being carried out by the grass roots institutions. This article slightly moved from their earlier one and it establishes linkages between women empowerment and Local governance. The whole process has been analyzed in the context of transformation that Indian society undergoes at present. It also focus its attention on the intention of decentralization and the actual practice of decentralization. Based on the field work the problems of women empowerment and decentralization have been analyzed in this article.

M.S. Swaminathan Foundation's article "Decentralization of Child Care Services" underlines the role and responsibilities of the local bodies in child care services and brings out the conditions in which these services are being provided. The foundation has indicated the steps to be taken for effective delivery of such services through local bodies. It is a manual providing all the details of the management of the institutions to deliver the services.

Celine Rani, in her article entitled "Emerging Pattern of Rural Women Leadership in Panchayati Raj Institution in Tamil Nadu", examined the emerging pattern of rural women leadership in Panchayati Raj Institutions with reference to Gram Panchayats in Tamil Nadu. The author has analysed the contributory factors for the successful emergence of women leadership in grass root institutions. She has analysed the factors responsible for the emergence of the women leaders in a given social, economic and political environment against the backdrop of a theoretical framework. She has extensively analysed the power bases of these leaders while utilizing the opportunity to emerge as leaders in grass roots institutions.

Lalitha's article "Women in Panchayat Raj System: Empowerment through Self Help Groups" points to yet another dimension in the empowerment of women. The author has brought to light the active linkage between SHGs and the Panchayati Raj Institutions. She has also indicated the ongoing process by which she has underlined the movement of the SHGs towards the Panchayats, wherein the SHGs move beyond credit and economic activities.

Pazhani's article "Panchayati Raj and Empowerment of Women: A Case Study of Kanyakumari District in Tamil Nadu" analyses the socio-economic conditions of the women participating in Panchayati Raj Institutions, the factors responsible for active participation of women in Panchayati Raj Institutions and the involvement of women in Panchayati Raj Institutions with reference to Kanayakumari District as the district is known for its high literacy rate. The author has analysed the problems of the women in Panchayati Raj Institutions while handling power and suggested ways and means to overcome the same.

"Addressing Gender Needs through Panchayats: A Study in Tamil Nadu" by Nagabhushana Rao discusses the drinking water and sanitation project assisted by the Danish International Development Agency in Tamil Nadu. The basic idea of this paper is to analyse the gender needs addressed through the Panchayats and the participation of women in planning, implementation and maintenance of drinking water supply and sanitation projects. The author has selected two cases from the project areas. From the case studies of two Gram Panchayats the objectives have been analysed.

Palanithurai's article "Empowerment Process: Experience of the Elected Women Representatives in Grass Roots Institutions in Tamil Nadu" is an outcome of the training programme conducted for the elected women representatives of local bodies. This article brings to light the problems, barriers and obstacles faced by the elected women representatives in managing Panchayati institutions. It further indicates the need of these leaders to overcome such barriers.

Palanithurai and Ragupathy in their article "Building Alliances and Capabilities among the Elected Women Representatives of Grass Roots Institutions" analyses the process of the emergence of grass roots level women leaders' movement to perform the critical function in the society by this newly created critical mass, namely the elected women Panchayat leaders. The article traces the process of building a women's movement through the grass roots institutions to tackle the problems of women in the society. It is the document of a project carried out in Tamil Nadu.

G. PALANITHURAI

1

# DEVELOPMENT PLANNING FOR AND BY WOMEN

## Over Five Decades Of The Indian Experience

DEVAKI JAIN AND C.P. SUJAYA

This chapter attempts to trace the contours of State-sponsored "planning for women" as it has evolved over the post- Independence period and to examine the extent to which the women themselves have been involved in the exercise. The chapter is divided into four parts. The first part tracks the planning experiments of the initial social welfare and community development era right up to the beginning of the Ninth Five-Year Plan, with the increasing emphasis being placed on women's plans, earmarking of resources for women and fixation of physical and financial targets for women beneficiaries. The second part questions the rationale and the model of planning adopted by the State for women in the light of field realities. The third part examines the extent to which the Mahila component plan strategy announced in the Ninth Five-Year Plan, by itself, has the potential of giving women political power. It explores the need for the component plan to be yoked to the process of decentralisation and devolution of powers and functions to local government bodies so that planning and decision making at the local level can meaningfully involve the women. The fourth part of the chapter presents a case study of Kerala's PPC (People's Plan Campaign) where the concept of earmarking of local funds to women has been put into practice for the last four years. The positive and negative points of this experiment are then highlighted along with remedial suggestions. The concluding part of the chapter sums up the main issues arising from the experiences of planning and emphasizes the need for planning to become a part of the restructuring of the economic polity.

## PART I

### HOW "PLANNING FOR WOMEN" EVOLVED FROM THE FIRST TO THE BEGINNING OF THE NINTH FIVE YEAR PLAN

National planning systems in India have historically relegated women to the margins of the development resource allocation processes. This neglect applied as much to women as the "subject" or "target" of development planning as to women as the "agent" of development, to women's access to decision making and their participation in the management of development planning. Thus, on the one hand, women in the aggregate received a small piece of the development cake; and on the other, they had very little say on how the cake was apportioned and to whom. This double bind in which women were placed was an index of their weak bargaining power and political invisibility.

Decisions were taken by men, who largely dominated the development administration, on behalf of both men and women, as to how and for whom public moneys were to be spent. Women did not have agency. Allocation of resources to women was largely made for activities which male decision-makers considered fit and appropriate for women.

It is not that women did not receive plan resources from the Government budgets. The early years of development planning after Independence saw allocation of funds to the "social sector", to "social welfare services" and to "Applied Nutrition" in the Community Development Programme, all of which catered to certain "perceived" needs of women in different situations [by policy planners].

## Social Sector and Social Welfare Services

The programmes under the category "Social welfare services" were aimed at reaching a large number of "vulnerable" groups which included women and children along with orphans, the aged, the infirm, the beggars, the prostitutes, the physically disabled, the destitute and others. Dubey (1973) classified them under the –

- socially underprivileged,
- socially maladjusted,
- physically and mentally handicapped, and
- economically underprivileged

sections of society to whose welfare and protection the State was committed. Amongst the category of women, therefore, widows, unmarried women, women "in moral danger", aged, infirm and destitute women and "fallen" women received more attention. Underlined in this typology was the absence of the male breadwinner, the lack of male protection and the familial support system.

The categories of programmes under the "social sector" were more numerous and wider ranging than "social welfare services", covering education, public health, medical services, housing, welfare of backward classes, labour, labour welfare etc. They included school feeding schemes and maternity and child welfare centres. Illiterate women, malnourished mothers, girls who dropped out from school, the groups socially and economically discriminated against by traditional caste and other societal norms, the economically deprived groups such as the homeless were covered under the social sector umbrella .

> The First Five Year Plan allocated Rs. 340 crores to the Social Sector while a very small amount of Rs. 4 crores were allocated to Social Welfare Services. Women formed a significant part of the clientele of the social sector programmes.

## Community Development Programme and Women

The Community Development Programme (launched in 1951) concentrated on the rural areas and the rural population. The ambitious objective of this venture was, in the words of S. Gopal, the biographer of Pandit Nehru, "to change the whole face of rural India and to raise the level of the vast majority of our population". (Vina Mazumdar 1998)

> In Nehru's own words, "I will not rest content unless every man, woman and child in this country has a fair deal and attains a minimum standard of living". *Speech at Sholapur 30 April 1953* (Vina Mazumdar, 1998)

Within a few years of the start of the Community Development initiative, a women's "component" was started as an integral part of the programme. The Government kept on adding various activities from time to time to help the rural women. The basic underlying concept was the importance of home to the development of community. (Shanti Chakravarti, 1977) They included nutrition education, food production, feeding of pre-school children, mahila mandals and nutrition to pregnant and nursing mothers. The women who received the benefits of these programmes were the wives, the mothers, the daughter-in-laws, the daughters, in short, those who were members of the rural households. The sweep of the CD programme was, therefore, much wider than the earlier 'social welfare' programmes. The stress was on increasing the skills and knowledge base of these women within the families. The planners saw home science, food storage and preparation, child welfare, food processing, environment education, sanitation, etc. as important subjects for women because they were responsible for the welfare of the household members. The planners recognised the instrumental value of women in terms of their crucial roles in household welfare. At the same time the programme overlooked the economic ventures in which the village women were engaged in and failed to cater to these needs. (Indira Chakravarti, retired woman Deputy Director, Panchayat and Community Development, Assam, 2000)

However, the Community Development Programme did create cadres of women extension workers such as the Gram Sevikas who were from rural and agricultural backgrounds and who developed personal contacts with the village women. (Indira Chakravarti, 2000) The Gram Sevikas ran Balwadis, organised meetings of women, and helped them with information, demonstrations on various topics to propagate a better way of life. There was less emphasis on food production and more on family life improvement. (Padmasini Asuri, 2000)

Institutions of rural women such as the Mahila Mandals were also started during this programme at a later stage, for which the Mukhya Sevika's posts were created. It was at this time, as Padmasini says, that sewing machines were distributed to rural women, in the assumption that following this urban-oriented vocation, they would be able to increase their earnings; other programmes such as Applied Nutrition, Associated Women Workers' Training Schemes, Farmers' Training and Education Scheme, etc. were introduced from time to time. But they did not succeed in strengthening the agency of women in any sustainable manner. Shanti Chakravarti observes that inadequate infrastructure was provided to the new extension agency, their coverage was insignificant, they had restricted mobility and technical supervision and guidance. (Seminar on Women and Development, Anand, November 1977).

In 1980, a country review of the role and participation of women in agriculture observed, "The review of major programmes for rural development reveals that the role and contribution of women were ignored virtually in all the sectors and aspects of rural economy such as production, processing and distribution".

> The Committee on the Status of Women in India (1974) observed that "though some member of the Mahila Mandals have acquired both interests and experience in developmental activities, their purely voluntary and non-representative status denied them recognition from local statutory self-governing institutions". Their effectiveness, however, varied sharply from State to State. Reviews and evaluations have commented on their vagueness of objectives and lack of resources.

Whether it was the social welfare or the components of the social sector schemes or the community development programmes, the quantum of resources actually reaching women was comparatively very small. Decision making powers were not vested with women in any significant way. Yet these initiatives raised some very important issues related to women's roles, the need for education as an intervention to change women's lives and the importance of extending sustained support to cadres of women workers in the rural areas. Some of the women workers emerged as role models, in doing pioneering work, in spite of various impediments and challenges.

**The Setting up of the Central Social Welfare Board**

The setting up of the Central Social Welfare Board (1953) was an experiment and an innovation of a very different kind. It gave women agency and enabled them to have a say in resource allocation, planning and implementation. For the first eleven years of its existence, (1953-1964) the Board was the sole, dedicated institutional planning and delivery system for women and children at the national level. It enjoyed a pre-eminent position under the leadership of Durgabai Deshmukh who managed to achieve an enviable level of co-ordination with the other contemporary development actors and institutions such as the community development effort, the social sector programmes, the handicrafts and handloom boards, etc. To enable it to carry out its enlarged role of co-ordinating social welfare activities with the other arms of Government, the Chairperson of the Board was included on the major Boards and National Committees set up by the Government such as All India Handicrafts Board, National Committee on Family Planning, National Committee on Adult Education, Working Group on Employment of Women, National Committee on Children, etc.

> The Board was fully funded by the Government. The fund allocations made to the Board in 1954-55 were Rs. 63 lakhs. By 1985-86, it had increased to Rs. 16.27 crores.

Durgabai, who was sensitive to the roles, contributions and the multiple needs of women and had plenty of organisational drive, also encouraged institution building by and for women at the grass roots level, the building of leadership of women in order to foster social development and the creating and managing of institutions and mechanisms for the effective delivery of services to women and children though people's efforts. The Board was an influential and powerful organisation which, though situated outside the Government, functioned on behalf of the State with a degree of autonomy. This balance was fractured in the mid-sixties when the Ministry for Social Welfare and Security was set up to look after, among other subjects, social welfare. The Board had a broad mandate, consisting of –

- assessment of the needs and requirements of social welfare organisations,
- co-ordination of Central and State Ministries funding social welfare activities,
- evaluation of the programmes and projects of aided agencies,
- promotion of social welfare organisations on a voluntary basis in places where none exist,
- rendering financial aid to deserving organisations or institutions.

Over the decades, the Board tended to concentrate its efforts and energy on only one of these objectives, namely, that of providing grants, to the exclusion of its promotional, catalytic, watch dog and co-ordinating roles. The Board did not also seize the opportunity of playing a decisive role in resource allocation and planning in the social welfare and social development sector, in spite of Durgabai's early initiatives in this regard. This was certainly case of an opportunity missed.

We conclude by observing that Social Welfare, Community Development, education, health and other basic needs—these were the components which helped ,the tentative contours of "plans for women" to take shape in the first two decades of development planning in India.

## The Logic of 'Special Programmes' for Women

Why were special programmes for women thought to be necessary? On the one hand, Article 14 lays down equality before the law between men and women as a fundamental right. Article 15 abjures all discriminatory practices on the basis of sex. Yet in the very same Article, that is Article 15(3), the Constitution legitimised positive discrimination in favour of women and children "nothing shall prevent the State from making special provisions for women and children". Was it not the basic premise of the Constitution that these 'special provisions' were necessary for enabling women to successfully claim the fundamental right to equality?

The same logic appears in relation to the right to equality irrespective of caste. Article 15(1) prohibits discrimination on the basis of caste, but Article 15(4) empowers the State to make "special provisions" for scheduled castes, scheduled tribes and socially and educationally backward classes.

In other words, it was accepted that women's historically disadvantaged position could not be converted to one of equality with men purely through the Constitutional-legal framework. Positive discrimination, affirmative action, special schemes, programmes, resources, all had to be added to strengthen and provide ballast to the legal framework of gender equality.

The provisions of Article 15(3) regarding positive discrimination in favour of women and children were added later to the Constitution through the First Constitutional Amendment in the early fifties. A judicial verdict of 1951 had pronounced preferential treatment to weaker sections as discriminatory. The Constitutional Amendment was then carried out to enable the Government to introduce special measures for the upliftment of women. This was in line with the strategy, of the Government to use State intervention to confront institutionalised discrimination. (Vina Mazumdar, 1998)

A suggestion for reservation of seats for women in elective bodies, for example, was proposed as long back as the Constituent Assembly was turned down by the women members of the Assembly on the grounds that it went against the principal of equality of the sexes! We have certainly travelled a long way since!

But was equal attention paid to the identification of the roots of inequality and to attacking the structural infirmities and defects that had led to women being unequal partners in society? This is a question that must be asked and has been indeed asked from time to time by the women's movement.

### The 1970s–The Committee on the Status of Women in India, the United Nations Decade for Women and New Research under Women's Studies

The publication of the report of the Committee on the Status of Women in India (CSWI) (1974), the International Women's Year (1975) and the declaration of the International Women's Decade

(1976-85) were the milestones of the seventies. The CSWI's report "Towards Equality", was commissioned by the Government. It served its purpose in raising the women's question in relation to the direction that planned development had taken in the first two post-Independence decades *vis-a-vis* the realisation of the promise of and commitment to gender equality that the framers of the Constitution had made to the women of India.

Empirical research conducted during this period had gone into areas hitherto untouched, such as women's work, intra-household disparities, satisfaction of basic needs, violence against women, women's health and survival, lack of legal protection and vulnerability to oppression and discrimination both in the private and public sphere.

A time-allocation study conducted in 1976-77 by Devaki Jain and Malini Chand (ISST, New Delhi)verified the hypothesis that female work participation rate was under enumerated because of the nature of female work and wages. The statistical invisibility of women's work has now become part of conventional wisdom. The study, which was done in 6 villages in Rajasthan and West Bengal, identified the various determinants of female labour supply, regrouped productive and non-productive activities against the conventional logic and defined gainful activity on the basis of evidence.

The hitherto unacknowledged economic contribution of poor women to the survival and welfare of their households was highlighted through these studies even as the anti-poverty programmes made their first appearance on the agenda of the national government.

> The invisibility of poor women's work, their multiple and overlapping roles, their discontinuous engagements in the labour force and many other factors ensured that it would take another decade before the Government finally realised that addressing the household would not automatically reach programme benefits to the women in it. IRDP was launched in the mid-seventies and DWCRA in 1981-82

The information that emerged through research helped to foster a new understanding of women's roles and contributions which now broadened and deepened considerably from what it was in the fifties and sixties. Amidst the emerging debate and the search for answers to old as well as new questions, the responsibility of the State as the prime mover for social change was re-emphasised, even as the stark contrast between statements of gender equality and the structures in place through which women were to be empowered for social change became more and more apparent.

The "internationalisation" of the issue of women's status through the agency of the UN also helped in focusing attention on the structures within national governments which were responsible for ensuring the advancement of women. With the inception of the International Women's Decade, the 'national machinery' became an officially sanctioned and legitimate concept, the preoccupation with which has continued ever since.

## The Gradual Emergence of "Plans for Women"

Along with this, the sanctity of formulating a 'plan of action' for women was also globally acknowledged. It was first depicted in the "World Plan of Action" for women, which emerged from the first International Conference for Women in Mexico in 1975. The Government of India came out in 1976 with its own National Plan of Action for women, a 36 page document partly inspired by the World Plan of Action, partly based on the suggestions of the 1974 report of the CSWI and borrowing from certain parts of the approach to the Fifth Five Year Plan. The National Plan of Action consisted of five separate chapters on

1. Education
2. Health, Family Planning and Nutrition
3. Social Welfare,
4. Employment
5. Legislative Provisions

There were certain dichotomies and contradictions in the Plan of Action which are indicative of the difficult transition that was being negotiated from viewing women as consumers of welfare and protective services or household nurturers to productive persons in their own right.

> The National Plan of Action recommended setting up structures comprising of what the global discourse termed the 'National Machinery' .These were set up within the Government of India in the mid-seventies.
>
> The National Committee on Women (headed by the Prime Minister) and the Women's Welfare and Development Bureau within the Department of Social Welfare. The National Committee then created a Steering Committee, which in turn constituted an inter-departmental committee consisting of representatives of most of the Ministries functioning in areas considered important for women.

Each of the five chapters of the National Plan of Action contained a separate Action Plan, covering particular sectors. The National Plan of Action contained a large number of suggestions and recommendations. In fact, one of the functions of the Steering Committee, which was the creation of the National Committee on women, (see box above) was to cull out the items requiring immediate attention and action from the National Plan of Action and indicate as to how these may be implemented. (It is another matter that the proceedings of the Steering Committee do not show any great pre-occupation of the Committee members with following up this particular theme).

What is important to note here is that, post-CSWI and post-Mexico World Conference on Women, the Government of India took the first tentative step to frame a document which was an aggregation of schemes, programmes, suggestions for reform, etc. which had several ingredients of a "component" approach. The reasons for its lack of sustainability were several. One was the failure to allocate resources on a matching and secure basis. In other words, the plan-design exercise was not matched with a resource allocation process. The NPA stood outside the budgetary process of the Government of India and no effort was made to dovetail the two. Another reason was the lack of an accountability mechanism.

However, at this time, the demands for component plans and separate allocations for women's programmes were simultaneously being voiced from other locations.

- The Working Group on Employment of Women set up by the Planning Commission (chaired by Prof. Ashok Mitra, with Prof. Raj Krishna as the member-in-charge, Employment, Planning

Commission) as a preparatory exercise to feed into the Sixth Five Year Plan produced a report that recommended a special plan for women within every sectoral and area plan. It recommended the delegation of responsibility of women's advancement to each of the Ministries implementing its own plan of action for women. No longer were women to be the responsibility or the constituency of only one or two Ministries. Henceforth women were the subject matter of all government agencies and formations.

- The National Committee on Women in its first (and only) meeting held in April 1978 passed a resolution that all departments should ensure that their plans and policies should not adversely affect the opportunities for women but should actively safeguard and support them. These special steps were to be documented and presented to Parliament.
- The Steering Committee, (the creation of the National Committee on women) in its second meeting, decided that the Minister for Social Welfare would address a letter to his Cabinet colleagues on the need for:

  "a deliberate policy to promote women's integration in all sectors of economic and social policy in the development plans of every sector, I would therefore suggest that a beginning should be made in all sectors of the Plan of your Ministry. A reasonable *percentage of allocation may be earmarked for programmes relating to women and may be separately monitored."* (emphasis added)

Here is the germ of the component plan for women. It emerged from divergent locations, voiced by different sets of people, all within the broad category of spokespersons or agencies for social development within the national government. The emphasis was three-fold.

- one was the need to broad base the women's question, moving it away from its centre in social welfare to spread it out amongst many agencies within the government. This "burgeoning" was the reflection of the new internalisation (based on empirical data and research) of women's productive roles, their contribution, both actual and potential, to national development.

- the other was to allocate specific resources for women in each of these agencies from out of their existing budgets. This came out of the collective realisation by development agencies that in spite of the right to gender equality to women and prohibition of discrimination on the basis of sex contained in the Constitution, women's traditional and accumulated handicaps effectively prevented them from enjoying these benefits without the weight of affirmative action. Thus, "gender neutral" strategies or mechanisms adopted by the State, such as budgeting and planning for the families, households, communities (or the general population) as a unit, had failed to reach the women in these categories.
- the third was the insistence that each government agency should manage and monitor its own investments in women, that they had to own up to this responsibility themselves. This went counter to the conventional wisdom, which had ruled in the bureaucracy hitherto, that apportioned the field of development and administration into discrete jurisdictions amongst the various State agencies. Women as a cross cutting theme or subject were a new paradigm that had to be grappled with by the State structures.

In spite of these pronouncements by the organs of the State and by the influential working groups of the Planning Commission, the Component Plan for Women did not take any concrete, system-wide shape for the next two decades. There were some exceptions, however, where the idea of earmarking resources for women within a larger programme meant for the 'general population' did catch the imagination of the political masters and the policy makers. These then took shape as directives in certain programmes, sectors and ministries. Prominent amongst them was the range of anti- poverty programmes, which were introduced in the seventies and eighties.

ANTI-POVERTY PROGRAMMES AND WOMEN

The Integrated Rural Development Programme (IRDP) targetted families, which meant, overwhelmingly, the male heads of families or other male members. But not the women. The number of women beneficiaries covered by IRDP, as per figures furnished by the Government itself, was infinitesimally small. Development of Women and Children in Rural Areas (DWCRA) was therefore started as a sub-scheme of the IRDP, solely for women (and children). It was launched in 1981-82 on pilot basis in a few blocks, later on taken up in all the States as a major programme for poor women. But in 1985, the Government also took a decision that one-third of the IRDP beneficiaries shall be women. One-third of the beneficiaries of TRYSEM (Training of Rural Youth in Self... Employment) were also to be women. Jawahar Rozgar Yojana had also a stated preference for women. Most of these anti-poverty programmes have 30-40% of benefits reserved for women. The Indira Awas Yojana has a special component in which dwelling units are constructed for the poorest women-headed households.

In addition to the Ministry of Rural Development with its focus on women in poverty, many other agencies of the Government of India took up both 'women-specific' programme initiatives as well as strategies to benefit women in a targetted way through 'general' programmes. This trend picked up steadily through the Five-Year Plans. The Sixth Five Year Plan (1980–85) emphasised women as a specific development sector and a planning priority. The Seventh Plan (1985–90) identified and promoted 'beneficiary oriented programmes' with the objective of extending direct benefits to the women. The Eighth Five Year Plan (1992-97) emphasised that the "benefits of development from different sectors should not bypass women". "Special Programmes are to be implemented to complement the general development programmes. The flow 0f benefits to women in the three core sectors of education, health and employment are to be monitored vigilantly". By the nineties, the thrust on women's development had resulted in a perceptible increase in resources allocated in the budgets of certain Ministries and Departments under the broad rubric women's development. The approaches followed were mainly, two fold, one, special programmes for women, the 'women-only' programmes, and, two, the quota or component approach, whereby a part of the total budgetary resources of general programmes were earmarked for women, or a specific percentage of beneficiaries were mandated to be women.

**The Ninth Plan and the Resurrection of the Component Plan for Women**

The Report of the Working Group on Women's Development set up in January 1996 by the Planning Commission to help prepare for the Ninth Five Year Plan (1997–2001), while reviewing the programmes for women undertaken during the Eighth Plan had this to say about the performance of programmes for women-

> "Although many beneficiary oriented programmes have a portion of the targets earmarked for women, the experience so far has been that the share of the women in the funds of those schemes is not satisfactory. Keeping in view this fact, a separate women's component will be kept aside in funds of all these schemes to ensure the utilisation of that portion of funds for the women beneficiaries only. It is, therefore, proposed to earmark the women's component in every central and centrally sponsored scheme from the first year of the IX Plan. The monitoring of these funds will be undertaken through the Indira Mahila Yojana. Similarly from the first year of the IX Plan, a separate women's component will be insisted in the State plans as well. After the 73rd amendment to the Constitution, a large number of women are now being represented in the Panchayati Raj Institutions. *As the immediate consequential step in the process of power to the people, there is an urgent need to involve women in the decentralised planning process*. Indira Mahila Yojana will be an instrument in this direction and through this scheme, the women will be organised into groups, they will articulate their felt needs and prioritise these needs *which will subsequently become the district level women's sub-plan*. It is very urgent, therefore, that the Indira Mahila Yojana follows the Panchayat Raj process in every State immediately taken into consideration". (emphasis added)
>
> (Ninth Five Year Plan (1997-2001) Report of the Working Group on Women's Development, Department of WCD, 1996)

> This recommendation of the Working Group is unique in one striking respect. It has yoked the component plan strategy with a crucial and dynamic concept, namely, that of decentralised planning.

Even before the Working Group's recommendations, the Department of Women and Child Development had requested the Planning Commission (in late 1995) to introduce a Mahila Plan component in the Ninth Plan. The Ninth Plan exercises were starting at the time, discussions on the draft Plan with the States/Union Territories and the Central Ministries and Departments would be taking place. This was the appropriate time to introduce new planning concepts and ideas and get them discussed in the working groups.

The suggestion from the Women's Department was that the Planning Commission should emphasise with all these agencies to identify 'specific quantifiable Mahila Plan component in each scheme/programme' before they come for the meetings with the Planning Commission on the Ninth Plan. While certain programmes have already specific earmarking for women (such as IRDP and some of the other anti-poverty programmes), the Women's Department wanted the Planning Commission to consider earmarking of funds for women in other programmes and Ministries such as Agriculture, Animal Husbandry, Wasteland Development, Employment, etc. It went on to suggest that the quantum, the percentages, the number of women beneficiaries and the benefits accruing should be specifically indicated in the Mahila Plan component. The responsibility for doing this should be vested in the concerned agencies of the Central and State Government. The Women's Department also wanted the Planning Commission and the Ministry of Finance to give incentives (by way of additional Central funds) to those States who would give emphasis to the Mahila Plan component 'by providing targets in excess of the prescribed minimum percentages'. The monitoring of the performance of the Mahila Plan component was suggested to be carried out by the Planning Commission and the Programme Implementation Department.
(Quotes from the letter dated 12-12-95 from Secretary WCD to the Member-Secretary, Planning Commission).

"Expectedly, the internal notes of the Planning Commission showed their identification of the concept of the Mahila Plan component with that of the Special Component Plan (and also the Tribal Sub-Plan) [See subsequent part of the paper for these two]. While addressing the advisers of the various divisions within the Planning Commission, the Plan Co- ordination Division explained, "the Sub-Plan for women, as visualised, should be operative under all women related developmental sectors, both at Central and State levels, just as on the lines of Special Component Plan (SCP) for SC's and Tribal Sub-PLan (TSP) for ST's wherein a certain percentage of both physical and financial targets are earmarked for the women".

(Note of the Planning Commission dated 20-5-96)

The Planning Commission took about a year to respond to the request of the Department of Women and Child Development. In October 1996, it sent a comprehensive communication to all Ministries and Departments of the Government of India sharing the general thinking in the Planning Commission on important issues related to the formulation of the Ninth Plan. The issues dealt with include–

- *Plan priorities* (agriculture, rural development, rural infrastructure, seven basic minimum services, poverty alleviation, public sector reform).
- *Delivery and implementation* (creation and strengthening of institutions of participatory development, involvement of panchayats, co-operatives, self help groups, workers' associations, partnership with the voluntary sector).
- *Decentralisation* (need to devolve more 'social welfare measures' to the Panchayats, encouraging local bodies to raise resources, greater autonomy to the States).
- *Continuation of existing schemes and new schemes* (need to review the entirety of ongoing schemes to retain only those which have impact, dropping of schemes and projects where only 5 per cent of expenditure has been incurred even after 60 per cent of the gestation period is over, high priority to be given to SC/ST welfare through adequate earmarking of schemes with direct benefit potential for Scheduled Castes and Scheduled Tribes, under the Special Component Plan and the Tribal Sub-Plan, etc.)

It is under this last section that we find a reference to the Mahila Plan component idea. "For the Ninth Plan, it may also be desirable to identify a women's component in the various schemes and programmes of the States and Central Ministries" observes the Member-Secretary.

The Ninth Plan began in 1997 and will go on to 2002. Information on follow-up action by the agencies involved in the Mahila Plan component is scarce and difficult to obtain. Informally, we learn that the earmarking of 'Mahila Plan components' by most of the Central Ministries has not yet actually taken place. As far as the States are concerned, similarly, we learn that Karnataka, Rajasthan and Madhya Pradesh have taken certain steps to institutionalise the Mahila Plan component in the State Plans. It is also not clear what kind of monitoring of the progress is taking place and what are the results of the monitoring, where the bottlenecks are, etc.

## Some earlier initiatives in women's plans

Long before the Ninth Plan, the mechanism of "Action Plans for Women" had been tried in some States. Madhya Pradesh, for example was one of the early initiators.

Karnataka made an effort in 1993 to work towards an institutional model of planning for women. The objective was to identify those sectors where women's participation has been traditionally greater and to suggest strategies for development of women in these sectors. For a start, six broad sectors were identified. These were land and housing, agriculture and allied services, rural development, education, health, industry with focus on sericulture, KVIC, VISHWA, etc. The senior policy makers and administrators (including the Finance Department) then held department-wise discussions–

"(a)to identify schemes which would lead towards empowerment of women by recognising activities in which they participate and enabling them to have a controlling voice in such activities,

(b) to facilitate diversification of production activities through training, skill upgradation, access to credit,

(c) create a sustained programme for education and health". The document prepared by the Government of Karnataka states the following-

'Women's development cannot be a programme of one department alone. Viewed thus' women would continue to be relegated to a separate stream, rather than being integrated into the mainstream of development and economy. Women's development can only succeed if all sectors of Government are adequately sensitive to the needs of women and focus their programmes on women' ".

*Contd......*

> One noticeable feature of the Karnataka model was that the recommendations made included policy changes, amendments to laws, improvement of procedures, increasing representation of women in committees, etc. and not only earmarking quantum of benefits to women or allocating percentages of the funds to women or percentages of women beneficiaries. Both qualitative and quantitative aspects were included.
>
> Government of Karnataka paper "Women's Development Programme 1993").

The "women in agriculture", "women in sericulture", "women in dairying", "women in fisheries" etc. genre of projects made their appearance in the seventies and eighties and have remained with us ever since. Most of these are still being funded externally, i.e., from outside the mainstream Ministry budget and plan. The group of Agriculture projects have been the earliest to be taken up (Karnataka, 1983). This was followed by a number of other externally funded projects of similar nature in other States such as Tamil Nadu, Orissa, Madhya Pradesh etc. In the Eighth Plan, the Ministry of Agriculture launched a pilot scheme of Women in Agriculture in seven States in the country and this has now been continued in the Ninth Plan on an expanded basis. This initiative has meant that the Government plan funds for agriculture are being invested, for the first time, in a "women's component". There have been few evaluations of these projects from a focussed gender perspective. The available evaluations and reviews show that the focus is primarily on training for higher productivity and income. While highlighting the pioneering and innovative nature of these projects and stressing their positive impact in the Eighth Plan, improvement in access to technology and extension have been stressed as resulting in "empowerment" of the target group women. (Ministry of Agriculture) There is no reference in these evaluations to equity issues, legal literacy,ownership rights, land rights, titles, control and access issues, wages, mobilisation, gender issues within the State agencies, etc.

In the Seventh Plan, the Department of Women and Child Development launched the STEP programme (Support to Training and Employment) in which informal sector women workers falling in the seven or eight "sheds" such, as agriculture, small animal husbandry, dairying, fisheries, handlooms, handicrafts, etc. are supported to avail of information and services to upgrade incomes and skills through the strategy of groups, such as co-operatives. Cumulatively, these sectors contain the largest number of women of the unorganised sector. The Annual Report of the Department of Women and Child Development (1998-99) shows that a total of 72 Projects have so far been launched, with a coverage of 4.16 lakhs women. (Out of this number, the majority of women, 3.47 lakhs are covered by dairy projects) The women's organisations built up under this project were to be linked with and supported by the huge parastatals or public sector agencies, boards, commissions, etc. that exist in the line Ministries of each of the sectors. No evaluation is available to see the extent to which the interests of these informal sector workers have been "mainstreamed" in the line Ministries.

## PART II

## THE "EARMARKED FUNDS" APPROACH TO PLANNING FOR WOMEN—A CLOSER LOOK

### Top down and Centralised

So far, within the Government, the idea of the "plans for women" or the "component plan for women" or the "mahila component" had evolved and taken shape within the conventional milieu of centralised and top-down planning that has been the common feature of all Five Year Plans of India.

> D. Bandhyopadhyay (1999) quotes E.M.S. Namboodiripad's dissenting note to the Ashok Mehta Committee Report "Democracy at the Central and State levels, but bureaucracy at all lower levels—that is the essence of Indian polity as spelt out in the Constitution". D.B. says "prior to the 73rd Amendment, there was an almost non-accountable bureaucratic administration, the officers were not accountable to those over whom they exercised power and authority".

The dominant feature of the component approach was the earmarking of resources for women at macro or national or aggregate level, since that was where the plans were prepared and finalised. This was accompanied in most cases by allocation of "physical" targets to be achieved with the help of the earmarked funds. These targets were decided upon, right at the top, that is, at the central level. The effort was to ensure that women got a "fair" share of the development outlays in the plans/budgets each year by mandatory executive action at the policy, planning and programme levels. These interventions were assumed to satisfy the requirements of women both in terms of their needs and the requirements of "planning for women". But no effort was made to question the direction of planning itself. It was also assumed that women would have no problem in receiving these benefits through the same general delivery system. The implementation of these centrally planned programmes was done by a centrally directed bureaucracy which, through the years, had proliferated from the capitals right down to the village in myriad forms.

Commenting on the generic failure of Indian planning in estimating people's initiative and response as a political force for change, a biographer of Nehru observes that "planning made them mere beneficiaries. And since the benefits that was due to them came through a line of intermediaries, even this largesse was imperfectly distributed by imperfect people in an imperfect way" (Dhavan and Paul 1992). This was all the more true of women as the "beneficiaries" of planning .

The earmarking of resources, the identification of plans, programmes and schemes for women, the designing of "quotas" for women within beneficiary oriented programmes aimed at both men and women, all these processes and activities were carried out in a centralised fashion, at the national level or at the State government levels. The prime mover was the government and its various organs. The influence of groups outside the government, the women's movement, the women's studies discipline, organisations of civil society, community based agencies, etc. on the process of designing State plans, programmes and schemes was marginal in so far as the directional issue went, though it was considerable in other substantive matters.

Consultations with some of these groups did take place with increasing frequency from the seventies and eighties onwards. But even they took place it was more to fulfil an obligation to "meet women's groups", for example, or to institute "participatory processes" or "to get feed-back from the field" and less to have serious policy dialogues on the planning paradigms and processes. The government still played a proactive role, the discussions were held at its instance, at times, locations and on occasions decided by it. Consultations with outside groups, however, did become a part of the State planning culture in so far as the plans related to women.

Secondly, these interactions did not directly involve the majority of the population, i.e. the poor women in the rural areas, [or the women in the urban slums] for whom these planning exercises were actually being carried out. Their voices, or the voices of their representatives, were not heard first-hand in these meetings. At the most, their needs and voices were heard at second hand, through the agency of the women's groups, most of which worked closely with them and were sensitive to their needs. At the same time, muted criticism was often voiced that the articulate urban or semi-urban women who found their way to these meetings did not really represent the mass of rural women. But neither was any effort made to evolve a system of representation that would enable the vast majority of women in the country to feel satisfied that their views were being heard. The millions of poor rural and urban women had no agency in the planning process, had no legal and effective representation in the discourse.

## The lack of attention to gender in planning

The "earmarked funds" experiments and initiatives quickly became part of the mainstream planning culture as far as women were concerned. But evaluations and impact assessments of women-targetted schemes carried out from outside the government had been throwing up evidence that their outreach to the poor, especially to the women, was very minimal. A number of weaknesses and defects were revealed in the studies–

- Local functionaries approached their tasks mechanically, were more bound by procedures and targets rather than by the needs of the women "beneficiaries".
- Acute lack of village level data, on households, assets, income, etc. leading to wrong targetting.
- Women did not find it easy to deal with male functionaries or with the largely male-oriented systems in place in the village.

- Women found it difficult to organise themselves in collectives, such as co-operatives of workers etc., due to cumbersome procedures and lack of technical and official support. Mahila Mandals [the only ubiquitous form of women's organisations in the villages] suffered from a number of systemic faults and were not able to represent the needs of most needy rural women.
- Whether the earmarked benefits had the potential to change women's traditionally disadvantaged gendered position and what were the issues that these interventions were addressing did not receive much attention, as the priority was on reaching the benefits to them.
- Crucial aspects of gender planning, such as redefinition of categories, reform of information systems, time budgeting of women, area-wise [or "sector-wise" or "work- shed-wise"] design of programmes etc. were not part of the planning design. These gaps resulted in distortions in design, difficulties in measuring impact, etc. Lack of the planners' exposure to the emerging discipline of women's studies led to failure to expose inadequacies in concepts and definitions, to discover new tools of analysis, such as survey methodologies using time-use data, methods for measuring energy inputs and outputs of women, etc.
- Lack of attention to gender and related aspects led to continued prevalence of sex-stereotyping, neglect of women's basic survival strategies in programme design and content.
- There was no delivery system for gender. The interventions were an add-on, grafted on the mainframe plan design.
- (ISST, Bangalore)

**Absence or Devolution to Local Governments**

Decentralisation of both planning and implementation, which reduces the distance between the planners, implementers and the beneficiaries, was missing. So was local accountability. Local communities of women, or of the poor, were rarely aware of government plans. Local governments and local organisations were not involved in planning or implementing national programmes, except to a very peripheral extent, as for example, in the identification of beneficiaries in the anti-poverty programmes. No effective feedback was possible, as there was no space for it in the planning cycle. Mid-course corrections could not be done. This inhibited the process of adaptability to local conditions and exacerbated women's lack of awareness, absence of training and other facilities. Thus, the blue-print approach of many national programmes did not show sensitivity to State-by-State variations.

## Representative Bodies of Women—Lack of Authority and Neglect of "Mobilisation" as a Process

The persistence of many adverse features of this dominant planning paradigm over the last four decades had in fact, invited the ire of development specialists, activists, women's groups, social workers and many others. The failure to involve women's representative groups in planning became, in fact, a common critique of government programmes. The Indian women's movement along with the women's studies movement, had convincingly established the argument over these years of centralised planning that "women, particularly from the poorer households, need their own organisation to help them break the barriers of inequality, invisibility and powerlessness and expand the base for participatory development" [Kumud Sharma]. Beyond the Indian voices, at global level, the various international conferences convened by the different agencies of the UN were saying the same thing. [Mexico, Copenhagen, Nairobi, ESCAP, ILO, NAM, etc.]

These proponents of mobilisation posited the building up of organisations of women through mobilisation of groups at grass roots as a counter to the welfarist ideology that still dominated government thinking in the planning and the delivery of services and programmes for women—namely, one which saw women as the 'beneficiary' or the 'target' rather than the 'active agent'. Groups of women, as opposed to individual women, had collective strength, bargaining power and the ability to articulate their views and their needs. They could build effective leadership, could facilitate participatory approaches to planning and implementation and could bring planning closer to the people. As far back as 1974, the CSWI Report "Towards Equality" had made recommendations for ensuring greater collective voice for women in local planning. The Committee had recommended the setting up of statutory all-women's Panchayats to ensure greater collective participation by women in the political process. The Committee on Panchayati Raj structure (1977) had recommended village level women's organisations to improve the quality of planning at the local level.

The Mahila Mandals promoted by the government in the fifties were seen to be comparatively ineffective in achieving these objectives (due to a variety of reasons) .

A study carried out by ISST New Delhi in 1992 looked at Mahila Mandals, cooperatives and Panchayats in tandem as institutions introduced in rural areas "for ensuring local participation in the task of socio-economic transformation". The study postulates the pre-conditions for Mahila Mandals to flourish as the increasing growth of Panchayats and the decreasing control of official machinery over rural development programmes. It is only under such conditions that the planning and implementation of such programmes as are capable of being managed locally can be looked after by representative bodies of women supported by Panchayats. The study found, after examining the position in two States, that such conditions were not fulfilled, rather, they were reversed. The role of Panchayats was weakening and the bureaucratization and control over even locally manageable rural development programmes was increasing. The Mahila Mandals were almost never associated with the planning and design of locally manageable schemes, not even where a percentage of benefits is earmarked for women, as in IRDP and JRY, or even DWCRA which is an exclusive programme for women. Mahila Mandals are therefore handicapped for lack of information about formal structures, their scopes and functions. It is only when the supportive hand of an NGO is there that the study found the Mahila mandals to be active and functional.

The Seventh Five-Year Plan (1980-85) urged that organisations of women be promoted to ensure the elimination of weaknesses in programme implementation. The "group approach" was recommended for improving the quality and access of government services.

DWCRA (Development of Women and Children in Rural Areas) had in fact, incorporated the group approach in its design. But the 'art' of mobilisation of women, the gender ideology and commitment, the attention to 'process' were missing in the programme design. Mobilisation of women, especially poor women, takes time. It cannot be made to order. As observed by a feminist-economist, poverty alleviation was a time consuming process, it is expensive. Its durable success depends on both external support and internal motivation. Above all, the poor must have the room to devise choices of their own. Within a tightly woven project format, with main emphasis on reaching earmarked benefits to women, "the group approach" could not be taken beyond a point to its intended conclusion. (Devaki Jain, 1988)

In a recent interaction, Ela Bhatt (September 2000) made a distinction between the process of "mobilisation" and the process of building up an "organisation". This distinction is very often lost sight of, in the government programmes, where the two are treated as one.

Yet the "group approach" did find its way to the government planning lexicon, with all its imperfections, by the mid- eighties, as evidenced by the Chapter in the Seventh Five- Year Plan document. Some of the government programmes that have been launched in the last two decades have incorporated this feature [STEP, CAPART's programme of organisation of beneficiaries, the Revised Programme of Action of the National Policy of Education (1992)]. The Indira Mahila Yojana is based on the setting up of self-help groups at the sub-Block level. The National Perspective Plan for Women (1988-2000), Shramshakti (1988) [The Report of the National Commission on Self-Employed Women and Women in the Informal Sector] both emphasized the importance of women's representative organizations in programmes for women.

Meanwhile, new government initiatives such as the Women's Development Programme in Rajasthan in the early eighties and the Mahila Samakhya Projects in several States of the country in the late eighties and nineties [both of which used the mobilising of poor women as an article of faith] became very influential in propagating the success of this approach. The inputs and the thinking of women activists and researchers shaped these two initiatives, though both were launched by the government. The implementation, monitoring, evaluation and measurement of impact of these programmes were also designed in a participatory, gender sensitive and equity based way in which the women of the groups were central to planning.

Most often, there was a wide gap between the group approach as adopted by the government and the mobilization conscientisation-awareness-raising efforts made by women's organisations. It was the difference between a strategy that depended on a top down implementation direction, on a target approach that saw women as needy and weak, but not strong enough to know how to organise themselves and ask for information and services and an approach that took women in the context of their power dynamics and encouraged them to think of their own self-determination and self-definition. The group approach in the State-sponsored programmes is taken up as part of the project design, where an organisation of women is needed as part of the delivery mechanism. The stage of mobilisation, where issues of concern to the women are identified and a slow process of building a collective identity is built up using empowerment strategies is missing here.

## Lack of Gender-sensitiveness in the Implementation Machinery

The lack of sensitivity on the part of the top administrators and bureaucrats, the middle level managers, the technical and specialised cadres, the extension staff in the field, the officials at the 'cutting edge' level, etc. was another adverse characteristic of the top down planning and delivery model. The strategy of "earmarked funds" for women did not change this environment. The "quota" for women meant that the same extension workers had to be in position in the field. Bias towards women was more pronounced in the case of poorer women, especially those of *dalit* and *adivasi* communities.

A Task Force was set up in 1985 by the Ministry of Rural Development to suggest ways of sensitisation of government officials in the wake of the government decision to earmark quotas for women in anti-poverty programmes. It expressed concern at the poor recognition of the issues concerning women's development at various levels of the administration. While on the one hand the government was taking steps to increase the access to development resources by women, their effective implementation required a proper understanding of the specific issues involved as well as sensitivity towards the situation of women in a larger context. The Task Force made a number of important recommendations regarding training programmes for various levels of officials in rural development. These included pilot camps-cum-workshops in DWCRA districts, introducing new features such as participatory analysis of key issues, face-to-face dialogue with groups of rural women and formulation of action plans by the trainees.

Gender training programmes became part of training establishments' repertoire from the mid-eighties onwards and have subsequently been taken up on a regular basis in many State training institutions, but their effectiveness and even their consistency varies sharply across the country. More attention is paid to the planning, policy and mid-level officials and less on the "cutting edge" extension machinery in these training sessions. A common experience was that it was more difficult to change attitudes through training than to convey information or impart skills in gender analysis, especially when conventional methodology was used. In training institutions dealing with "technical" disciplines , the priority tends to be on dissemination of technology and technology applications, in the interest of making women "catch up". The training then becomes narrowly focused and productivity or growth oriented in the technical sense. Equity issues, whether related to gender or class, legal literacy, ownership issues, land rights, titles, control and access problems, wage issues, mobilisation, overlapping hierarchies within the training situation, etc. do not get much attention and sometimes, are totally ignored.

**Parallels with the Scheduled Caste Component Plan and the Tribal Sub-Plan Experiences**

The experience of the Special Component Plan for the Scheduled Castes since the Sixth Five-Year Plan (1980-85) contains lessons for the present initiative to earmark resources for women through the mechanism of a component plan. The parallels between the State responses to planning for women and planning for Scheduled Castes are indeed striking. Like women, the Constitution gives the highest priority to the development—educational, social and economic of the members of the Scheduled Caste communities. A number of safeguards have been built into the Constitution to enable the members of these communities to catch up with the rest of the population. They include, but are not confined to, legal instruments for the removal of disabilities, for punishment of discriminatory acts of commission and omission and mandatory provisions for reservations in public services.

However, by the end of the seventies, it was apparent that these efforts were too meagre to make a significant impact on the socio-economic status of these communities. Low literacy levels, grinding poverty, landlessness and socially discriminatory practices such as untouchability persisted in these communities. Whatever benefits accrued, such as in reservations in public services, were cornered by what came to be termed later as the "creamy layer" of the target population.

The Planning Commission then initiated a major affirmative action programme. It first set up a Working Group with broad terms of reference to review the status of developmental programmes for Scheduled Castes/other weaker sections in their entirety and formulate concrete proposals for a new development perspective along with recommendations for effective administrative arrangements. A sub-Working Group was constituted exclusively for Scheduled Castes.

Based on the recommendations of the Working Group, the mechanism of the Special Component Plan was introduced in the Sixth Five-Year Plan (1980-85) .The Special Component Plan for Scheduled Castes launched by the government in 1980 is designed to channelise the flow of benefits and financial outlays from the general sectors in the plans of all the States and the Central Ministries for the development of these communities. These flows were of three types, namely, flows from existing schemes, flows from reoriented/modified existing schemes and, finally, flows from new schemes. The SCP is essentially a strategy of earmarking benefits to the Scheduled Castes in physical and financial terms in the relevant sectors. In concrete terms, physical goals along with the financial outlays required to achieve these goals were to be spelt out in the SCP document. The responsibility for drawing up comprehensive programmes or plans, earmarking funds from the sectoral budgets, etc. was vested in the Ministries and Departments in the Government of India (for the Central budget) and in the State administration (for the State budget). The Sixth Plan was able to invest an amount of Rs. 3,533 crores under the Special Component Plan in 20 States and Union territories as compared to a cumulative amount of Rs. 433 crores spent in the earlier five plans.

The Sub-Plan for tribals had been initiated even earlier. Unlike the Scheduled Caste Component plan, the Tribal Sub-Plan was mainly spatially based, choosing the geographically contiguous areas in which tribals resided.

In October 1999, the Planning Commission, on the basis of a review of the "special strategies" of the Scheduled Caste Component Plan and the Tribal Sub-Plan, both at Centre and State levels, owned that the plans have become routinised and suffer from qualitative and quantitative deficiencies. The Central government has, as a consequence of this finding, set up Standing Tripartite Committees at Centre and State level to look into all policy-related matters and issues for effective implementation of these plans (Letter from Member-Secretary Planning Commission in October 1999 conveying the decision to all State governments).

Commenting on the lessons learned from the earmarking resources for weaker sections without accompanying shifts in the established planning paradigm, Devaki Jain, (1988) remarks–

"Intensive earmarked support for tribal populations [like women, identified as disadvantaged] by designing and executing tribal sub-plans which were area specific—had failed to decrease the immiserisation of the tribals—examination of the process of planning and delivery of the programmes revealed that they were handed down from above to functionaries issues of gender had to take a back seat to implementation—both in terms of the conceptual framework and of the mechanism of implementation. In short the method [top-down] by which the development scheme was designed and implemented, prevailed over the aims and objectives. This had little to do with who in government or NGO was doing the implementing, or for whom [men or women] or with the package being delivered.

**Conclusion**

The effort to move away from "exclusively women's" projects, resulted in locating an alternative planning format, one where women would be ensured a fair share of the benefits of general infrastructure, local developmental opportunities and composite developmental programmes, with all linkages and inputs. These two formats have dominated the mainstream planning agenda ever since. The latter model was based on the assumption that women beneficiaries would find it as easy as the male beneficiaries to access the earmarked benefits. While emphasising the need to "mainstream" women into mainframe planning, the Department of Women and Child Development has continued to launch new programmes exclusively for women in subsequent Five-Year Plans, while at the same time, pursuing the case with other ministries to take women "on board".

## PART III

## LEARNING FROM EXPERIENCE—THE WAY FORWARD

### Can the Component Plan for Women be a Stand-alone?

The several approaches used from time to time to integrate and institutionalise planning for women and development within the State systems have been described above. We see that there has always been a tendency to focus on the perceived needs of women, through special schemes, programmes and plans. The impetus for such pro-active planning came both from within the country–a welfare State, bound by Constitutional obligations to women's development and equality—and later on, after the internationalisation of the women's question, from the global forums, such as Mexico, Copenhagen, Nairobi and Beijing. The presence of the women's lobbies, the women's movement, the community-based organisations, the representative associations of women, the research disciplines such as the social sciences, women's studies, the educational institutions and other civil society organisations within the country had all influenced the thinking of the State to various degrees in the process of planning for women.

From a purely "welfare" preoccupation with "vulnerable" women, the canvas widened to include other broad constituencies, such as "rural women", "women workers", "poor women" and women seeking political power. Women were seen as instrumental in the reaching of socially acceptable national goals such as literacy, health small families, protection of environment and many others. Programme interventions by the State attempted to involve women in these important sectors.

These initiatives, however, placed as they were within the prevailing planning and policy environment and context, exhibited the typical features of the mainstream top down Indian planning model in philosophy and practice. Having had its roots in the welfare model, the idea of a paternalistic State having to think of the needs of the different groups of the population continued to be very strong. While action plans and component plans for women came to be hammered out with increasing refinement from the mid-seventies onwards, they all partook of the same planning ethos. *Plans for women, in other words, could not strike out a pioneering path on their own, nor make a brave departure from the general direction of other mainstream planning exercises.*

The idea of the component plan, as we have seen, was first mooted in the mid-seventies, but was not taken on board by the government in a generic sense. Earmarking of quotas for women, however, was made in many of the anti-poverty programmes from the eighties onwards. The component plan was revived in the context of the exercises done for the Ninth Five-Year Plan, as brought out in the earlier part of the chapter. The content of the directions issued by the Planning Commission in its 1996 letter was to identify a women's component in existing schemes and programmes.

> While the Working Group on Women's Development set up for the Ninth Five-Year Plan (1996) had emphasised the linking of the Mahila component plan with decentralised planning, the directives and guidelines issued by the Planning Commission to all the Government of India's Ministries, Departments, allied agencies, etc. regarding the component plan were deficient in this very important aspect. No mention was made of decentralised planning in the guidelines.

It would seem that the objective of recommending this kind of identification process to be undertaken by the governments is mainly to ensure that women get a fair share of the development cake in quantifiable terms. This anxiety arose from the hitherto poor utilisation of resources by women from State budgets and plans. Instead of adding on more and more "women-specific" schemes or schemes and programmes "only for women", the approach was to ensure that general developmental programmes catered for both men and women. This was impossible if no earmarking was done and no targets or specific outlays were fixed for women.

The fixation with figures and quantification, as we have noticed, is part of the conventional way of measuring progress or of evaluating satisfactory implementation in planning terms. The reality of poor, rural women's lives however, is indicative of many social, economic, cultural and environmental obstacles that prevent them from enjoying their due share of resources, services, facilities and benefits. Unless women are given opportunities to break through these obstacles, are able to access information, technology, challenge unequal power relations through individual and collective empowerment strategies, the gains accruing from the earmarking of resources in plans and budgets cannot benefit them except marginally.

Apart from urging a system-wide earmarking of budget funds, the Working Group on Women's Development had also made a recommendation (quoted in the earlier part of this chapter) that for women to be involved in the decentralised planning process, they should be organised into groups (through the agency of the Indira Mahila Yojana), that women should articulate and prioritise their needs and that this process should lead to a district level "women's sub-plan".

The Indira Mahila Yojana (IMY) (recast) has been described as an integrated programme for women's development, which seeks to build an organisational base for women throughout the country. It aims to converge all the social development programmes and integrate sectoral allocations at the district level to address women's needs. The lowest rung of the organisational structure consists of Indira Mahila Kendras at the Anganwadi level. These groups, along with other similar groups constituted under various health, education and other social development programmes, would federate at Block level. The Indira Mahila Kendras are basically self help groups. They are expected to access various programmes implemented by the Rural Development, Urban Development, Education and Health sectors as well as others dealing with economic and production activities. The Women's Department conceives of Indira Mahila Yojana as an important constituent or conduit of the Mahila Component plan. However, this Yojana is still pending final clearance of the government. In the meanwhile, activities had started in about 200 Blocks some years ago and the Planning Commission has recently reviewed these. How far the agency of the IMY will be able to involve grass roots women in local decision making, only time will tell.

A joint evaluation report prepared by the Department of Women and Child Development and the Planning Commission in 1997-98 arrived at the following–findings–

- Though IMY has a potential to use women's groups as an instrument of women's empowerment, there are many operational problems such as lack of training, funding for income generation and convergence activity, lack of animators, etc.
- The absence of co-ordinating officers in the district and the failure to draw up district plans has affected the implementation.

Based on the findings of the joint evaluation, the Yojana was recast with new featuers, such as greater flexibility for women to form groups, participation of members of local Panchayats and officials as facilitators, preparation of district plans by IMY which will reflect women's priorities, active involvement of NGO's to assist in group formation devolution of planning powers for Block level projects to the local administration, etc.

From the original 200 Blocks, it was decided to expand IMY to 900 Blocks in the Ninth Five-Year Plan.

The concern with quantification, with expenditure, with utilisation of funds within a prescribed time limit, with counting of beneficiaries, with reaching targets set at the beginning of the Plan period and other easily measurable indices have been part of the stock in trade of government programmes. The component plan, by itself, is a further illustration of this methodology. By itself, without the help of strategies of empowerment, participation, mobilisation and sustained support, the component plan approach would not be able to counter the factors responsible for the unequal status of women.

The instrumentality of the component plan therefore, needs a set of empowerment and participation strategies to enable transfer of political power to women, to enable them to take charge of planning changes in their own lives. A basic requirement would seem to be the over-turning of the hierarchy of present day planning, of the top-down model. A window of opportunity has opened with the promise of *devolution of powers and decentralisation of functions* to the three-tiered Panchayats at village and sub-district and district levels.

*Strategic partnerships* between elected women in Panchayats, local community women's groups and those resource organisations who are committed to women's political, economic and social empowerment would be another critical requirement. Such partnerships are already much in evidence. A large number of resource organisations are engaged in networking in different parts of the country, taking up a variety of activities in collaboration with women in the community and the elected women in the Panchayats. Issues taken up include credit, capacity building, employment, shelter, savings and credit, communication of information and other innovations. Problems of violence, health, education, local corruption, lack of accountability of local governments, etc. are tackled through building a supportive environment which will allow institutional solutions to be handled by the women themselves.

> Swayam Shikshan Prayog, a voluntary organisation based in Maharashtra, working in such a mode since 1995, has now built an alliance of women's collectives and elected women of the Panchayats and claims that this has emerged as a new kind of leadership which "is changing the face of local governance", "transforming Gram Panchayats to become accountable and transparent and building an informed and active constituency". The synergistic alliances between the community women and the elected representatives help mobilize communities to participate in local development, improve access of all to infrastructural facilities, help eliminate middle-men and corruption and keep the community well-informed through regular interactions.

If we were to use such a multi-levelled and synergistic approach to women's involvement in local planning, the component plan would then not be a stand-alone, but would be an enabling mechanism to extend women's outreach to development resources and goals, defined in their own tongues.

## How to Change the Direction of Planning?

The only significant change, post-independence, to have occurred in the planning prototype took place in 1993 with the 73rd and 74th Constitutional amendments. This has found an echo in the report of the Ninth Plan Working Group already referred to.

The Working Group's deliberations and approach were influenced by the 73rd Amendment to the Constitution of India. After these amendments became part of the Constitution in 1991 and were followed by new Panchayat laws passed in each State, Indian development planning and administration, theoretically at least, could never be the same. Twenty-nine different kinds of development and regulatory activities had now to be transferred to the Panchayats as units of local government. This was a mandatory provision, not an optional one. The subjects included social sector priorities such as education, drinking water, women and child development, etc., economic priorities such as the anti-poverty programmes, production oriented activities such as agriculture and allied subjects forestry, infrastructure such as community assets, etc.

The Working Group was clear that the component plan had to be hitched to decentralised planning if the promises made to the women were to be actualised. It was no longer enough for plans, programmes, allocations and schemes to be made in the government offices at Central or even State levels. They had to be made by women, where they were situated, where they were located. It was for the local bodies (including the urban bodies) to decide what are the kind of schemes that the women needed and demanded, how much funds were required to be allocated, how they were to be spent, how the monitoring was to be done.

With the move towards decentralised planning, fresh interest has been generated in planning not only for women, but also for women in the units of local governance. Article 40 of the Constitution had already envisaged Panchayats as units of local government. But this provision remained on paper for long, not being legally enforceable. Though Panchayats have been in existence even before Independence, they 'were invariably denied any meaningful powers and authority and, worst of all, the elections were seldom held at five-year intervals'. (Devaki Jain, UNDP)

The entry of elected women into the Panchayats in large numbers in the mid-nineties onwards signalled the start of a complex, multi-faceted and politically nuanced process of power dynamics. By the time the first Panchayat elections had been held in the States and the women had time to settle themselves in their new positions, the pattern of struggle became apparent. On the one hand, women have to fight the backlash that has been mounted against them, questioning their credentials, legitimacy, capability, motivation and sense of responsibility to occupy these offices. On the other hand, the process of devolution of powers from the two higher tiers of government, namely the State and the National Government, to the third tier of the Panchayats has been, to say the least, long drawn out and laggard. There emerged a not-so-hidden agenda, on the part of the government, of unwillingness to share power with the Panchayats as the grass roots units of governance, which is continued to be played out in different manifestations and strategies.

Elected women have, therefore, to fight on several fronts at the same time. They have to fight for their own place in the sun in the Panchayats *vis-a-vis* the patriarchal forces arraigned against them and at the same time, they have to fight the political and bureaucratic State agencies for according a greater role in governance to the Panchayats.

> A senior bureaucrat reminded the participants of a recent workshop convened at Bangalore to debate on the theme of empowerment of elected women members of Panchayats that for women to be truly empowered as members of PRI's, it is essential that the PRI's themselves must work well. Women interests cannot be viewed in isolation from the functioning of the Panchayats as a whole. He further said that those do not believe in women's participation in Panchayats or it a problem are those who themselves do not believe in Panchayats.

In spite of these tremendous odds, many of those who, from the outside, are working with Panchayats have no hesitation in agreeing that the difference women are making to local government is becoming evident in new priorities and new values. Women are not merely participating in the Panchayati Raj process but they are questioning the system itself. (L.C. Jain)

The challenge is to build up elected women's capabilities through information, through legal awareness and supports at local level. The challenge is to build enabling mechanisms, which can initiate planning by women, that is, bottom up planning. The committees of the Panchayat are examples of these mechanisms.

The scenario, as we take a look across India, is not very promising. Panchayats are still seen in most States as extension agencies, as bodies or organisations which will help the government to discharge its developmental and regulatory functions more efficiently through the use of a better delivery system which is closer to the grass roots and to the people. In other words, they are deemed to work as extension agencies, rather than as people's representative organisations. Decisions, especially the major ones dealing with control of resources and shaping of policies, still rest with the old ruling classes. The Panchayats political profile and genesis mandated in the 73rd Amendment to the Constitution is most often overlooked, especially at the lowest tier, where because the elections are to be fought on non-party lines, the Gram Panchayats are seen as necessarily 'non-political'. The identification of the word 'political' with the political parties of the day has helped to create this false negative. As such, the Panchayats, except in a few States, have not been involved meaningfully in the exercise of planning from the grass roots. At the most, they can nibble at the margin of the hand-me-down projects received from the State or national capitals in the form of programmes and schemes (their roles are limited to identification of beneficiaries for programmes designed elsewhere, to supervision of local works planned and constructed by offices over whom the elected members have no authority or control, etc.)

According to the 1999 South Asia Human Development Report, some of the most basic features of a decentralised democracy should include guaranteed political autonomy and specific powers to local bodies in the State, including delivery of public services, natural resource management and law and order. Other essential features include providing local bodies with the power of tax collection up to a specified percentage and devolving a certain portion of national and State revenues to them.

The debate on the changes to be brought about in the power structure is long and never-ending. The issues are not simple nor is the environment static. "Power is not something people give away. It has to be negotiated and sometimes wrested from the powerful": (Devaki Jain 1999) . But elected women have enough answers to most of the questions. They know what are the factors which impede them and what supports, inputs and services they need to go ahead. Among the former they included the following:

- inability to articulate
- lack of self esteem and confidence
- lack of information
- restricted physical mobility
- patriarchal controls
- double burden of work
- corrupt system
- lacunae in laws relating to PRIs
- no freedom for decision making

Among the latter, they listed:

- the need to organise and express solidarity
- the need for training and exposure
- right to information, education and economic independence
- more of women functionaries and officials at local levels
- gender sensitisation of elected male members and functionaries
- representation in all committees
- amendments in party politics to encourage women's entry into politics (Asha Ramesh and Bharti Ali, undated)

In seeking to access these resources and services from outside, the elected women in the Panchayats can readily call upon a large number of support organisations from various locations within civil society.

The women's movement has been one of the greatest proponents of women's empowerment through political participation and decision making. Since the introduction of the 73rd Amendment, many other organisations of civil society falling under the broad banner of social change, have also been engaged in a continuous process of helping the elected women in the Panchayats to transform the existing political culture by promoting democratic freedom and the rights of the marginalised groups. There are numerous examples of local action initiated by the elected women in the Panchayats with the help of voluntary organisations, educational institutions, activist groups, grass roots or community based organisations and even government programmes. When assessing the resources of women in Panchayats, therefore, we should think of. the synergistic combination of these elected women and the support organisations outside the Panchayats as a continuing source of their potential strengths.

The example of Mahila Samakhya is only one of such efforts made in various parts of India to forge a link between women in the community and the elected women in the Panchayats.

Through the formations of village level collectives of women, Mahila Samakhya provides a continuing source of support to the elected women. The *sanghas,* in fact, become a reference point for the elected women, as they can take all the issues relating to governance to these collectives. Validation and legitimacy are provided to the elected women through this agency. This ensures that the interests of poor women are watched over. The Swayam Shikshan Prayog works in Maharashtra, partnering with community women's groups and Panchayati Raj institutions. Again, this synergistic link helps the elected women to get into the gendered debate on credit, violence, health, education, etc. at the community level. These interactions also help the community women's groups by enhancing their knowledge and awareness about the electoral processes of local governance. There are countless other efforts of this type which are too numerous to be recounted here.

The short point that is being sought to be made here is that planning at the grass roots level can be entrusted to the elected women even at this rather fragile and indeterminate stage of the devolution of State powers and functions to the Panchayats, in view of the availability of strong support organisations in the field. Perhaps women can lead the way, by transforming and transmuting the macro-level commitment of earmarked funds via the Component Plan through the nuts and bolts of local level planning to achievements on the ground.

## PART IV

### THE KERALA CASE STUDY (PEOPLE'S PLANNING CAMPAIGN)

Among the States which have progressed ahead *vis-a-vis* others in the devolution of powers, finances and function to the Panchayats are Kerala, West Bengal and Madhya Pradesh. The following is a case study based on a brief summation of the Kerala experience from a gender perspective. (Prepared by Aleyamma Vijayan of *Sakhi*, Trivandrum, 2000)

Kerala has gone a step further than the other States. Not only has it devolved 40 per cent of the budget directly to the Panchayats and urban local bodies, it has also earmarked 10 per cent of these devolved funds for projects exclusively for women, that is, for projects which directly benefit women.

The macro-context in which the government took these initiatives was the general environment of disillusionment with what came to be known as the Kerala model of development in the seventies. Though Kerala has a high human development index (HDI) notwithstanding its low per capita income, as evidenced by high literacy levels, low birth rates, high life expectancy and low infant mortality, the State has been performing very poorly in its economic sectors, mainly agriculture and manufacturing. The adverse economic repercussions include economic stagnation, very high levels of unemployment and budget deficits. On the social arena, there was increasing incidence of violence against women and high/increasing suicide rates. There were also sharp regional and intra-district inequalities as well, which were leading to social tension .

Another disturbing feature of this most literate State in the country is the very poor participation of women in formal political institutions and processes. The highest percentage of women in the State assembly never exceeded 10 per cent The position of women in decision making in trade unions, political parties, service organisations was even worse.

A year after the elections under the new State Panchayati Raj Act took place in 1995, the Left Democratic Front government was voted into power. It was decided to mount a campaign strategy to make the decentralisation process into a popular programme. The lead was taken by the Planning Board, where a cell was created to oversee the activities. Against 990 Gram Panchayats, 152 Block Panchayats and 14 district Panchayats, 3,954, 564 and 105 women respectively, won in the elections.

Local level planning was initiated in the wards, that is, at the sub-Gram Panchayat level. (Kerala Panchayats had high population densities, average being above 25,000). The Ward Sabhas met mandatorily twice a year and arrived at a consensus on what their needs are and how the resources could be mobilised. With the help of expert committees at the Panchayat level and development seminars, each Gram Panchayat prepared a development report which were then transformed into project proposals. These projects were then sent to the district planning committee for approval. The funds were directly passed on to the local bodies. A voluntary technical core team operated at each Panchayat level, to ensure technical feasibility and financial viability of the projects.

The positive indicators of women's participation, based on four years' experiences with Panchayati Raj in Kerala, are as follows:

- Women participated in Panchayati Raj not only through their candidatures for elections, but as convenors of task forces, as key resource persons etc.
- Women attained a degree of visibility that had not been there before.
- There was general acceptance and recognition of the roles played by the women and the work done by them.
- The Planning Board included topics and issues relating to women in the training schedules right from the beginning. The training handbooks brought out by the Planning Board contained directions to involve women in execution of development projects. A minimum 30 per cent quota was prescribed for women's participation in the training programmes at all three levels.
- The Planning Board played a pro-active role in ensuring that the expenditure on women's projects did not fall below 10 per cent from the second year onwards. The Board ensured this by placing an embargo on all sanctions by the District Planning Committees unless the expenditure on women's projects reached the minimum prescribed. The Board thus played the role of a watchdog to ensure women's interests.
- The Board prescribed a mandatory gender impact assessment when carrying out cost benefit analysis of all projects.
- Special efforts were put in to ensure good participation and involvement of women in the Gram Sabha meetings.

- A special effort was made to mobilise poor women through the agency of the Anganwadi workers.

The negative indicators of the experience are as follows :

- In spite of all-out efforts, the participation of women in the Gram Sabha never exceeded an average of 20 per cent. The women who attended these meetings mostly belonged to the economically backward classes.
- In the Gram Sabha meetings, the women generally attended concentrated in the women's development group only, or the groups in charge of social inputs like water, sanitation, education, etc. in spite of the fact that there was no such restriction on their attendance.
- Lack of data on women inhibited the preparation of a comprehensive development report on women. This was in striking contrast to the reports written on the other sectors, where collection of data was successfully done, with full involvement of the members.
- Women's attendance in the training programmes was disappointingly low. There were many drop-outs.
- There was a lack of women resource persons, especially for training programmes at the lower levels.
- The preparation of projects for women suffered because of inadequate training on development and planning issues, lack of experts on gender and limited number of women volunteers. There was all-round lack of familiarity with the basics of gender planning.
- In the first year of the campaign, the preparation of projects for women, against the earmarked component of 10 per cent funds, was unsatisfactory. One view was that most of these projects could not be deemed to be women's projects. These projects included roads, bridges, sanitation, drinking water, minor irrigation and electricity. Others included beneficiary schemes such as animal husbandry, poultry etc., where, though the assets were in the women's names, there was no safeguard that the control or ownership was actually in women's hands.

- There were other systemic defects such as poor marketing, unsatisfactory health care cover for animals, etc.
- The elected women representatives carried a double and triple burden of responsibilities and work covering professional and household spheres. This greatly added to their stress. They had to face slander and criticism from families and outsiders. Many of them did not want to contest a second time for this reason.

**Conclusions reached in the Case Study**

*In Aleyamma's words*

"The experiences of Kerala shows that attempts to bring about effective and good governance does not automatically address the question of gender inequality.

"If good governance is about equity and equality, gender and gender equity has to be major concerns in development.

"For example, it is important to analyse how needs are perceived, voiced and understood? How resources are generated and allocated? How the differences of power and privileges between men and women influence upon this process?

"The last four years of experience makes it very clear that women as a group lack the social and economic and political power.

"The final control over resources and the decision making capacity is still with men. Many times in discussions, comparison is made between the scarce resources and whether it should be spent for drinking water or cycling for women!

"Many are aware of the issues of women but not of the potentials of gender-based planning and development.

"The experience in Kerala makes it very clear that just by decentralising power or allocating funds or putting certain mechanisms in place, gender equity cannot be addressed. Kerala has taken a step in the right direction but it needs conscious intervention to progress further. Patriarchy as a system has deep roots of society and sustained and long struggles, systematic intervention of all concerned persons, especially of women's organisations and movements only can bring lasting changes."

## Some Questions and Answers on the Kerala Experience

*What are the missing links (from the gender perspective) in the PPC (People's Plan Campaign) carried out in Kerala for the last four years? What are the conscious interventions that will have to be introduced to make the plan campaign stronger in gender articulation?*

1. Lack of ownership of the programmes by women in their collective strength. Who defines what are the projects which 'directly benefit women'? The formal involvement of women at the policy making level is minimal. The Planning Board itself does not have any woman member. Political space is still to be occupied by women in spite of their presence in the Panchayats in such large numbers.

2. Men are still the decision-makers. Women do not still enjoy political power. The women's projects are generally chosen by those in position of authority and deemed to be appropriate for women. In several places, where women made their choices, these were not implemented. Women wanted mobile libraries, it was not agreed to. When choosing self-defence training, women wanted to go the whole way in *karate,* up to the black belt. This was not deemed necessary.

3. Gender planning is both political and technical. It is not enough to incorporate women's needs into existing planning disciplines without re-ordering the context and the rationale of the current planning tradition. Neither the political nor the technical dimension is in evidence in the Kerala context. Therefore, the question of what constitutes a "women's project" within the "women's component plan" is left wide open. As one of the elected women put it, the money in the component plan is spent without understanding the "problems, needs, potentials and limitations" of women locally. The money is spent on pre-determined projects, artificially termed as "women's projects" by tagging on the word "women" (women' s cowshed, women's milch cattle) .

4. How do we introduce gender into local level planning? How do we ensure that women's entry into political life has empowered them?

Moving towards gender equality, as the 1995 UNDP HDR reminds us, is not a technocratic goal—it is a political process.

> HDRs have introduced some indices to help measure progress towards reaching gender equality. "These indices were useful since they gave an opportunity to develop more interesting ways of monitoring attempts towards equality than the usual breakdown of activities by sex and numbers in social indicators, such as literacy rates, infant mortality, etc." (Devaki Jain, 1999). But in the context of the countries of the developing world, it is necessary to go beyond these indicators and include, instead, indicators linked to certain characteristics of poor countries. Key issues such as disparities, unequal opportunities, access, participation (as differentiated from membership only), poverty, etc. would be used to evolve a gender audit mechanism which in turn would lead to better implementation and monitoring of locally planned programmes and their impacts.

Gender planning has been defined as a transformative planning tradition, which has as its goal, the emancipation of women and their release from subordination. While it is not a theoretical construct, nor has any universally applicable procedures or broad generalised assumptions, it does have components of planning practice, tools, methodologies, built on extensive research and literature on women and gender in the first and third worlds. (Carolyn Moser).

Some of the basic conceptual issues underlying gender planning tradition are the differentiation between sex and gender, between practical and strategic gender needs, between gender relations approach and women-in-development approach, etc. Many of the 'women's projects' taken up under the 10 per cent component plan for women cater to women's practical gender needs, but do not take things further. Thus, increased income generation for women may be at the cost of their increased drudgery, without bringing in any space for questioning the perpetuation of unequal sexual division of labour. The case study shows that opportunities for increasing women's income have been identified in such a way that women can combine them with household responsibilities! Questions such as ownership, control, management of assets were also not always addressed. If strategic gender needs had been addressed, the projects would have worked on different assumptions, while taking the acknowledged need for increased income by the poor women as a starting point. Similarly, access to Anganwadi centres by women was not ensured, though the construction of these centres was taken up under the women's component. Increased mobility for hitherto housebound women (through cycling) adds to women's self-confidence and power, which is a strategic gender need, but has been contrasted with the practical or basic need of drinking water by the general population. Above all, the fact that unspent money lying with the Panchayats at the end of the year was mostly from the women's component plan is clinching evidence of the gap in the gender planning input in the PPC.

Another issue of concern is the finding that while their participation in the PPC has drained many of the elected women (especially the younger ones) of their energy and time, that they suffered from mental tensions, had to put up with double and triple burdens, the system itself has not responded to this adverse impact. It is clear that the gender relations aspect is unfavourable to women in Panchayats and that the patriarchal forces have landed the women into a stressful situation. External support to the elected women has not been forthcoming. On the whole, however, the train blazed by Kerala by devolving finances to the Panchayats and further earmarking a percentage of these funds to women's development is unique in the current history of post 1991 decentralized planning.

*It combines the effort for effective decentralisation of planning to the Panchayats with the effort to earmark resources for women through the Mahila plan component approach at the grass roots level.* This strategy of combining the two elements will ultimately give more power to the women, place resources within their reach and ensure women's control over them for bringing political, social and economic change. But the absence of a gender strategy in the PPC is an inhibiting factor at present.

While the PPC women's "component" is closer to the people than the "Mahila component plan" introduced in the Ninth Plan by the Department of Women and Child Development and the Planning Commission, both need to bring women into power by correcting an unjust and unrepresentative system through sustaining the link between women and the political process.

## Conclusion

The chapter has attempted to describe the various efforts made in the last five decades to institutionalize planning for and by women in India, "to give it a local habitation and a name" by evolving mechanisms which are effective and sustainable. We have experimented with programmes and schemes grouped under categories such as welfare, community development, anti-poverty, to Action Plans which comprise of a range of programmes covering different activities, to the component or earmarked model of planning, where a mandatory percentage is set aside for women in general programme budgets. There have also been initiatives such as Mahila Samakhya and the Women's Development Programme (Rajasthan) which have followed vastly different strategies but have been taken up under the government budgets.

One feature of the scene traversed by this chapter is that we have looked primarily at the one instrumentality of "schemes", "programmes", and "projects". Planning, in the State lexicon, must yield programmes and projects, and these invariably deal with discrete activities.

Even here, we have concentrated on certain sectors, which the State has prioritised, such as those with income earning potential or social welfare sectors. We have not discussed housing, environment, even health or education (and many more). But the instrumentality of the "project" or the "programme" would still dominate in these areas as well.

The "special provisions for women and children" in Article 15(3), which prevails even over the gender equality provisions of the Constitution, is the fountain head of the "plans for women".

Hence, development planning "for plans, programmes, schemes, projects" has been put under the microscope here.

Under the State aegis, planning is done in the sectoral mode. The format of plan documents, the demand for plan funds, their allocation and distribution, all follow a sectoral approach. The implementing structures such as departments, technical bodies, field cadres, monitoring systems, are also designed along sectoral divisions.

Planning for women, on the other hand, need "integrative strategies" (Moser). This has been one never-ending search within the State systems, one that has yielded little good result. "Nodal agencies" or "national machinery" have been designated or set up to give chase to this ideal, but they have faced difficulties, which are of the nature of organisational barriers.

Within the State structures planning is more of a technical and administrative business. It is more management- managerial, techno-administrative, an exercise that has its own set of rules, jargon, its procedures, numbers, norms, guidelines, etc. It has its own internal logic and its justification. The links between it and the reality of women's lives are difficult to forge and preserve.

In other words, the milieu of planning is not woman- friendly. This refers to the whole milieu. The State efforts have been to find little oases, or corners, which will have a different ethos, within the gigantic apparatus of the State.

Yet, the State has persevered and gone ahead, may be haltingly and slowly, often repetitively and routinely. What is most urgent is for the planners to realise that planning is political and not merely "technical". That the "end- product" is not a set of operational plans, targets and numbers, but the emancipation of women and their release from subordination through their own strengthening, their collective efforts. Schemes, targets, numbers, etc. can be only a means to the end product. This can take place, not only through material changes in the condition of women, but through a shift in the balance of power between not only men and women, but between the powerful and the less powerful and more marginalised and the excluded of which women form a major part. In spite of all efforts, "patriarchy, as a system, still defines the relations between men and women in society as well as the entire developmental process" (Nalini Nayak).

If the political roots of planning are to be restored, we need to shift the emphasis more to encouraging wider representation of women in all public institutions, community-based, representative, membership based, economic, social and others. Kerala, with its enviable social development indicators, has a very low participation of women not only in the State Legislative Assembly, but also in party structures, in trade unions, in professional associations, etc. This is a poser for those who equate literacy, awareness and political awareness with women's political strength and agency.

> In Kerala, where the PPC has become synonymous with the political party in power, hence a potent electoral issue, questions are being posed about the future direction of people's planning. "How can the gains of the first phase of this campaign be consolidated to counter consumerism and its consequences the people as a whole falling victims to the vagaries of the market place—apart from the evident objectification of women?" Hindu, 24th September, 2000). This sentiment was echoed by an activist who recently spoke of the contrast between the Kerala Planning Board's emphasis on the primary and secondary sectors in the PPC (in the interest of building up employment avenues) while the global and market forces were decimating whatever opportunities for work were still available in the State.

We recall Gandhi's words that the real change in India will come when women begin to affect the political deliberations of the nation.

We also need to recognise planning for women as a specific planning approach. Too often, women's plans have been an add-on, a component, grafted on the mainframe. Issues such as elimination of stereo types, ownership, access and control, abolition of unjust division of labour based on sex, drudgery, removal of discrimination, measures against violence, etc. are the basic conceptual rationale, the gender interests, which are rarely taken into consideration when preparing plans for women according to the current planning tradition. The problems which the PPC women's component faced in Kerala are an instance of how, even when decentralization, devolution, women's components, were all present, the absence of knowledge of gender planning showed up in the type of activities planned for women.

2

# ROLE OF WOMEN IN DECENTRALIZATION

C.P. SUJAYA AND DEVAKI JAIN

SECTION I

## Introduction and Summary

While much has been said and can be said about decentralization especially as conceived by the 73rd and 74th Amendment to the Constitution of India, and what it has done for women's inclusion in politics and administration; much more can be said and needs to be said about what women bring to the understanding and improvement of the system of local government.

Thus, this chapter argues that women's experience of local government and Panchayats cannot and should not be used only in a limited for gender focused way to enhance the participation of women; or to ease their way through the political undergrowth, or even to improve women's contribution to the Panchayat's product. It must be usefully utilized to redesign the very substance of the decentralization system and process.

What are some of these pointers that women's participation in local government in India are making? Given below is a summary of the items which have been identified by the women, the elected women, as points for attention. These will be further supported with references to studies, reports, meetings and several articles in the rest of the chapter:

1. While quota has in fact been an important breakthrough for women's participation in politics, it has also been able to yield, out of ground level experience, ideas for reform of the very system. An elected woman in Andhra Pradesh, at a conference called by the Department of Political Science of Osmania University in February 2000 said "the quota system for women has become a policy of reservation for men".

   What she meant was that beyond the 33-1/3 per cent reservation, all other spaces now are "reserved", i.e. held on for and by men (M. Meera, ISST, 2000). In other words, women are contained into that quota, and are not permitted to enter the unreserved constituencies because of the rules as well as because of the entrenched male power as part of a project to associate women politicians into a federation at the local level.

   At a consultation with elected members of the Zilla Parishad in Tumkur district, (Karnataka) convened by the SSF (Singamma Sreenivasan Foundation) May 2, 2000 in collaboration with the Tumkur Zilla Panchayat and the Chief Executive Officer, the vice-president of the Zilla Panchayat whose five-year term was over said that "Five years ago I was in the kitchen, and I only knew the four walls of the kitchen, today I am able to chair a meeting like this one and know how to handle administration and the public. Tomorrow I will be back in the kitchen for the rest of my life" — because the system devised for reservation namely the roster is such that she cannot be renominated to the same constituency or even renominated to stand for elections.

2. At consultations on May 2nd and 3rd, 2000 in Karnataka (Ref. SSF Report) women pointed to, what could be called, the hard core of entrenched political patronage systems which had been developed over decades and which still rule the political processes including selection of candidates, support systems etc. Thus one of the important aspects of women's advice to political processes in India is the need to reconsider the present

electoral system. They have many recommendations which need to be addressed to the Election Commission in its rules, procedures including to the People's Representation Act. "Women want to transform politics" (Revathi Narayanan, Mahila Samakhya, 2000).

3. Another area to which women's experience points and which can be considered more theoretical is the role of politics based on identity. Many women who have come through the quota, perceive themselves as representing the area and not necessarily women. While this attitude is legitimate, it also invites criticism as whether it is women. *Dalits* or backward caste, reservation is supposed to enhance the representation of that particular group be it women, *dalit,* backward caste or minorities. If the representatives or the person who takes that ticket does not necessarily identify themselves with that particular social category , it is perceived to be "unrepresentative". The question of politics based on "identity", its positives and negatives is debated in several layers of political discourse and this experience of local women politicians needs to be taken note of in the discourse. We need new yardsticks to measure performance. (Revathi Narayanan, Mahila Samakhya).

4. A fourth finding or pointer, in a sense, speaks to the earlier point but also contradicts it. Where women have found that they are able to assert their voice whether it is a voice for an issue or for woman kind, analysis reveals that this is either due to the effective availability and access to support structures such as proximate women's organisations, proximate women's awareness programmes or sustained interaction with training orientation programmes. (Mahila Samakhya, SEARCH, ISST) where they operate in isolation, they are truly alone. Thus the cushioning of the elected person whether it is *dalit,* woman or minority—by support structures derived from the same social categories, seems to be an 'enabling necessity'.

5. Further broadening this point, it also seems that for the voices of these groups which have had historical discrimination to have what can be called the transforming impact namely to redress

or rearrange the hierarchies in politics, the hierarchies of power, backup is necessary from the broader social and political movements or struggles. Struggles which are fighting for the rights of *dalits,* or women or displaced persons or tribals—socio-political struggles which attract the attention of the political leadership if they ally themselves with these groups who are fighting for a voice of these groups within the local government structures, can become more powerful. Therefore, the pointer here is to form an alliance between these political personnel and the broader struggles of power of the historically subordinated groups.

6. A sixth pointer coming out of the women's experience is one which has also been affirmed and elaborated by many of those who are working in the field of decentralized government, namely that the current structure of devolution is inadequate. In a brilliant paper, Nirmala Buch (ISI, April 2000) describes the fault line in the very Bill and Act which led to the 73rd and 74th Amendment. She points to the lack of clarity in the handing over of funds and powers for administration to the local government. Further (*Search* 2000) the only schemes which are truly in the hands of the Gram Panchayat are infrastructure schemes. Since this is all that is given to them, whether it is men or women, they are involved in the implementation of infrastructure. This has two flip sides. One, the limitation of not being able to participate in the design and implementation of social development and anti poverty schemes. Two, the accusation from the "non-believers" in Panchayat Raj that the elected representatives in local government are not interested in development but only interested in contracts because it gives space for corruption. A trap.

   It is interesting that in Kerala the people's campaign for decentralisation has in fact taken this point already on board in the sense that the science movement is the partner to the movement for decentralisation and in the districts, it is the members of the People's Science Movement and other volunteers who are providing technical services to the elected persons in their efforts to design and manage the funds which have been devolved uniquely in Kerala. However, the fault line in Kerala is that the movements which have been harnessed for enabling local government do not include the women's movement and other such struggles. Thus Kerala which is often acclaimed for its social evenness as reflected in the human development indicators and indices such as GDI and GEM is unfortunately notorious for the socially deprived status of its women.

Whether it is Suguna Kumari of the State Commission on Women or Aleyamma Vijayan of *Sakhi* or other social scientists and activists, the appalling powerlessness of Kerala's women, the high rate of suicides, the high rate of dowries, the low participation in leadership and governance, raises the significant question or the proposition that gender equity while it is a necessary condition, is not a sufficient condition to recast hierarchies of power-domination and subjugation. The relations of power, the scope for affirmation of rights, especially autonomy, and what can be called real equality are not completely provided by merely having equality in education, health status or even earnings.

The hard rock of patriarchy historically embedded, requires a greater knock than levelling social development. This is starkly revealed in the Kerala experience.

7. At another level of debate—where ideas such as subsidiarity are discussed, women's experience cuts across the "whys and buts". Proximity of place of work, of agencies of governance, of social amenities to place of residence, is clearly preferred by women for the obvious reason, that they are still (despite so many changes in rhetoric and perception), home-makers, careers. Hence a government, especially an elected council, a people's agency, proximity is an undiluted value. In addition, its powers in women's perception have to be broader and deeper, rather than distracted with conceptual constraints. For example, representatives of the anti-*arrack* movement in Andhra Pradesh recommended that the district government (Zilla Parishad in Karnataka) be imbued with judicial powers to arrest *arrack*

vendors, rather than go to a court (NCW 1996). Similar suggestions have come from other "sectors" such as those working to reduce domestic violence against women (ICRW 2000) or those working to provide social security including worker land security to home based workers, and others in the informal economy (SSA, 2000).

8. Women are pointing to the importance of working out the linkages between institutions outside of the local self government itself, such as cooperatives, trade unions, Mahila Mandals, other registered societies, educational institutions and sector specific associations and the elected body suggesting that these have to be more specifically worked out so that the skills of these agencies can be of use to the elected agencies. (Renana Jhabvala, SSA, New Delhi, 2000).

9. Women's experience is pointing to the need for new yardsticks to measure progress, new methods of using monitoring frameworks for stimulating progress towards social justice (gender Audit) monitoring frameworks, measures of equity and inequity as now being used are not adequate, nor appropriate for measuring the democratization of government.

10. The contradictions between local and global (WDR 1999) are also being "melted down" by women's efforts. In an area called Ulloor in Kerala, women had taken credit and started producing what are called basic consumer products like soap, processed foods—like pickles and *papads.* These conventional foods often get competed out in the market because of the larger food manufacturers, who have a better marketing and packaging skills and who invade all the super markets. I was surprised that they had survived. I was told by the District Collector, who is the civil servant in charge of a district, that they had survived and expanded because they were doing mutual support networking in the neighbourhoods. In other words, one neighbourhood group decides to produce certain items and the other neighbourhood group decides to only buy from them. So by making the production-consumption cycle amongst themselves, they have managed to quadruple their initial financial turnover

from 12,000 to 50,000 within one year on the basis of the first credit that was given to them in the beginning of the year.

Even the Collector and of course the economists who are doing research on this project, were surprised, as was I, because we all believed that producing conventional products like soap and semi-processed traditional foodstuffs, garments, leather bags, leather shoes from local leather would all be competed out by the mass produced goods in the markets.

11. People led, people centered localizing government — these terms and their aspirations, need the backing of stakeholders: and what is more stakeholders who are organized into collectivities who can make that claim, backed by numbers, — themselves and allies.

    Women more than men, by the very domain they occupy in the social and economic landscaped, have appeared as the most vivid, interested "parties" in this effort—from their own experience of working in the Panchayati Raj system in India.

12. International experience or the experience of other countries, reveal women's interest in proximate government, in quotas to ensure their presence (UNDP, International Conference on Women's role in politics, New Delhi, 1999).

In the following pages, we give evidence from a wide range of sources to support there propositions.

SECTION II

**Review**

There has been a quantum jump in women's representation in rural local bodies following the 73rd Constitutional amendment. From a miniscule 2 per cent to 4 per cent overall in the country, women have now reached impressive percentages ranging between 33 per cent to 40 per cent In terms of absolute numbers, they constitute a mind-boggling figure of next million. When the Constitution was being amended for this purpose, there were many non- believers as well as those who wanted to believe in women's roles in local governance, but had too many doubts, who scoffingly asked "But where are the women?" Today, we are told that hundreds of women in a few districts in Karnataka want to contest elections, have offered their candidatures, but have not been able to get into the fray for a variety of reasons related to the mechanics of the electoral process, but not for want of trying.

Could these women have entered these elected bodies in such a large numbers, without the reservations of seats, and there considerable pressure is put on the parties to field women candidates? There is evidence to suggest that women would not have entered the councils in these numbers were it not for this constitutional mandate. It was the pressure of national law, combined with the political imperative of winning elections, that changed political parties perception of women limited capacity for public office.

### PRI: Transforming Women

Women's experience of PRI has transformed many of them. The elements of this transformation include empowerment, self confidence, political awareness and affirmation of identity.

### Empowering Women

Women have gained a sense of empowerment by asserting control over resources, officials and most of all, by challenging men (Jain 1980, *Anveshi* 1993).

Men and their habits, long outside the relam of female influence, seem to be a major concern of elected women. For example, Deviramma, a 50 years old woman from the Golla or cowherd community, kept cattle and sold curd until recently. Today she is president of the Yeliyur Gram Panchayat, one of the 5,611 Gram Panchayats constituted in December 1993 under the Karnataka Panchayat Raj Act 1993. As quoted by Raj *et al.* ( 1995), she states:

> "If we are outspoken they, the men, call us brazen and dub us shameless. But now we don't care because we know we have access to people who will have to hear us. The day we have our Gram Panchayat meeting, the men and the people at home mock us—that's when we bring out books and show them what we know".

Nevetheless, Devirramma report that: "Our secretary , who is a male, doesn't let us talk at the meeting", a complaint that she has already made to the Deputy Commissioner. Similarly, 50 years old Subamma caste member of the Brahmasahra Gram Panchayat, she says (Rai *et al.*, 1995):

> "The men have always ridiculed us, and perceived us as incapable of the management of public affairs, we now make up one-third of the councils. This adds to our sense of strength. We must be 50 per cent or more. We must overpower them with our numbers."

Women are also aware that their strength comes not only from their numbers but also from their knowledge and skill, for example literacy. Thus, women see training as an important part of their empowerment. Many NGOs have sized on this as fundamental issue and have begun to focus on the training of women. Clearly this is necessary , but the danger of too narrow a focus is to suggest that it is only women who need training. What the presence of women politicians has done is to invert the conventional hierarchies as to who are the teachers and who are the taughts. Such women are making it clear that it is the male extension officers who need training, and not just the female representatives. This is an important message for donors and other funders of training, who have tended to assume in the past that the objects of their support must be women.

Women's empowerment challenges traditional ideas of male authority and supremacy. It is unsurprising, then, that PRI has been opposed by some men. Ratanprabha Chive (Ratna) is the Sarpanch (head) of the seven hamlets that comprise the Ghera Purandar Panchayat. Ratna was beaten up as soon as she assumed office by her rival who could not accept the fact that a female had outwitted him (Rai *et al.*, 1995). Today Ratna puts forward proposals in this male-dominated office and poses questions when she is unsatisfied. She says:

> "Whenever there is any tension in the villages, they come to me and I have learnt how to sort out the problem. Many people have realised that it is indeed a waste of time to make a complaint to the police chowki (station)."

She has launched programmes for adult education, digging wells for drinking water and repairing school building. She seems to have tackled the political and bureaucratic system which is complicated for a woman who has studied only upto standard seven (the public education system runs from standard 1-12). As Ratna says:

> "It is not the education that matters so much here. It is the grit and determination, which a woman has in plenty."

Self-confidence gained through belonging to local organisations seems critical to enabling women to step out of unequal relationships (Antrobus 1985; ISST 1992). This sense of freedom is even more profound when the group to which women belong is the PRI. This freedom is carried into the very activity of politics by these women. There is a visible difference, a sense of excitement, in the women of rural India.

> "We are better representatives than men, as we can always be found at home in the kitchen or in the nearby fields. Men wander about, they are either in the town or the beer shops."

Nagamma was an elected member, from a reserved constituency, but she won against a male scheduled caste member, which was a very unusual occurrence in the Panchayat Raj elections. The villagers in the area who were interviewed during this study were unanimous in their view that this woman was the most effective among all the female elected members of the Mandal, a view which was also shared by the Pradhan (the head of the village ).

Not all men have opposed PRI and the changes it has brought. Kultikori, a big village in West Bengal, elected an all-woman Panchayat in 1993. When it was time to decide on party candidates for the May 1993 elections, all the members of the male-dominated body stepped down. They asked their party, the CPI(M), to field the young women of the Ganatantrik Mahila Samiti (the women's wing of the party) who had done remarkable work in eradicating illiteracy in the village. The CPI(M) fielded women candidates in all 11 seats of the Panchayat, and they won (Rai *et al.*, 1995).

**Understanding Politics**

PRI has given many women a greater understanding of the workings of politics, in particular the importance of political parties. Vijayalakshmi was a Congress-I member of the Mandal, a homemaker, of Munnuru village. She wanted party politics be operated in the elections to Mandals because the party bureaucracy (at the State level) usually controls its members in the Mandals. Without the party, no one else would be able to control them. The party functionaries and the leaders are well-informed of the activities of the Mandal members, and they take some care to see that they function in such a way as not to jeopardize the outcome of elections, which since 1993, means that female members must be respected.

Kamalamma is a Scheduled Caste member and belonged to the Janata Party. She used to roll *beedis* to earn some money, and remained at home most of the time. She says: "The influence of the political parties is such that now persons from deprived groups have a better chance of being elected members. Earlier, only persons with money and of the upper castes could be elected to any position of importance".

## Affirming Identity

On the other hand, some women's involvement in PRI has helped them affirm their identity as women with particular and shared experiences. A woman at a Panchayat meeting in Karnataka stated (SSF 92):

> "When we meet we work together as women, for our lobby. We don't notice party identities."

Such women seem to be drawn to an identity above caste or party. This self- perception arises from two sources: from women's own sense of their shared experience and from attitudes and imagery imposed on them by the men. The men see these new political actors as women and not as party colleagues. Party politics, a necessary condition for classical democracy, is competitive, but the women bring a non-competitive or cooperative ethic as they are drawn to work together across party lines and seem to have similar interests. Gender can supersede class and party lines. Women have opened up the possibility for politics to have not only new faces but a new quality.

## Women changing Governance

PRI has helped to change local government beyond simply increasing the numerical presence of women. There is now a minority of women who are in politics because of their leadership qualities or feminist consciousness, for example, the women who were formerly part of the sanghas of the Mahila Samakhya Programme, an awareness-raising, group-based programme. Visible changes in the articulation of ideas and leadership qualities exhibited by this minority were noted in the survey between 1987, the first year, and 1990 (ISS, 1994). The difference women are making to local government is becoming evident in different priorities and different values (Jain, L.C., 1994).

## Changing Priorities

Some of the ways in which women, through PRI, are changing governance are evident in the issues they choose to tackle: water, alcohol abuse, education, health and domestic violence. For example, forty teams of women in Sonbhadra (Uttar Pradesh) area had carried out systematic *yatra,* or processions, covering ten villages each, or 400 villages in all, to explain the salient features of the 73rd Amendment and the place given in it to women. In the discussions that took place during these *yatras,* women voiced clear priorities. For nearly 90 per cent of the women, the top priority was water. They expressed a need for clean water for fields, for their cattle and for their families. They said life was unbearable and cultivation impossible. without developing the water resources of the area. Even as they were determined to prevent the outflow of water from their areas, they were equally determined to prevent the inflow of liquor into their area.

> "We have been ruined by liquor. We are being ruined day after day. The day's wages are drunk by the men-folk. There is no money for groceries hence no cooking."

Alochana, a centre for documentation and research of women in Pune, found that only two of the nine members in Bittargaon could sign their names. However, in this village which has a 16,000 population, Alochana found out that the women have "learnt to keep accounts from the local school teachers and the Gram Sevaks (rural workers). They have put an end to gambling and have come down heavily on liquor dens". The policy they adopted was to "shut the door on every drunken husband". Any protest made by them or children is met by physical assault.

> "We will not bear it, Once we acquire some position and power, we will fight it out, We know that it is not going to be easy because this battle will be carried out in each home. But the fact that the Panchayats will have a minimum number of women we will use that strength for mobilising women at large and keep liquor out, as a priority."

Women are also taking action against child marriage and child domestic labour, whilst promoting girl-child education, as is evident from the many success stories from Nellore, the heart of the successful anti-*arrack* struggle (Rohde 1994; Anveshi 1993).

But the enormous expansion of women's representation in decentralized government structures has highlighted the advantages of proximity, namely the redress of grievance and (most important of all) the ability to mobilize struggle at a local level where it is most meaningful, for example, the anti *arrack* movement.

> "We want education for our children. There are schools and teachers who draw their salaries regularly. They mark the attendance of non-existence students in their registers. But they scarcely come to the schools. With this sorry state of affairs, how can you have education for your children ? We are going to tell those teachers: either teach or go."

As with education, women have used their elected authority to address quality health care as a critical issue. In Maharashtra, the Indian School of Political Economy organised 60 workshops at Pune under the project of "Leadership Training for Rural Women". The chief conclusion of these workshops was that family planning, drinking water, schools and bio-gas plants are the priorities of women, rather than the TV set or temple (Manipal1994). Women too, have brought domestic violence onto the agendas of political campaigns. In theses and other ways, the issues women choose differ from conventional [illegible]tical platforms, which are usually caste/ ethnic/ religion-ba[illegible]

But not only do women choose different issues, they appear to choose less corrupt practices as well. Kogendranath Mohato. Panchayat secretary of Kultikori, says:

"The men I had worked under formally passed on their expenses in cigarettes and paan(betel) to the Panchyats, But the didies (sisters) here are not only clean on this score, they are more dedicated."

Women value proximity, whether it be to a drinking water source, a fuel source, a creche, a health centre, a court of justice or an office of administration. Poor woman have to walk to access these facilities. Which is exhausting and consumes valuable time. Moreover when there was an attack, a rape, a burning, a witch hunt or other violence against a woman, seeking redress from councils. Which are located far away, may not be feasible, But if these Councils and the people in them are near, the chances or redress and effective action are greater.

The decentralization of government structures has, however, been regarded with suspicion and anxiety by progressive groups. Decentralization can exacerbate lack of local resources and perpetuate regional disparities. It has often been misused by Central government to offload social security provision. It has also been misused politically by dictators or single authority regimes to control from the Centre through decentralized mechanisms.

But the enormous expansion of women's representation in decentralized government structure has highlighted the advantages of proximity, namely the redress of grievance and (most important of all) the ability to mobilise struggle at a local level where it is most meaningful, for example, the anti-*arrack* movement. Thus women critique of macro-economic policies is about equity, then what better responses can there be but to put political power in the hands of those most in equitably treated, namely women? In this sense, PRI may be conceived as a macro-political adjustment whose effects are felt at the micro-level.

Women are beginning to change not only the issues and values of governance but are also adopting different methods to those of men. They do not let official protocol stand in their way Narayanan (1993) recounts the story of one Panchayat official, Suman:

> "According to them (the officials) the area was not a catchment area and hence not suitable to construct a tank. They could not think anything beyond that. But Suman wanted to keep up her promise to the electorates of reviving the old tank. She mobilized necessary resources through other sources, and was able to fulfil her promise. After a good monsoon, the tank was flooded with water much against the scientific thinking of the bureaucracy."

SECTION III

## Some Questions and Answers

How well equipped are the women to take part in this act of administrative reconstruction? One unanimous feedback received from the field during the electoral experiences of the last six to seven years is that women have learned to look at themselves in a new light. They are more confident. (what does this mean, how is it seen and measured? A recent story heard is that elected women representatives from very poor communities have started using coconut oil to rub into their hair, and not remnants of used cooking oil as heretofore. (record of documentation committee meeting of KWIRC Project, (Laxmi Krishnamurthy's statement) Another woman (Susheela Kaushik's study of Haryana) said that even her adversary in the village has sent her an invitation to a marriage in the adversary's family. This was seen as a status jump. Other stories refer to *dalit* women raising their voices when talking to upper caste men of the same village, whom they would not have even dared to address directly in the past. Many other stories are available, which speak of personal transformations within the psyches of women as a consequence of working in local government).

Many women, when confronted with the question of their own capabilities, turn round and blame the external environment (their lack of powers, authority, financial resources, information, less exposure to training, etc.) for their not being more successful in their work—it i[illegible]ly that these have a poor self image of themselves as Pan[illegible] or Sarpanches; nor do they feel they do not have the inherent capability for carrying on the work of the Panchayats. They feel that if most, or at least some of these external constraints are removed, they would be able to function better, even

within the constraints of their social situation. These external constraints have been generally articulated as lack of co-operation and devolution of powers from the State, lack of finances, lack of information, lack of legal powers and authority and non-involvement (at the best) and enmity and friction of the local bureaucracy and Panchayat staff (Susheela Kaushik). The Haryana study showed an interesting correlation between women's feeling no change in status even after the elections to the non-devolution of powers from the State government. Some women in Haryana (same study) went further. They explained that they did not feel a rise in status after their elections but they felt it was because their husbands did not allow them to participate in the Panchayat meetings!
(In other words, their participation means their status rises)

Grass roots research have helped to invalidate the many myths that have sprung up in the last decade about the quality of women's participation in running the Panchayats.

Nirmala Buch (Women's Experience in new Panchayats: The emerging leadership of Rural Women—Occasional Paper No. 35, CWDS, 2000), surveying three large States of India, has produced figures of elected women's awareness and knowledge about Panchayat related matters, of elected men's and women's attendance in Panchayat meetings, on weekly time spent by elected men and women in Panchayat work, on efforts made by women representatives to solve problems presented to them in Panchyats, on efforts made by the elected women to carry their view point in meetings, etc. Her findings are that the level of participation of women is quite high, while not reaching the performance levels of the men. In the three States (Madhya Pradesh, Rajasthan and Uttar Pradesh), for example, the women's attendance in the Panchayat meetings ranged from 55.5 to 74.4 as against the men's attendance range of 68.7 to 95.6. The findings relating to the other quality aspects of women's work, similarly, brought out that women were by no means laggardly, ignorant or lazy. Majority of the women surveyed had a good awareness level and knowledge about the working of the Panchayat. A substantial proportion of the women devoted time to Panchayat activities. In order to argue their views strongly and to convince the Panchayats in the meetings, they took other members into confidence, held informal discussions, repeated these efforts, took help of others, including husbands, etc.

A study from Tamil Nadu (Women's Participation in Panchayati Raj: A case study from Tamil Nadu—V.B. Athreya and K.S. Rajeswari, paper presented at the IX National Conference on Women's Studies, 8-11 January 2000, Hyderabad) where the sample was 100 women from District Panchayats in two districts, showed that 95 per cent of the women studied, stated that they had actively participated in the meetings. Sixty-three per cent of the women responded that they also spoke in community meetings and put forward suggestions.

Elected women keenly feel the lack of what is termed (for want of a better and more inclusive word) "training" or "capacity building". They invariably express their felt need for this type of support. Wherever elected women have received the benefit of innovative training and support, their performance has exceeded expectations, collectively, as a group.

Swayam Shikshan Prayog, which works in Maharashtra with grass roots women and communities on issues of economic empowerment and local governance, reports that alliances between elected women and women's collectives, which are strengthened through focused training, result in new institutional arrangements for improved governance. As a result, women are participating in village assemblies and Gram Sabhas in larger numbers, demanding greater accountability from all elected members. Village women and elected members participate in dialogue platforms at Block and district levels so as to give feedback to local officials. SSP believes that capacity building exercises should involve State officials and planners so that they recognize women's capacities to participate in governance.

Mahila Samakhya in Karnataka, has provided an accountability mechanism to the elected women who were earlier, Sangha members. The elected woman treats the Sangha as its reference and validation point. Where the elected woman does not break her trust with the Sangha, she gets benefited, as the women of the Sangha constantly support her with information of what issues she should take up in the meetings of the Panchayats, what are the burning issues in the village/ward which affect the women collectively and which need intervention at the local government level. The Sangha guides the elected woman in this way, a hand-holding and step-by-step consultation process where the Sangha's collective energies are at the disposal of the elected woman.

The training efforts of RUWSEC based in Chingleput, Tamil Nadu, helped the elected women to prioritise reproductive health concerns of the women in the community. Such a concern for their own bodies and reproductive matters did not come naturally to them. Women are used to neglecting their bodies because of their own perceptions of low value attached to their bodies. The training received has now challenged the elected women to think of activating the Panchayat structure to make it accountable to the people.

Do the elected women affirm their collective identity as women, do they push for a women's need-based agenda and programme? There appears to be a quality difference between the priorities of elected men and elected women. Dr. Shanta Mohan (National Institute of Advanced Studies) found that the elected men wanted immediately "do-able" things such as taking up construction activities, building of local infrastructure. These items were not only visible, they were costly and caught the attention of the public quickly. The elected women wanted different things, they could be lack of water, dealing with alcoholism in the area, increasing the access of children to schools, coping with domestic violence and marital conflict. She found that generally, the women's prioritized programmes had a longer time perspective than those of the men. The immediacy and the visibility of the men' s suggestions, however, generally carried the day and, therefore, she found that the men's programmes generally subsumed those of the women.

Anti-liquor campaigns in Haryana and Andhra were spear-headed by women. 84 out of 100 women in Haryana who were studied by Susheela Kaushik, proudly said that they took up the liquor issue in their constituencies and Panchayats.

Is there a danger of women being type-cast, or getting stereo-typed as a "woman Panch"? One Zilla Parishad Pradhan in Haryana said (Susheela Kaushik) "Women can only speak to women". Whom do women represent? Sutra in Himachal found, somewhat to their surprise and concern, a commonality in elected women's perceptions just after they were elected. The women felt that they represented only the ward in which they stood for elections. They did not feel responsible for the Gram Panchayat as a whole. They were wary of stepping into the other wards. They called themselves 'ward members' and not Panchs or members of the Panchayat. Similarly, do women feel that only women's issues should concern them?

The evidence from the field is a resounding no. Women may not yet have the space to think out their own priorities slowly and carefully, but they have no intention of getting type cast. But here, the dominant culture of Panchayati politics and administration also play a role, both for shaping men's as well as women's day-to-day 'bread and butter issues'.

ISEC study (1982) on Panchayats in Karnataka in fact, showed that both men and women elected representatives, spent more time on items of infrastructure such as roads, lighting, drainage, other civic amenities than on more basic concerns, say, poverty or employment creation or micro-planning.

Many other studies show that women are not really happy to be restrained into a 'woman-and-child' folder or box. They would like to be involved in all the activities in the Panchayat. It is another matter and a rather significant one at that, that mostly all Gram Panchayats as well as the other two tiers are given the responsibility of infrastructure works rather than planning and development of the Panchayat as a whole, or social justice or employment or agricultural, horticultural or animal husbandry production. The old habit of entrusting only local civil or physical works to the Panchayats is still very much around.

Thus the working orientation of the Panchayats in general, has had the inevitable effect on the elected members, both men and women. There is an overwhelming focus on 'village works' being taken up. This prevents the women (and the men) from getting into the more crucial area of planning for the village as a unit, into the complexities of natural resource management, etc.

But here and there, we hear of many women being led by their intrinsic concerns with depleting resources. *Uma Prachar* [September 1995] recounts the story of an elected, member of a Gram Panchayat in Bangalore (Rural) who is also, simultaneously,

President of a local self-help thrift group as well as a member of the Water Management Cooperative Society involved in a participatory tank rehabilitation scheme since many years. This woman is deeply concerned with the degradation of village resources and sees clearly that the *gomal* cannot support grazing activities much longer, since the vegetation, the trees, etc. are fast disappearing. According to Madhav Gadgil, [see interview in the same issue of *Uma Prachar*], the village level institutions [i.e., the water management society, in this case] should be properly linked up to the Panchayati Raj institutions. It is the concern of women over the fast depleting natural resources, [water, trees and grass] that can bring in these different frames of reference and these institutional linkages into action and planning.

In a study of Rajasthan Panchayats and women's participation in them (1995, ISST), it was found that elected women and village women have responded to mobilisation round food, water, work, housing, violence, etc. This study notes that there are more women's groups in Rajasthan than men's groups or mixed groups.

Another story from Andhra Pradesh, to show the synergy that is created with the linking of different institutions through the agency of women. The concern here is food security in a poverty context. Neela Mukherjee stresses the point that the indigenous knowledge about the varied dimensions of food-livelihood security lies with the local communities. It is the local-level Panchayat which can initiate and implement plans along with the local community for appropriate interventions in approaching food-livelihood security at the local level.

Women's good management of grain banks has been exemplified in the experiences of Agragamee in Kashipur and Gram Vikas in Kalahandi, both in Orissa, a State vulnerable to food shortages and natural calamities.

A poor semi-literate woman farmer, who is the Sarpanch of the Gram Panchayat in Medak District has built up an impressive food security scheme in the village with the help of an NGO which has encouraged the setting up of Sanghams, or women's organizations. She became a member of the Sangham and attends the weekly meetings regularly. Thus, a three-way relationship has developed amongst the Volag, the women's group and the PRI.

'Food Security and Panchayati Raj', pages 219-221)

The women's movement has the biggest stake in building up powerful and dynamic leadership of women in Panchayati Raj Institutions. The 'empowerment' of grass roots women (though the word itself was coined later) has been an imperative with the women's movement ever since the renewed debate on the women's question started in the seventies. The debate threw up various models of grass roots organizations, of which one of the important were the Mahila Mandals, which had been legitimised by the government already, in the Community Devlopment programme. But they were seen as inherently weak in both functioning and coverage.

In 1974, when the Report of the Committee on the Status of Women recommended statutory all-women's Panchayats, it was as a transitional measure to ensure greater participation by women in the political process, especially in the area of development planning. This suggestion did not find favour and today, all women's Panchayats are found in very isolated numbers, in just a few States. (Grass Roots Empowerment (1975–1990) A discussion paper by N.K. Bannerjee, CWDS)

Today, a large number of women's organisations and women's Volags support the elected women in Panchayati Raj structures, mainly in the areas of capacity building and awareness raising. Compared with the lakhs of women who are holding elected office, even these efforts are very thinly spread. Nirmala Buch has found that the training resources go in a reverse order to the actual training needs the village Panchayats get the least, the intermediary level gets more and the district Parishads take the lions' share (Marg Workshop). The voluntary sector has, on the whole, been successful in forging linkages with the elected representatives. The other movements such as the trade union, the workers' movements, etc. are able to find linkages only through the committed work of voluntary organizations or when they themselves act as link organizations.

Neither the women's lobbies nor any of the other people's movements or the workers' movements or campaigns have been able to prevail upon the State in the form of a sustained force or campaign, to fulfil the constitutional commitments it has made in

1993 of turning Panchayats into effective units of local government. This is perhaps the biggest failure of the movement.

The basics of "planning from below", that is the crucial exercise of integrating the plans prepared by the Panchayats at district level into a district plan, has still not got off the drawing board. Pointing out this as a very serious gap in the Ninth Plan between commitment and practice, D. Bandhyopadhyay terms it as a "wilful disregard of the third tier of governance at the district level". ["Planning from below–Is Planning Commission Performing its Role?" *EPW* March 18, 2000] Many of the elected women have echoed their unhappiness on the irrelevance and uselessness of many of the schemes and the general lack of congruence between them and the needs of the villages (Asha Ramesh's study). It is not just a change from co-option or nomination to election, that has taken place in the quality of women's representation. A change in mind set has taken place in the country between the fifties and the nineties on what exactly Panchayats stand for. It has been summarised as a change from the search for a more efficient delivery system to a basic change in administration, whereby a non-representative autocratic and bureaucratic regime is being replaced with a representative and responsive elected system of governance. [D. Bandhyopadhyay–*(Man and Development)*, December 1999] "Exercise of power was downwards and the nominal accountability upwards". This was sought to be reversed.

The unwillingness to part with power is nowhere more graphically illustrated that in the institution of the district collector and the collectorate. The 73rd amendment to the Constitution has brought in a third tier of government, below the State government. But no review or redefinition of the collector's role *vis-a-vis* the Panchayati Raj institutions has taken place so far. The collector has so far, since the British era, been the "pivot of the district administration". But with so many functions having been now decentralized and devolved under Article 243 of the Constitution, a new look at the old institutions is very much over due. (*Pioneer*, 4th December 1999, *Collector versus Panchayat* by Rahul Arun and Samir Arun.)

Another upcoming debate is whether "decentralization" as a

concept, takes us far enough. Writing in the *Hindu* on this theme, Vinayak N. Srivastava points out that "decentralisation" refers only to the transfer of 'functions' and not transfer of 'power' whereas "devolution" encapsulates transfer of functions as well as of powers. ("Decentralisation without devolution is meaningless" *Hindu*, 23rd February 1999)

The framework of the Act and Rules of the Panchayat can be tested on the touchstone of women's experiences, especially in those States where the second elections have taken place. Euphoria has given place to disillusion. The roster, first hailed as an effective mechanism to bring in large numbers of women into the electoral fray, is now being exposed as vulnerable to misuse, to the disadvantage of women. Large numbers of women who have completed one term, are unable to continue their engagement with local governance. (meeting of 3rd May)

The Act has been used as a "hold all" or a portmanteau to push in the government's priorities. The small family norm has been introduced to the greater disadvantage of women rather than men. More than half a dozen States in India have introduced this into the statutes. There are stories of men divorcing their wives, of families giving children away in adoption. (reference either *Marg* or *ISST*, to find out)

The "no confidence motion" is a black law that is contained in most of the State Acts. The women and the *dalit* Sarpanches have been at the receiving end. In Maharashtra, the law is so obtuse that the Sarpanch's vacancy caused by a woman sarpanch being asked to leave as a consequence of the no confidence motion, does not go to another woman for the remaining part of the term. It invariably goes to a man. (Rohini Gawankar in her Hyderabad paper)

In Karnataka, the posters put out by the government wrongly show that the seats not reserved for women, as per the roster, in the recently concluded Gram Panchayat elections, are 'reserved' for 'men'. The fact that women can offer their candidature against open seats along with men, is just suppressed by the election. machinery. No campaign has been mounted by local groups against this type of insidious propaganda by the organs of the State. (personal communication from Asha Ramesh).

Meera Saxena, Secretary, Women and Child, GOK, in the meeting on 20th March 2000 (SSF), hinted at field officials wanting only 'somewhat' literate women alone being made eligible to stand for elections. The failed experiment of restricting eligibility to contest elections to households having a latrine brings out the same tendency to use the Act to restrict the benefits to the asset-owning class. Women, who are at the bottom of the heap, have to constantly keep running if they have to stay at the same place.

Mainstream policies, such as those on population, total literacy, legal reform and others, proceed along conventional lines of reasoning and thinking.

## SECTION IV

The chapter has deliberately been called 'Role of women in decentralisation' and not 'experience of women in local self government' because we wish to make a larger point. We have already mentioned one aspect of this larger point, namely that women have been influencing the understanding and direction of decentralisation, that women are perhaps the stronger stakeholders in decentralisation. But what we wish to add here is to broaden the argument to include the discourse, even at the global level.

Some of the skepticism about local government and its value in terms of improving the possibility of achieving development with social justice; or put in another way, eradication of poverty and access to development rights by the 'people' etc. has been because of negative experiences, almost worldwide. Whether it is (Pinochet Chile, Ayub Khan Pakistan, Zia Bangladesh, Ujaama Nyerere, Commune China and many more) there have been hidden motives, or fault lines, where the local becomes a pawn or a system in order to strengthen central control; and in India the basic critique is that the civil servants, the bureaucracy and the politician at the higher level of elected council , are unwilling to disable their positions of power, patronage and direction this alliance with struggles for power, for wresting power from the traditional bastions becomes crucial for the achievement of the stated goals of local government, namely a more participatory and perhaps more efficient if not more equitable system of government. The notion of enabling power to develop at the local level has been abused. There have been hidden agendas and these have put people including those who have commitment to the idea of people led government of the idea of localising power into a skeptical mode. Other arguments are well known such as local is more conservative and central is more progressive. Feminists are worried about highly localised governance, as it gives space for conservative cultural, traditional attitudes and practices to be exercised at the village and community level.

These anxieties are genuine and to them one can also add, from the Indian experience, many negative notes. In the Indian case, as has been pointed out almost *ad nauseum,* devolution has not really taken place and most of the State governments have found innovative back door means to obstruct the localisation of government. The list of such experiences have been recorded in other forums of the same seminar, namely, bureaucracy and its unwillingness to hand over its patronage, State level and national level politicians unwilling to hand over patronage, the skepticism that elected persons do not represent the poor or the subordinate and in women's case that they are proxies for men. A further allegation is that local politicians do not necessarily represent local interest but sectional interest, which are nothing more than a clone of the problems at the national level.

Other scholars have pointed out the complete lack of devolution of development funds and schemes to the local government. Except for Kerala, no State government has passed on its development funds to be actually designed and implemented by local government. A study by Dr. Vinod Vyasulu made of two districts in Karnataka also emphasizes the impotence of the district in carving its own development. A report that was submitted to the Karnataka State Planning Board by one of the authors of this chapter, Devaki Jain, who was the Chairperson of a Sub-Committee set up by the Government of Karnataka to look at district level planning for social development also pointed out that not only were there no devolution of finance, but the departmental schemes which try to reach out to the village were so multitudinous and so tied up with the departmental accounting systems, that no locally elected body could possibly have any space for design. This Committee made several significant recommendations ranging from the importance of rationalizing the schemes to the importance of giving what is called untied funds, to be utilized by the elected body. This is what Kerala has already done namely to give funds to the locally elected body and have them design it for their own use with the help of volunteers. Unfortunately in Karnataka, even though this recommendation was made and the P.R. Nayak Committee on Panchayati Raj also recommended the same procedure, the State government has continued to hold all the strings in its hands.

A study conducted by the ISEC in Bangalore on an experiment to give funds without specification to the Gram Sabhas has revealed that the choices made by a local council have not only greater relevance, but also mobilize greater resources than when a scheme is handed down–("Gram Panchayats have the wisdom to manage their own funds", *Indian Express*, dated April 16th, 2000)

Thus it could be argued that by and large the aspiration of localizing government has not been achieved, except perhaps with a few flaws in Kerala.

Yet in the World Development Report 1999, the themes are local and global and economist such as Stiglitz laud the importance of people led government, which means local self-government. They argue that it is only local led government which can be efficient, which can provide growth with equity, which can reduce disparities, which can provide the institutional framework for globalization with justice. However, the same document also flags the importance of a liberalized political economy without showing the design by which a federation of local self government can in fact be a challenge to the careless invasion of globalization into a country.

The importance of participation by 'People' is highlighted in the WDR 1999, in Stiglitz 1998, in Bhagwati 1999, in Norgaard 1999 and the Human Development Report 1999. The intention of this inclusion may vary from those who see it as more just, to those who see it as promoting more efficiency, to those who are interested in preventing breakdown and civic instability. But the accommodation of "people" is seen as a necessary component even for the hard headed single mind, "growth" generation. The 1999 WDR has two pillars, globlisation and localization. is valuable for participation, and for the *Ownership,* claiming what Stiglitz talks about. But as the report also admits, globalization disconnects with the "local" often trampling over it. Localization can create problems for what is called national consensus on say the fiscal deficits. And yet national consensus on such items as fiscal deficit is almost a necessary conditions for the foreign Direct Investments (FDI) and Multinational Corporation (MNC).

Yet, there is an example from the State of Kerala in India, where women's groups have actually dealt with this disjunction and used localization to deal with what are called the market forces of globlisation.

Responding to this black hole in the discourse on decentralisation, the importance of local government, four institutions in the four States of southern India have set up a programme to build a Federation of local women politicians—a clone of the Indian Federation of Women Lawyers or Women Journalists. This will be a Southern Indian Federation of Women politicians in local government.

It is hoped that through such Federations such collectivities of political personnel who have a freshness, and a stake in redesigning development there will be one more important actor to pull down State structures which are impeding local government.

It is hoped that this Federation will also inform itself of not only technical skills like budgeting, designing fiscal policy, utilizing funds such as the component plan for women, use new promoting framework like the Gender Audit but will start a process of revisiting or redesigning development with women. It might be called women designing or redesigning development planning and implementation through the local self government institutions (see SSF Project Report)

The Gender Audit, a module a Proforma which can be used every three years (or two years) by the local administration to collect fresh data on some crucial variables, derive indices like from them, which can monitor development impact. G-D-I & G-E-M disparities (SSF : the gender audit 2000). Thus audit can be made into a *dalit* audit also.

It is such initiative which might in fact "pull up" Local government into a key player in development with social justice.

**Notes**

In Kerala, they have launched in support of their local self-government programme a people's campaign for preparing a five year plan. There is a gazette notification by the State government to this effect. The elements of people's campaign are as follows:

- They have formed neighbourhood associations, called in Malayalam, 'Ayil Koottam'. 'koottam' is gathering. Neighbourhood gatherings which take place almost every week.
- They have employed resource persons from the area, retired school teachers, engineers, nurses, civil servants, functionaries, even students, post graduates working towards their Ph.D., unemployed as volunteers.

There are key resource persons, conveyors of neighbourhood groups, members of task force. For every village which could be in Kerala a population of 10,000 to 15,000 there is a Panchayat, namely a local elected body with these 'enablers' who are the volunteers.

The neighbourhood group discusses what they think are their needs, the issues in terms of development and sets out a plan of action. Every month, the Conveyor and co-conveyor of the neighbourhood group meet together in something like a conference at the village level, in which they are divided into task forces according to sector. Then in the afternoon, it is summated by the chairperson of the Gram Panchayat. The minutes of this conference are then carried forward to a district level meeting for district planning, convened by the chairperson who is an elected person and that prepares the district level plan. Parallel to this process of designing what are called the nuts and bolts of development, namely budgetary allocation, there is a process of accountability. If a particular work, what is called civil works has been sanctioned after this process, the actual detailed expenditure allocations are written by hand in a big chart and nailed to a tree; wherever the neighbourhood group meets, as well as on all the boards of the Panchayat for everyone to see what is the expenditure. Second, there are beneficiary committees in every village. We have what is called BPL which is "below poverty line", where we define the poverty line as being something like US $ 150. The Beneficiary Committees are composed only of these BPL households and individuals. They decide who should have the priority in getting the benefits of a development programme, whether it is an animal, a house, credit, pension, according to the budgetary allocations under these heads. In other words, the beneficiaries decide on what they want as benefits and in the order of ranking in terms of who comes first.

One of the resource persons I met is a man who owns and runs a private college for 700 students. He comes from the area which is a tribal hilly area. I asked him why he is doing this full time unpaid job. He said he loves it because it makes him feel he is participating in a social justice movement. He in turn is a product of another movement which took place in Kerala, which is the People's Science Movement. The People's Science Movement (KSSP) was one of those "walks" which is very common in India, where a leader decides to walk *(padayatra)* from one part of a province to all over the province with some message, stopping overnight as a guest with free hospitality for himself and his fellow marchers. Gandhi's salt march which many of you have seen on the screen, Vinoba Bhave's land gift *(bhoodan)* walk are part of our tradition: as I know they are of yours. The great march of your kings and chiefs.

This march for the KSSP carried with it scientific knowledge, —knowledge about land, water, traditional medicine, both natural resource and technological skills. They would stop in villages and demonstrate through posters, talks, audiovisuals and as they moved from place to place, more people gathered to join them. It was of course a political ideology driven movement namely to level up knowledge and ensure that science and technology should not be the privilege of the technocrats and the elite. That shared information on scientific and technical knowledge can be the most powerful tool for people for building equity .This movement was so successful that it inspired a national movement called the Literacy Movement in India, which was also one of those, walks, where the movement believes in what is called peripatetic or mobile 'march' type processes to mobilize people.

Most of the "volunteers", resource persons whom I met were people who had come out of these movements and who had seen both the effect of this movement on those for whom it was meant, but it also inspired them to stay with it, as it was to them, a way of serving the people. Three post graduate students joined a neighbourhood group when I was there, and this neighbourhood group was mainly composed of women, who seem to represent all the classes that we have in rural areas, from the very rich to the very poor, including the single old woman who is the widow, left behind by everybody else. I could not believe that 100 such women could sit and listen under a tree for nearly one hour in sweltering heat of 40 degree centigrade to a man who was explaining to them a new programme called '*kutumba sthree*', i.e. woman of the household.

This programme is a financial assistance programme where if a group of women, minimum ten, decide what they would like to do, the district level government will give them all the necessary support—finance and technical help. I asked these three young men who were sitting there, who they were. They said 'we are local students'. I asked them 'why are you here'. They said that 'we are interested in seeing that these programmes are put on the ground. We are inspired by the enthusiasm of the people to learn and to do and we would like to be involved in that'.

Some of the innovative projects that the beneficiaries have chosen and which the district elected persons had implemented were even for me, first time. For example, one women's group was running a tiny 'hotel'. Hotel in India does not necessary mean residential accommodation, but something more like a cafe. They were giving coffee, tea and one square meal, It was run by a group of "BPL" women. The local government had given them money for putting up a small building on private land and the owner of the private land had leased it out for five years at rent which the women paid out of their profits. This shack or the little building: was the grant given by the local government. Within two months, the cafe was beginning to attract 100 customers a day. The customers were drawn by the fact that when women run a kitchen, it was assumed that the food would be tasty and would be 'authentic'. The woman who was keeping the accounts was a nurse and she had given up a lucrative nursing job and joined these other nine women to run the 'hotel'.

Another was there a women's group packed into a bag all the ingredients that were required for the seasoning of food for a family for one week. There were little packets of all these spices including the Indian favourite red chilly. These packets were sold for 15 rupees, which is 30 cents of a US dollar and was vended on a bicycle in a basket. Housewives found it a great relief just to pick up that packet, rather than to struggle for the small quantities they require for their weekly needs of about 8 or 9 'spices' or condiments.

## REFERENCES

Ambika Menon, Thirteen–*Women, Food Security and Panchayati Raj.*

"And who will make the *chapatis*?"–A study of all-women Panchayats in Mahrashtra, Edited by Bishakha Datta, 1998.

Arun, Rahul and Samir Arun, Collector *Vs* Panchayat–strengthen local self-governing bodies to increase popular participation in administration, *Pioneer*, 4 December 1998.

Asha Rarnesh and Bharti Ali, Towards Political empowerment -Profiling women elected to the rural and urban bodies in Karnataka and Gujarat.

Athreya V. B and K.S. Rajeswari, *Uma Prachar, Newsletter* -March -May 1995. Women's participation in Panchayati Raj : A case study from Tamil Nadu, paper presented at the IX National Conference on Women's Studies, 8-11 January 2000.

Bhave, Pushpa Censorship and Silençe Perspective on Freedom of Expression, Review of Women Studies, Ws-2, *EPW*, Vol XXXV, April 29th, 2000.

Bella Abzug and Devaki Jain, *Women Leadership and the Ethics of Development*, August 1996, Gender in Development Monograph Series #4, UNDP.

Banerjee, N.K Grassroot empowerment (1975 -1990). – A Discussion Paper– Occasional Paper No, 22-1995.

Buch, Nirmal Women's experiences in New Panchayat: the emerging leadership of rural women, Occasional Paper No. 35, 2000.

Changing the Text of Local Governance–grassroots women's leadership in governance–women and political participation 21st century challenges.

*Deccan Herald*, Hegde for consensus on women's quota bill, A newspaper clipping, May 17th, 2000.

Devaki Jain, Centre for Gender and Development Studies, University of the West Indies, Nuancing globalisation or mainstreaming the downstream or reforming reform, working paper No. 3, May 2000.

Devaki Jain, *Home Thoughts From Abroad*. University of Westville, Durban, May 15, 1999.

Devaki Jain, How Important is the Private Public Dichotomy —the case of the EWRs, Seminar–women in Panchayat Raj, 27-28 April 2000, New Delhi.

Devaki Jain, *Panchayat Raj — Women Changing Governance*, September 1996, Gender in Development Monograph Series #4, UNDP .

Devaki Jain, *Participation of Women in Panchayati Raj*, December 1998.

Garg, Mridula Word as Censor. Review of Women Studies, Ws-7, *EPW*, Vol. XXXV, April 29th, 2000.

Gayatri, A. Menon & Suranjana Gupta, From Margin to Mainstream - Building stakes in the SHG-BANK linkage Programme-*Swayam Shikshan Prayog*, October 1999.

Gopal K.S. and Shashi Kumar. Twenty- seven, *Towards A Village Food Security in Rainfed Areas : A Case Study.*

*Grassroots*–Vol. I. No. 4 (12). April 2000.

*Grassroots*–Vol. I, No. 3 (11). March 2000.

*Grassroots*–Vol. I, No. 2 (10). February 2000.

*Grassroots*–Vol. I, No. 1 (9). January 2000.

Gupta, Shashi Prabha *Fourteen Panchayati Raj–The Key to Food Security and Nutrition*, Minutes of the meeting of the documentation team–April 26th, 2000.

Kannabiran, Vasanth Censorship And Silence—Review of Women Studies, Ws-2, *EPW*, Vol. XXXV. April 29th, 2000.

Menon, Ritu Structured Silences of Women, Review of Women Studies, WS-3 - *EPW*, Vol. XXXV, April 29th, 2000.

Mukherjee, Neela *Ten -Food -Livelihood Security at the Community Level and Role of Panchayati Raj Institutions.*

*Panchayati Raj Update*, Institute of Social Sciences, June 1994.

*Panchayati Raj Update*, Institute of Social Sciences, September 1995,

*Panchayati Raj Update*, Institute of Social Sciences, July 1999.

Panchayats and Development Elite's *Vs* Dalits, *Man & Development*, December 1999.

Planning from Below Is Planning Commission Performing its Role?, *EPW*, March 2000.

Shikshan Prayog's, Note on Swayam Efforts with PRIs.

Sujaya, C.P. Towards a New synergy in Political Consciousness.–Paper (work in progress) prepared for associating elected women representative in PRI Institutions–one day consultations with Karnataka based organisation, March 20. 2000.

Thakkar Usha and Rohini Gawankar, Women Sarpanches–Empowered Or Disempowered ? (A study of women Sarpanches in Maharashtra).

Uma Chakravarthy, State, Market and Freedom of Expression: Women and Electronic Media, Review of Women Studies, Ws-2, *EPW*, Vol. XXXV. April 29th, 2000.

*UNDP*, Towards Just Development Identifying Meaningful Indicators, South Africa, 1999.

*Uma Prachar, Newsletter*, September 1995.

Vinayak, N. Srivastava, Decentralisation without devolution is meaningless, *The Hindu*, 23 February, 1999.

Volga, To Censor or Not to Censor: Film and Public Policy, Review of Women Studies, Ws-2, *EPW*, Vol., XXXV, April 29th, 2000.

3

# WOMEN IN LOCAL GOVERNANCE EXPERIENCE IN ANDHRA PRADESH

P. MANIKYAMBA

The revitalization stage of Panchayati Raj , which had set in the late 70s , brought about several structural and functional changes in the system. One significant change is the passing of the 73rd Constitutional Amendment in 1993 which provided for reservation of not less than one-third of seats and chair-positions to women in the Panchayati Raj bodies. The amendment, which could be regarded as one of the important achievements of the Indian Women's Movement, created high hopes among all those concerned about the increased and active involvement of women in grass roots politics, especially in decision-making. The expectation is that reservations to women could facilitate 'bigger and better share' to them in the whole process, 'infuse democratic way of functioning' in local government, help for decline in corruption and provide a space for women in the male dominated political sphere[1]. Reservations are also considered to be responsible for offsetting and unsetting the *status quo* and for beginning the process of bringing out simple women in the task of governance[2].

This chapter would focus on the pattern of recruitment and performance of women members and chair-persons in Panchayati Raj institutions in Andhra Pradesh experience of the writer in awareness generation, information dissemination and training of women in general and elected women members in particular; identification of future trends and the strategies for the political empowerment of rural women.

**Experience**

Andhra Pradesh is one of the few States to introduce the system of Panchayati Raj as early as 1959. The component of the present three-tier system are Zilla Parishads, Mandal Parishads and Gram Panchayats. The Mandal Parishads are smaller units than the former and Panchayat Samithis and the Mandal Parishads are organised with the objective of "going nearer to the door steps of the rural public: Andhra Pradesh is the first State to provide early in 1986 reservation of chair-positions to women in Panchayati Raj bodies. The Andhra Pradesh Mandala Praja Parishads, Zilla Praja Parishads and Zilla Pranalika Abrivruddhi Sameeksha Mandals Act, 1986 provided reservation of 9 per cent of the total number of offices of chairman of Zilla Praja Parishads and Presidents of Mandala Praja Parishads to women"[3]. This Act is important in that it ensured representation to women in key positions. The State is implementing the provisions of the 73rd Constitutional Amendment and one generation of women members and chair-persons have completed their term.

Seven years have passed since the passing of the Constitutional Amendment and it is appropriate to take stock of the experiences to plan for the future. The male dominated social setting, including the political has been strongly against the sharing of power by men and women. In a large number of cases, caste, familial or social nearness to the presidents of Panchayat bodies have been given greatest importance in the recruitment process[4]. Hence the quality of membership got heavily compromised in the first-two decades of the implementation of the system of Panchayati Raj in general. Significant variations between the attendance in records and actual attendance were present. While the above had been the general trend, some women, though very few in number, had made real contributions. They moved resolutions and participated in deliberations and decisions. Women in key positions with interest and talent could play considerably important roles in decision-making. Sitamahalakshmi, who served as Sarpanch of Mukkamala

Gram Panchayat in early sixties was a very active and promising woman and her Sarpanchship provided a source of inspiration to other women. She had several achievements to her credit, but was later forced to surrender her office. Threats, deadlocks, challenges, non-cooperation by officials and traditional objections—all have had their impact on the forced surrender of the office by this woman[5]. During the period when 9 per cent reservation of chair-positions was in operation, two women became Zilla Parishad presidents and 101 women served as presidents of Mandal Parishads. Of the 101 women Presidents of Mandal Parishads, three got elected to positions unreserved for women. These figures indicate a quantitative increase in respect of women's position in leadership roles and this was because of reservations. Selection of capable women must have led to qualitative improvement. It is needless to say that all sorts of manipulations have had their play in the choice of women candidates. But micro level studies made very clear that a new and young women's leadership had emerged. This is a sign of revitalization in the context of women's participation in the Panchayati Raj bodies. In a study conducted by the writer in 1989, it was found that not a negligible percentage of women (12%) contested for and assumed leadership roles. It is personal interest and initiative that had contributed to their decision to contest. Familial connections continued to have influence on recruitment but the impact was less than what it was in the 60s and 70s. Thirty two per cent of the women elected as presidents, though nominally inducted, performed effective roles with the help of family members and in some cases with the very active cooperation of husbands. Twenty-eight per cent of the women presidents were endowed with the ability to perform independent roles[6].

Ganta Deenamma, former president of Yelamanchili Mandal Parishad, West Godavari District; Subbalakshmi, former president of Undi Mandal Parishad in West Godavari District; Nagamani, former president of Bashirabad Mandal in Ranga Reddi District; Mallela Gouri, former president of Bikkavolu Mandal Parishad in East Godavari District; Parvati, former president of Anaparty Mandal Parishad in East Godavari District; Nalini Ram, former president of Kuppam Mandal Parishad in Chittoor District; Amudavalli, former president of Pichatur Mandal Parishad in

Chittoor District; Gandu Savitramma, former president, Kesamudram Mandal Parishad in Warangal District and presently, member, State Commission for Women, Andhra Pradesh; Subhadramma, former president of Jammalamadugu Mandal Parishad in Cuddapa District are among the efficient women who served as chair-persons at the middle level institutions. Mrinalini, former president, Srikakulam Zilla Parishad; Rajeswari, former president of West Godavari Zilla Parishad; Geeta, former president of East Godavari Zilla Parishad have been successful women presidents at the district level institutions. Very recently, Geeta has been elected to Rajya Sabha. The role of nominal performers was over shadowed by the officials or husbands thereby defeating the purpose of reservation.

**Post Amendment Scenario**

The post amendment phase proved beyond doubt that the women in Panchayati Raj moved from peripheral to leadership roles. In fact young and new women's leadership has increased which is made clear by field investigations in Andhra Pradesh. Several success stories have also come to lime light. A few examples could be given here. Karuna who had completed her term very recently contested and won a general seat in Chimvenla Mandal of Nalgonda District and later got elected as Mandal President, which position was reserved to Scheduled Caste women. This young woman's experience has been one of struggle and confrontation with officials, party leadership and the government at higher level. Cutting across several barriers, she could get benefits to her Mandal, concentrating on problems of drinking water, irrigation and education. She successfully fought against misappropriation, erring officials and a manipulated no-confidence motion. She carried the struggle with remarkable confidence and succeeded both in protecting her dignity and promoting democratic values[7].

Srinivasa Kumari, Sarpanch, Tadepalli village in Guntur District worked in a totally different atmosphere. This committed young woman has been a very efficient persuader, problem solver, and administrator. With a planned and phased programme, she repaid the loan left by her predecessor and mobilized funds for development works. Her focus has been on education, irrigation and other amenities to the villagers. She strongly feels that women are honest and could provide good politics. She said that women concentrate more on meeting the needs than on power, but for men power occupies top priority[8].

In her recent field trip on 9th, 10 th and 11 th of April 2000, the writer interviewed women presidents of 14 Mandals in the East Godavari District of Andhra Pradesh. A high proportion of these women are young, educated and are new entrants in respect of political involvement. Six of them have a very clear perception of their role and six have a reasonably good view. This is really an encouraging trend. An improvement in the quality of membership and an increase in the number of interested women are clearly visible. Of the remaining two women, one is ignorant and the other has a very limited perception of her role. Male domination in the case of three women and male interference in the performance of seven women were noticed. The remaining four women presidents have been independently performing their roles. As regards educational levels, two are graduates, two had education up to intermediate level, eight have secondary level education and those with elementary educational qualifications are two.

Kamidi Sitamahalakshmi of Karapa, Alamanda Vijayalakshmi of Tuni, Pechetti Vijayalakshmi of Ainavilli, Busi Jayalakshmi of Kothapeta and Sridevi of Mummidivaram are important among the Mandal presidents who have successfully completed their term very recently. Extensive interviews with these women revealed that commitment, honesty, service orientation and dedication are their cardinal virtues .Twenty-eight year old Sita Mahalakshmi said "I have accepted the position not for the sake of status and power but to serve people. I strongly feel that development does not come all of a sudden, but takes place in stages"[9]. "Am I not competent to contest? is the question that every women is now posing to herself", said Vijayalakshmi of Tuni Mandal[10]. Within a short period of assuming office, this woman picked up courage and feels that there is a lot to be done for women by women. Thirty-five years old Pechetti Vijayalakshmi, emphasizing on the need for women's participation in the political process and for purposeful implementation of reservation told the writer that with increasing awareness, women are definitely going to be active in the political process. “I have the satisfaction that I performed my duties to the best of my capacity and my work is recognized in each of the villages in my Mandal”, she concluded[11]. Sridevi of Mummidivaram faced tough opposition from the local party leadership for being honest and committed. But her courage and the support of colleagues as well as public enabled her to successfully fight against four no confidence motions[12]. Busi Jayalakshmi, the wife of a staunch TDP party worker in Kothapeta has shown concern for the development of her Mandal and a special concern for promoting the interests of Scheduled Castes. She regularly conducted Gram Sabhas and earned reputation as a powerful mobilizer of public support. Pointing out that women’s presence makes a difference, she said that the kind of politics men and women play would be markedly different. “For women, respect and reputation are important, but men prefer conflicts and money making”, she added. She is interested in contesting a second time and emphatically said “I had established positive influence on the people, and am confident that they would support me. I was always and am available to the people. Whenever they called, I went to help them and cooperated with them. I worked for equitable and fair distribution of favours and resources whether it be pensions for old aged or other benefits. The identification of needy people is done in Gram Sabhas. The women members of the Mandal and other women also have worked without Party considerations and are making the best use of the available opportunities”, she said[13].

Fatimabee, former Sarpanch of Kalva village, Orvakal Mandal, Kurnool District received the best Sarpanch award of the State government for her exemplary work in improving the conditions of her village. She also received the Fight Against Poverty Award sponsored by the United Nations Organizations. This 39 years old ‘tough as steel and soft as silk’ lady was initially hesitant and even terrified to take up the role of Sarpanch. When interviewed after becoming Sarpanch, she said “I had never seen a city before, never sat in a room full of men, much less spoken in the presence of others”[14]. But participation in orientation programmes brought about marked changes in her attitude and approach. She gained enormous confidence and has worked for the development of her village. Behind the success of Fatimabee, are the concerted and continuous efforts of a voluntary organization called Proddu, meaning Sun Rise, headed by Sankaramma.

The above would suggest that the Constitutional Amendment has facilitated the entry of a large number of women in Panchayati Raj bodies and some of the women have been effective power partners. In places where young and energetic women assumed chair-positions, special attention is paid to promote income generating activities to rural women. Sitamahalakshmi of Karapa Mandal motivated a begging community called Budagajangalu to take up self-employment and engage in small business. This Mandal president could get the cooperation of the Women Welfare Department, Nodal Officer and the officials in the collectorate.

The success stories should not lead one to conclude that the outcome of the amendment has always been positive. Attempts to prevent capable women to enter the Panchayati Raj institutions have increased. New preventive dimensions emerged. These include kidnaps, forced withdrawals, illegal unseating, negative networking, harassment, subjugation and oppression. In a Mandal close to the capital of Andhra Pradesh, a woman was nominally placed in the role of president of a Mandal and functionally, it is the husband who is the president. He went to the extent of arranging for himself a chair next to that of his wife in her office. He goes through all the records and puts his initials on the official papers which he desires to be approved. The woman president, who was taught only to sign, fulfilled the formality of signing after seeing her husband's initial. This practice uninterruptedly continued. The members of the Mandal, other than the woman Sarpanch, officials and villagers never questioned the illegality. The Mandal Development Officer, who should function as the implementer of law allowed the practice to be continued. The point is, the officials, who should function as change agents, with exceptions, have become the perpetuators of male dominated political culture. The protectors of law have become supporters of illegal practices.

One of the unhealthy practices in the State of Andhra Pradesh is the constitution of All Women Panchayats to suit the needs of men. All Women Panchayats emerged in States like Maharashtra, Madhya Pradesh, West Bengal, Tripura, Karnataka and Andhra Pradesh. According to available sources, there are thirty All Women Panchayats in India. Maharashtra has the largest number of such Panchayats followed by Andhra Pradesh.

It is well known that the Committee on the Status of Women felt that one purposeful way encouraging rural women to enter politics is the constitution of All Women Panchayats and recommended accordingly. The committee clearly stated that the proposed statutory women's Panchayats are not meant to be parallel organizations to Gram Panchayats and that they are recommended as transitional measures to break through the traditional attitudes in rural society. The committee hoped that the All Women Panchayats would reduce inhibitions and encourage women to actively participate in local bodies. It should be pointed out that long before the committee's recommendations, some All Women Panchayats were experimented within the State. In the 70s, Mattupalli village in Kurnool District of Andhra Pradesh had an All Women Panchayat. In Gandhinagaram, a village in Warangal District, an All Women Panchayat was set up in 1981. The intention behind the formation of this Panchayat was definitely not encouraging women's participation in decision making. The major factors contributing to the formation of this Panchayat had been caste conflict, gender conflict and a spirit of compromise in the final analysis. It had merely a superficial stamp of all women and the decisions remained those of the village leaders. In the period following the implementation of the amendment, Andhra Pradesh had eight All Women Panchayats. The formation of these bodies was not preceded by real commitment.

**Interventions**

The writer is closely associated with a few organizations, in the State, working for awareness generation, information dissemination and training of women in general and elected women in particular. These associations include Ankuram, Young Women's Christian Association and Mahila Rajakiyadhikara Vedika. She is the Joint Secretary of Mahila Rajakiyadhikara Vedika. The Vedika conducted State level seminars and awareness generation camps in the districts of East Godavari, Nalgonda, Visakhapatnam, Krishna and Kurnool. The Vedika has been instrumental for the formation of Mahila Ikya Vedika (United Women's Forum) consisting of women's wing members of political parties, intellectuals and women's groups. The Vedika has also successfully conducted awareness generation camps in the nearby villages of Hyderabad. The members work both in their individual and collective capacities in the process of campaigning for political empowerment of women. The forum, which has completed six years of its existence, is awaiting registration.

The writer is a resource person for the training camps conducted by the Young Women's Christian Association, Secunderabad. The training module includes lectures, discussions, songs, games and role plays. The resource persons participate in role plays and project both meaningful and ineffective roles, thereby enabling the participants to choose the type of roles they like. They would be encouraged to identify problems and find ways and means of solving them. They would also be asked to play the roles. The songs composed by the resource persons are found to be useful information and interest generating sources.

A training camp to elected women representatives held at Anantapur in April 2000 by the Centre for Rural Action in collaboration with Ankuram where the writer participated as a resource person had produced very satisfactory results. A majority of the women who attended the camp were unaware of their membership in the Gram Panchayats. They only remembered that they were asked by village leaders to sign in some registers. The process of dialogue was used to give them information about the system, the nature of democratic institutions, rights, need for women's participation in Panchayati Raj institutions, the meaning of participation and other related matters. They had conducted model elections and model Panchayats after the training. More important than these is the formation of Saadhikara Mahila Samakhya, an association of empowered women representatives.

The efforts made so far are only limited and a lot more has to be done.

**Future Trends**

It is clear from the above that reservations to women opened up new areas. Women constituted a numerical minority in Panchayati Raj institutions but now one would be fascinated to see a big list of elected women to these bodies. The name boards on the front walls of the houses of some of these women definitely are status symbols.

When one enters the houses of these women for interviews, the hesitance prevailing some twenty years ago is now absent. The researchers are received with lot of enthusiasm and some women heads of Panchayats even told the writer that the visits of researchers would be a source of inspiration to them. These women proved beyond doubt that quantitative presence would lead to qualitative improvement.

Reservations had also opened up new techniques of oppression and exploitation in the context of women. This is not to say that the techniques are newly invented. These are not used earlier against women. Even promising women are kept at a distance from power positions. Despite the growth of preparedness to fight and assert, women, more importantly *dalit* women are subjected to several kinds of manipulations and preventive measures. Women heads of Gram Panchayats are often told that their only duty is that of signing on papers and nothing else. Some of them are asked in offices to fulfil the formality of signing. The local political leadership or the dominant male members of the Panchayats exercise real power. In essence, it is the numbers game that the patriarchal society would be interested to play. Women, as rightly pointed out by Kumud Sharma, need to go beyond the numbers game to expand their share in political power[15]. Women's movement should seriously question this practice and lodge a big protest. Extensive use of media and protest marches would be useful in this regard.

Experience in Andhra Pradesh and in several other States made clear that the device of no-confidence motion is frequently used to unseat women, especially young and assertive women. There are a good number of instances of *dalit* women being illegally unseated from their positions. Janaki Bai, a *dalit* woman who became the Sarpanch of Harpura village in Karnataka was allowed to continue in office for one year by the higher caste leadership because, according to the rules, no-confidence resolution could not be moved in first twelve months of the election. She was kidnapped on the day of illegal no-confidence vote against her. Her supporters hoping that there could not be no-confidence vote in the absence of quorum, went on a pilgrimage. But the pro-male and anti-*dalit* officials managed the show without quorum. She and her husband were beaten up and were freed only after the 'so called' no confidence motion was passed. A combination of caste and gender politics and gross violation of rules is very much evident here. As noted, Karuna, former president of Chimvenla Mandal and Sridevi, former president of Mummidivaram Mandal faced similar situations. It is necessary that women's groups should extend support to such women in challenging illegal acts.

The future of women in Panchayati Raj is going to be one of conflict between assertion and suppression, the conflict getting intensified especially when young and capable women enter these bodies. The conflict gets intensified both within and outside the family. Women's groups should and are going to give tough fight against manipulations outside the family. Parties play a prominent role in the selection of candidates, whether male or female. Conflict between party leadership and women's wings are bound to increase. This should be looked at as a positive sign in the process of accommodation and adjustment. This results in an increase in women's component in the decision-making structures of political parties.

Closely related to political power is economic power. Women heads of Panchayats are paying increasing attention for facilitating and promoting rural women's economic empowerment. Sitamahalakshmi, president of Karapa Mandal Parishad said that, "women have picked up confidence and courage through DWCRA schemes. There is change in their life style. Though the income generating schemes have not been useful for getting adequate earnings, women are learning the importance of living on their own, gaining courage and are developing a feeling that they can stand and work on equal terms with men." For making men effective partners in the development process reforms guaranteeing economic security to women are essential. Economic empowerment of women is going to be one of the top priority items on the agenda of women in Panchayati Raj.

Skill development is one of the prerequisites for effective role performance. It is all the more significant in the present context because of the considerable increase in the number of women representatives in rural local bodies. National and State institutes like the National Institute of Rural Development, Andhra Pradesh Academy of Rural Development, Rajiv Gandhi Institute, Tamil Nadu and Institute of Social Studies Trust, Karnataka and a large number of women's groups as well as other groups are engaged in awareness generation, information dissemination and training. But there seems to be a pressing need to rethink and to have a fresh look at the training modules and the items chosen for awareness generation and information dissemination. The modules identified and efforts put forth so far are varied and diversified. It is necessary to identify a broad training pattern for the country as a whole. Necessary modifications could be made depending on local requirements. Thus it is possible to strike a balance between uniformity and local needs. Awareness generation could focus on topics like social system, sub-systems, participatory democracy, government, rights, duties and local governance. Knowledge about women specific aspects such as women's status in general and rural women's status in particular, women's empowerment, urban-rural variations could form part of the awareness generation programme. It is very important to take elected women as resource persons as no other knowledge could be a real substitute to that gained out of experience. Training programme could focus on building confidence, promoting leadership qualities and preparing women for successful role performance. Networking based on large scale is another pressing need of the time. Women's political empowerment should occupy the position of top priority on the agenda of voluntary organizations committed for the promotion of women's cause. In addition to networking of voluntary organizations coordinated efforts of academics, activists, elected women representatives and women officials could bring about fruitful results.

Successful implementation of beneficiary programmes, depends among other factors, on the interest evinced by officials. Committed and service oriented women officials could be of added strength to women in Panchayati Raj bodies. Shashi Rekha, the Development Officer of Moinabad Mandal in the Ranga Reddy District of Andhra Pradesh received the best Mandal Development Officer award for her commendable work. She says that if the officers are correct, everything gets done well. She has been instrumental for the successful implementation of governmental schemes meant for women. Women's groups and all those concerned about the empowerment of women should launch a strong protest against the unjust media-print and audio-visual. Positive roles of women are either relegated to the background or wrongly magnified roles are projected. Both are unhealthy symptoms for society in general and women in particular. Therefore, careful watch on the media by women's associations is very much essential. Identification of success stories and spread of information relating to these is necessary to counter the argument that women have not been successful representatives. Current research should give priority to this aspect and try to expose the manipulations that are taking place. To make Women's Movement effective, its urban colour has to change and should spread to grass roots. To strengthen the role of women in Panchayati Raj should be the immediate task of all those concerned about grass roots development.

NOTES

1. Chrissie D'Costa, Women's Political Participation and Empowerment, *Panchayati Raj Interactive System*, The Foundation for Research in Community Health, Bombay, Vol. 2, No. 3, March 1996, p. 4.
2. *Ibid.* p. 7.
3. Section 5, sub-section 3, The Andhra Pradesh Panchayat Samithis, Zilla Parishads and Zilla Pranalika Abhivrudhi Sameeksha Mandals Act, 1986 as amended by Act 3 of 1987.
4. See also Sreeranjani Subba Rao K, Role of Women in Panchayati Raj Institutions: A Case Study of Visakhapatnam Zilla Parishad, Kasimkota, Ravikantam and Madugula Mandal Praja Parishads and Six Gram Panchayats, a paper presented at the IV National Conference of Women's Studies, Waltair, Andhra Pradesh (unpublished) 1988 and her Project Report (unpublished) on the same topic submitted to ICSSR, New Delhi.
5. Manikyamba, P., *Women in Panchayati Raj Structures*, Gian Publishing House, New Delhi, 1988, pp. 67-71.
6. (a) Manikyamba P., Women in Panchayati Raj Structures, *op. cit.* and (b) Women Presiding Officers at the Tertiary Political Levels: Patterns of Induction and Challenges in performance, *Journal of Rural Development*, Vol. 9 (6), Nov. 1990, National Institute of Rural Development, Hyderabad.
7. Karuna in her presentation of experiences at the seminar on Women in Panchayati Raj organised by the Department of Political Science, University of Hyderabad and UNICEF, 29-31, March, 2000.
8. Srinivasa Kumari, in her presentation of experience at the seminar cited above.

9. Interview dated 9th April, 2000 at Vemulawada, Karapa Mandal, East Godavari District, A.P.
10. Interview dated 9th April, 2000 at Tuni, Tuni Mandal, East Godavari District, A.P.
11. Interview dated 10th April, 2000 at Amalapuram, East Godavari District, A.P
12. Interview dated 10th April at Ainapuram, Mummidivaram Mandal, East Godavari District, A.P.
13. Interview dated 10th April 2000 at Kothapeta, East Godavari District, A.P.
14. (a) *Panchayati Raj Update*, April, 1997, Institute of Social Sciences, New Delhi, p.4; (b) Sakuntala Naraimham, Tough as Steel, Soft as Silk: Story of a Woman Sarpanch of Andhra Pradesh, *Panchayati Raj Update*, December, 1997, pp. 5-6; (c) *Eenadu*, Telugu Daily, 21st September, 1988.
15. Kumud Sharma, Transformative Politics: Dimensions of Women's Participation in Panchayati Raj, *Indian Journal of Gender Studies*, 5:1, 1998, Sage Publications, New Delhi, p. 44.

4

# POLITICAL EMPOWERMENT OF WOMEN AT THE GRASS ROOTS
## The Case of Karnataka

K. Subha and B.S. Bhargava

It is evident that women's oppression and discrimination have been built into the very systems and structure of the society. The absence of gender perspective in development was also observed in all domains of life. The central feature of feminism is, therefore, the consideration of women as the subject. Feminism is relatively a new term, which barely existed before the twentieth century and over a period of time the term has developed varied meanings. However, women are at the centre of the analysis and the concept of 'Womanhood' is placed centre stage and is based on the understanding of the women's point of view.

Dictionaries usually define feminism as the advocacy of women's rights based on a belief in the equality of sexes and in its broadest sense this refers to everyone who is aware of and seeking to end women's subordination in anyway and for any reason. Basically the movement seeks equal political and social rights for women as compared with men. So feminism could mean a perspective that seeks to eliminate the subordination, oppression, inequalities and injustices women suffer because of their sex.

## Three Major Traditions of Feminism

Three major traditions of feminism could be identified[1]. They are liberal, radical and Marxist/ Socialist Feminism. Liberal Feminism is the most widely known form of feminist thought which tries to explain women's position in society in terms of unequal rights to participation in the public world beyond the family and household. Here there is a focus on the public sphere, on legal, political and institutional struggles for the rights of individuals to compete in the public market place. Public citizenship and the attainment of equality with men in the public field is central to liberal feminism.

Radical Feminism pays attention to women's oppression as women in a social order dominated by men and the explanation for women's oppression is seen as lying in sexual oppression (because of their sex). This form of feminism stresses the interconnections between bodies and society and a crucial aspect of their agenda is for women to gain control over their bodies.

Third major feminist tradition, i.e., Marxist/ Socialist Feminism considers sexual oppression as a dimension of class power. This approach is oriented towards the public sphere and pays particular attention to women's position in relation to waged labour. It advocates a revolutionary approach in which the overthrow of capitalism is viewed as the necessary precondition to dismantling male privilege. The 'main enemy' in this form of analysis is the class system, which creates divisions between men and women. It shares with liberal feminism an enemy assumption that there is an underlying sameness between men and women.

Socialist feminism attempts to maintain some elements of Marxism regarding the significance of class distinctions and labour while incorporating the radical feminist view that sexual oppression is not historically a consequence of class division. Various versions of socialist feminism are identified by their views of the relationship between class and sex, i.e., the relationship between capitalism and patriarchy.

India was also experiencing the move towards equality between men and women. The influence of liberal feminism was becoming overt and the pressure on the government to give equal status to women was building up. As women demanded equal treatment and larger choices in various sectors, it became evident that the existing structure was insufficient. The first attempt in this direction was to give equal rights between men and women. Government of India appointed a committee on the status of women in India (CSWI) in 1977 to undertake a "comprehensive examination of all the questions relating to the rights and status of women". It had commented on the failure of an earlier policy to induct women into local government bodies through reservation of a few seats, as a form of tokenism, and recommended the establishment of statutory women's Panchayats at the village level to ensure greater participation in the political process.

The publication of the Report of the Committee on the Status of Women, the observance of International Women's Year in 1975, the formulation of a National Plan of Action for women, setting up of a National Committee with the Prime Minister as the head, proved the concern for women. Since then scholars and policy-makers diverted their attention to the issues of women which culminated in establishing a National Commission for Women in 1992 and the National Perspective Plan for Women (1988-2000).

It is since the mid 1980s that the women's movement and feminist scholarship have been exposing the unequal division of labour, power and resources between women and men and the different ways they are affected by policies and programmes which claim to offer equal benefits to everyone in the community. The women's movement has thus put gender relations at the centre in the analysis of social relations, which has led to the inclusion of gender in the development approach. The gender approach recognises women's subordinate position and inequalities in power distribution and aims at restructuring power, in favour of gender justice and equity.

Previous experiences show that women have rarely occupied leading positions and have not made much progress in spite of the laws that guarantee opportunity. There is thus a need for empowering women. Empowerment has different dimensions—political, social and economic. It is a process of redistribution of resources in the society in such a way that women get equal access and control over the resources and develop the capacity to influence decision-making process, planning, implementation and evaluation by integrating them into the political system. This implies political participation which includes right to vote, contest, campaign, party membership and representation in political offices at all levels and effectively influence decisions thereby leading to political empowerment.

It is now earnestly believed that developing countries have to build the society from the roots upwards with great emphasis on the concept of participation. One of the important indicators of political participation for women would be her share of representation in local bodies.

Reservation is one of the instruments of political empowerment as it guarantees representation. The passing of the Seventy-third and Seventy-fourth Constitutional Amendments can be considered as the greatest event for women's empowerment as one-third of the seats are reserved for women in the local bodies. The Constitution (Seventy-third Amendment) Act of 1993 which was brought into force from April 24, 1993, established India's Panchayati Raj Institutions on a sound footing. The Amendment gave the much-needed impetus to the concept of local self-government which till then suffered from lack of Constitutional protection. It envisages a polity where more powers are decentralised to the third level of government.

Decentralised governance reaches out to people and helps to improve human development by promoting participation and efficiency. Being closer to the people and more responsive to the local needs especially problems that concern women, it can be presumed as the level where women should participate more. In the Indian context the rural local body is the most important channel for popular participation in the process of development. As it deals with the day-to-day affairs of the rural folk it should keep close contact with the people and draw up ways and means to serve them. And can emerge as a model in incorporating women's talents in the light of the special nexus between women's concern and local issues and thereby enhance the status of women through political empowerment.

**Looking Back**

Indian environment is predominantly rural and the rural sector occupies an important place in the Indian economy. Even today, more than 70 per cent people live in rural areas. The focus on rural development started with the realization of the fact that the rural sector was underdeveloped economically, socially and politically and needed special attention of the government. The Community Development programme was launched in 1952 covering the entire nation. Later on the institutional arrangement that was made and came to be known as Panchayati Raj, was assigned the major task of uplifting the 'weaker sections' which included women. But when the system was introduced, very few women contested or got elected. It was the publication of the Report of the Committee on the status of women that there was a demand for representation of women in Panchayati Raj institutions by reservation. Having set the ball rolling, it is necessary to sketch the position of women in grass roots organization as it is the most approachable unit.

The Community Development Programme, unfortunately could not deliver much. The Balwant Rai Mehta Committee observed that the main factor that caused the failure of the Community Development Programme was the absence of people's participation. The Committee recommended the creation of three-tier system as the institutional arrangement to make people's participation meaningful and effective. Necessary legislation was to be enacted by every State to implement the Panchayati Raj system as a form of local self-government to perform developmental, administrative and political tasks. Rajasthan and Andhra Pradesh were the first States to adopt this system in 1959, followed by Karnataka and Orissa. Since then Karnataka has been at the forefront of decentralization.

A National Committee on Panchayati Raj Institutions, headed by Asoka Mehta was appointed in 1977 by the Janata Government, which was in power at the Centre. The report submitted in 1978 recommended a two-tier system of the rural local government, and emphasized the need for constitutional sanction to the Panchayati Raj institutions.

Most of the principles underlying the philosophy enunciated in Report became the basis of the Karnataka Zilla Parishads, Taluk

Panchayat Samitis, Mandal Panchayat and Nyaya Panchayat Act 1985. This was a 'radical change' brought about by the Janata Party which formed the government in Karnataka in 1983 under the Chief Ministership of Ramakrishna Hegde. It was implemented to give the highest priority to rural development, to eradicate poverty and to improve the rural economy through people's participation.

In addition to the Zilla Parishad at the District level followed by the Mandal Panchayat comprising of a group of villages, the Act provided for two other statutory bodies–the Taluk Panchayat Samiti at the Taluk/Block level, which was an advisory and co-ordinating body with no executive function and the Grama Sabha (Village Assembly) below the Mandal Panchayat. The Mandal Panchayat was the first elected tier located between the village and the taluk while the Zilla Parishad which was the second directly elected tier was a powerful body which administered schemes and programmes evolved by it and transferred to it. Cadres were maintained for manning the Zilla Parishad and the Mandal. Elections were held in January 1987. For the first time the elections were conducted on party lines.

Another significant feature of this Act was that, it realized women were inadequately represented in politics and an effort was made to do justice to them. Reservation upto 25 per cent was provided in the local bodies. Women's participation in the political process took a different turn in the history of Karnataka. Earlier when the Panchayati Raj system was introduced, very few women contested or got elected. The committees, which recommended the creation of Panchayati Raj Institutions (PRIs), did not say much about the role of women in these bodies. Balwantrai Mehta Committee recommended that in the constitution of Panchayats, provisions may be made for the co-option of two women members "who are interested in work among women and children". The Ashok Mehta Committee had mentioned that two women securing the highest number of votes among the women candidates in the election could take the seats reserved for them, a method of co-option by election. Though PRIs were established in almost all the States, women's representation did not exceed two or three. Consequent to the 1987 election women occupied twenty five per cent of the seats in all the districts. It became evident that women had made an entry into the political arena, which was till then left untouched to a great extent.

Almost half the population, which was excluded from the development process, was given a chance to participate in making decisions to determine their needs and priorities. However, a review of the working of the system gained from field experiences revealed some thought provoking problems. Recruitment of women was a problem in the absence of motivation and mobilization.

Political parties found it difficult to locate women who could contest for the two tiers. The numbers were so huge and the parties, who are the recruiting centres, were not prepared for a work of this magnitude. Only major parties, Janata and Congress, could succeed to some extent. Moreover, women rarely came on their own. Voluntary organisations could not come up to the situation to educate, enlighten or sensitize women or make them understand the subtle aspects of Panchayati Raj functioning. As a natural corollary to this, the people who were locally influential and belonged to the 'dominant castes' inducted their women into the Panchayats.

There is no comprehensive study on the basis of which one could conclude how Panchayati Raj members especially women members performed their role in Panchayati Raj Institutions, in the sub-committees, in decision making and formulation of rural development schemes. It is only on the basis of some reports published in the newspapers it can be inferred that in each Panchayati Raj Institution some women proved very assertive and active in decision making and to some extent work for the cause of women.

## The Present Scenario

The first five-year term of the Panchayats ended on January 1, 1992. Instead of holding elections, the Congress (I) government appointed administrators to Zilla Parishads and Mandal Panchayats. The 1985 Act was superseded by a new Act of the State–The Karnataka Panchayati Raj Act 1993, when the Congress (I) came to power after the 1989 Assembly elections. This Act incorporated the essential features of the 73rd Constitutional Amendment and established elected bodies at three tiers—the village, taluks and district levels—so that there is "greater participation of the people".

Among the salient features of the Act, it is worth noting that it establishes a three-tier Panchayati Raj system in the State based on the population as ascertained at the last preceding census of which the figures have been published. It envisages elected bodies at all the three levels; it provides for reservation of seats in favour of scheduled castes and scheduled tribes in proportion to their population and for reservation of one-third of the seats for women at all levels, it also provides for reservation of seats and offices of chair-persons at all the levels for the persons belonging to backward classes, scheduled castes, scheduled tribes and women.

The historic bill was introduced by the Karnataka Government in the legislative Assembly on April 1, 1993 to replace the then existing enactment. It was passed on April 7th. The legislative council unanimously passed the bill on April 13 and it came into force from May 18, 1993. There is now an elected three-tier structure of rural local government. The tiers are the Gram Panchayat, Taluk Panchayat and Zilla Panchayat. The Act also provides for a Gram Sabha.

*Grama Panchayats*

A Gram Panchayat is constituted for population not less than 5,000 and not more than 7,000; area or group of villages will be considered as a Panchayat area, and there will be one member for every 400.

Elections to 5,640 Grama Panchayats were held in December 1993. They consist of elected members each representing about 400 people. The average population of each Grama Panchayat is 5,300 according to 1991 census. Of the total number of 80,627 members in all the Grama Panchayat, 35,305 (43.8%) were women.

*Grama Sabha*

It is a body consisting of persons registered in the electoral rolls relating to a village comprised within the area of Grama Panchayat. It meets twice in a year. The Grama Sabha is a very important forum in which the annual statement of accounts, report of administration and the development works undertaken by the Grama Panchayat are reviewed. It also considers the development programmes proposed by the Grama Panchayat for the current year. It is responsible for identifying beneficiaries under different poverty alleviation and development programmes.

*Taluk Panchayat*

A Taluk Panchayat has been constituted for every revenue Taluk as the intermediate level in the Panchayat system. It consists of elected members at the rate of one member for every 10,000 population or part thereof. However, Taluks having a population of not exceeding 1.00 lakh have 11 elected members. Elections to all the 175 Taluk Panchayats in the State were held during 13th to 18th March, 1995, on party basis. The offices of Adhyaksha and Upadhyaksha of Taluk Panchayats have also been reserved for different categories.

*Zilla Panchayats*

There were 20 Zilla Panchayats in the State (presently 27) consisting of elected members at the rate of one member for every 40,000 population and part thereof (one member for every 30,000 population in Chickmagalur and Uttar Kannada Districts and one member for every 18,000 population in Kodagu District). Elections to all the Zilla Panchayat were held during March 1995 on party basis.

In all local government institutions the following reservation as shown in Table 4.1 is mandatory:

**Table 4.1:** SCs and STs Reservation of Seats

| | |
|---|---|
| Scheduled Castes and Scheduled Tribes | In proportion to their population |
| Other Backward Classes and Women | One-third of the total number of seats and one-third in each category for women, respectively. |

Election occupies the most central place in any modern political system. The State Election Commission was appointed in May 1993. Elections to all the three tiers were to be conducted in December 1993 on separate dates. The dates of elections to the Gram Panchayats was fixed on December 29th 1993 and Taluk Panchayats and Zilla Panchayats on 23rd January 1993. But only the elections to the Gram Panchayat were conducted and the other had been postponed indefinitely. Delimitations had to be done afresh as the previous Mandal Panchayats were to be delimited to form Gram Panchayats. Out of a total electorates of 2,06,36,782, there were 1,01,93,188 women.

Karnataka thus became the first State to bring the Panchayati Raj legislation in line with the Constitutional Amendment Act and to hold elections to the Panchayats under the new Act.

At the Gram Panchayat level, the elections were fought on a non-party basis with the intention of maintaining a better atmosphere in the village, to minimize conflicts and to assure full participation of the people. However, the Gram Panchayat election was an experience in itself. When the Panchayat elections were held in Karnataka in December 1993, there were no takers for the 1,239 seats mostly reserved for the backward classes, SC and ST women.

It is interesting to note that this time (unlike under 1985 Act) election to Gram Panchayat in 20 districts were conducted on a non-party basis. In many polling booths women outnumbered men. For example in Dharwar, Shimoga and Bidar there were large number of women. This could be attributed to the 33 per cent reservation. But it is sad that most seats were vacant due to lack of women candidates. Of the 200 seats reserved for women in North Canara, 162 seats were vacant.

The election to the office of the Adyaksha and Upadhyaksha was conducted in the first meeting of the Gram Panchayats on March 5th, 7th and 9th of 1994. Incidents of violent cashses, kidnapping of members including women and few deaths were reported. This law and order situation was shown as one of the basis for postponing elections to the other tiers as it was not conducive to conduct free and fair election.

**Table 4.2:** ZP ad TP Election Data 1995

| | Total No. | No. of Members | No. of Women Members |
|---|---|---|---|
| ZP | 20 | 919 | 335 |
| TP | 175 | 3340 | 1343 |

Table 4.2 shows that there are 175 Taluk Panchayats (TPs) and 20 Zilla Panchayats (ZPs) comprising 3,340 TP members and 919 ZP members. A total of 1343 (40%) seats in TP and 335 (36%) seats in ZP were reserved for woman. The elections were held in 3 phases on March 13,15 and 18 of 1995.

Elections were held for 914 ZP seats and 3,340 TP seats spread over 20 districts. Over 2.16 crore voters including 1.06 crore women were eligible to exercise their franchise in the elections.

The first Panchayat elections in the State after the amendment were thus completed in two phases—1993 and 1995. The 1993 Gram Panchayat elections were held under the 1993 Act as passed by the Assembly. The 1995 elections to the other two tiers (Taluk as passed by the Assembly). The 1995 elections to the other two tiers (Taluk and Zilla Panchayats) were also held under the 1993 Act but just with one amendment relating to the backward classes reservations. The amendment introduced two categories of Backward Classes - 'A' and 'B'. 'A' category was considered most bacward and 'B' category more backward. The former was given reservation to the extent of 26.6 per cent and the latter 6.4 per cent. Under category 'A' 190 castes were listed and nine castes under category 'B'. When the Panchayat elections were held in Karnataka in December 1993, there were no takers for the 1,239 seats mostly reserved for the backward classes, SC and ST women. Out of 8,0631 Gram Panchayat members, 35,160 (43.6%) are women members and of the total 5,640 Gram Panchayats, 1,878 (33%) are headed by women presidents and vice-presidents. An important outcome of the election process was, although the Act provides for 33 per cent reservation to women, the actual reservation for them became 43.6 per cent in the Gram Panchayats.

In 1995 the State Government appointed an Expert Committee to suggest amendments to the Karnataka Panchayati Raj Act 1993. The Committee worked under Chairmanship of P.R. Nayak, IAS (Retd), Former Additional Chief Secretary to State Government?[2] The Expert Committee reviewed the 1993 Act and finalized its report in March 1996. Among other significant recommendations are that the Adyakasha should be designated the Executive Head of the Taluk/Zilla Panchayat and the Executive/Chief Executive Officer should function subject to the Adhyaksha's overall supervision. The term of the office of Adhyakshas and Upadhyakshas should be in the region of 36 months. Women members of PRIs should represent on all standing committees at one-third of the total committee membership.

Keeping in view the recommendations of the P.R. Nayak committee and impressed by the need to make Panchayati Raj legislation blend with the changing requirements, the 1993 Act was substantially amended in 1997.

The Preamble to the Act expresses its basic tenet by declaring that PRIs should function as units of local self government. Among other changes achieving universal enrolment in primary schools, providing sanitary latrines, improving water supply, establish health and maternity centres and social forestry area to be among the priorities at each level.

The State Election Commission on 2nd February, 2000, issued a formal notification for the conduct of elections to 5,316 Gram Panchayats in two phases on February 23rd and 27th (for reservations, see, Appendix I) and on May 9th the two-phase elections to 27 Zilla Panchayats and 175 Taluk Panchayats in the State, wherein the elections were conducted on June 2, 2000 and June 6, 2000 respectively.

Out of the total 5,659 Gram Panchayats, only 5535 have gone to the polls, for remaining 124 Gram Panchayats polls would be held in the month of October 2000, because of the Lok Shbha by-elections.

The first phase was marked with high degree of enthusiasm among the rural electorates with more than 71.5 per cent of polling. In the second phase also there was a heavy turnout of 69 per cent. However, as many as 12 Gram Panchayat seats in six districts had no contestants and more than 26 per cent (19,751 seats of the total) Gram Panchayat members have been elected unopposed. The polling was by an large peaceful. The second election to the Gram Panchayat were thus conducted (see, Annexure II).

According to the break-up of voters furnished by the State Election Commission (SEC), 1,12,28,908 are men voters. The number of women eligible to vote were 1,11,29,513. Out of the 75,200 seats, the number reserved for the SCs is 13,908 (18.49 per cent), 6,932 for STs (9.22 per cent), 19,812 for Backward Class-A, 5,236 for Backward Class-B groups, while women from all categories will have 33,739 (44.87 per cent) reserved for them.

Of the 74,496 Gram Panchayat seats in 5,286 Gram Panchayats that went to polls on February 23rd and 27th, members have been elected unopposed for as many as 19,751 seats (26.5 per cent) as there was only one contestant for each of these seats.

The largest number of members elected unopposed is in Belgaum (2,453) and the lowest number of members elected unopposed is in Kodagu (144). In all, 1,38,215 contestants were left in the fray. The highest number of contestants was in Tumkur district where 11,734 candidates fought for 4,908 seats.

Interestingly, no one came forward to contest for as many as 585 seats. In all districts, except Udupi and Chamarajanagar, there were seats for which there were no contestants.

Salient features of the Gram Panchayat elections concerning women was that the rural women in Shimoga had 51 per cent seats reserved for them because of category-wise reservation of one-third of the total members. It was reported that 3 seats were auctioned (Yethambadi Gram Panchayat in Mandya District). Confusion was created during the filing of the nominations because of the 'compulsory of toilet rule'. The 'Toilet Rule' states that, nominations are accepted only with an affidavit from candidates affirming that they have toilets in their houses. A number of women who were otherwise interested in contesting did not come forward to file the nominations because of the compulsory toilet rule. More than one all women Gram Panchayat have emerged. The high votes turnout which was recorded in most places indicates greater interest among the people at the grass roots.

As the Zilla Panchayats and Taluk Panchayats elections are party based unlike the Gram Panchayat election all the political parties wanted to gain power. Women found it difficult to contest because of the rotation system followed. Even Gram Panchayat members were involved in campaigning. There were be 34,598 polling stations. Of them 9,521 have been categorized as sensitive and 7,545 as hypersensitive ones. There are 9,858 candidates in the fray in the Taluk Panchayat elections and 3,071 in the Zilla Panchayat elections. The ruling Congress swept the Taluk and Zilla parishad elections, wresting power in 135 of the 175 Taluk Panchayats and in 26 of the 27 Zilla Panchayats (also see, Annexure II). With results of two seats yet to be announced, the Congress won 2,099 seats, JD (U) 357, BJP 249, JD (S) 30, CPI (M) 7 and independents 238. In Zilla Parishads, the Congress won 649 seats while the JD (S) 80, JD(U) 73, BJP 41, CPI(M)4, BSP 1 and independents 41. The result of one ZP seats has been withheld by the State Election Commission owing to a court order and announced later. More than 60 per cent voters exercised their franchise in the elections that took place in two phases on 2nd and 6th June, 2000. Barring group clashes and booth capturing in several constituencies, polling went off peacefully. A large number of women have been elected to the Panchayati Raj Institutions as seen in Table 4.3.

**Table 4.3:** Women in PRIs, Elections 2000

| Tier | Total No. of Women Members | Reserved Category | | | | General |
|---|---|---|---|---|---|---|
| | | SC | ST | BC (A) | BC (B) | |
| Zilla Panchayat | 339 | 63 | 31 | 84 | 25 | 136 |
| Taluk Panchayat | 1375 | 252 | 182 | 361 | 71 | 509 |
| Gram Panchayat | 35187 | 7083 | 5759 | 10078 | 418 | 11849 |
| Total | 36901 | 7398 | 5972 | 10523 | 514 | 12494 |

*Source:* Office of the State Election Commission, Bangalore.

Total number of women Adhyakshas and women Upadhyakshas elected in the Zilla Panchayats are 18, in Taluk Panchayats 115 and in Gram Panchayats 4,291 are women office bearers. The reservation has thus brought into Panchayat a large proportion of women elected representatives.

Any people's movement is a struggle for the rights due to them. The women's movement too was the result of a strong desire to enjoy equal rights and freedom from suppression. In this background the 73rd Constitutional Amendment is a landmark as it envisages participation pushing sexual difference away from the mainstream paving the way for an egalitarian structure. It has provided more space for women in the political process. Reservation of seats and authority positions in local governments is an essential part of the democratizing process for women.

## Some Observations and Reflections

Karnataka can very well take pride in the fact that before the 73rd Amendment to the Constitution made, reservation of seats in favour of women under the 1985 Act was 25 per cent in Mandal Panchayats and Zilla Parishads. Now, reservation is also applicable to the offices of Adhyaksha (Chairperson) and Upadhyaksha (Vice Chairperson) at all levels. And it is in the same proportion as in the case of seats.

Reservation for these offices is on the basis of rotation among different categories.

The Panchayats had thus been formed and for the first time women made an entry in large numbers. But impressions from the field revealed that mostly illiterate women with no political background and having no knowledge of the functioning of the Panchayats had become Panchayat members (see, Annexure IV). During the elections (PRIs election 1993 and 1995), incidence of women being kidnapped and being forced to withdraw their nominations were plenty. However, there were exceptions where women have fought these forces and retained their seats.

Many of the Panchayat members were accompanied by a male member of the family who also participated in the deliberations. Some women members admitted that they felt uncomfortable to sit on the chair along with their male counterpart. Sometimes women were told not to sit with the men who are elders of the village as a sign of respect. In one village, a lady was elected as the Vice President of that Panchayat. But some men got together and managed to get the reservation cancelled. Accordingly, a male member became the Vice President[3].

It cannot be undermined that all talks on empowerment and equality becomes meaningless if it is not backed by access to political power and decision-making. This implies a need to develop gender aware political perspective. Women being half the population should participate in more number to bring about this perspective. The reservation has provided the basis as for the first time a large number of women were elected to the rural local bodies. At the national level, a total of 9,88,106 (35.9%) women have got elected as Gram Panchayat representatives; 59,688 women (40%) have been elected as Taluk Panchayat members; and 6,106 (39%) women have been elected as Zilla Panchayat members. However, Karnataka has the distinction of having the highest number of women elected at all levels—37,689 (46.7%) for Gram Panchayat, 1,343 (40.2%) for Taluk levels and 335 (36.45%) for the Zilla Panchayat. Karnataka also had an all-women Panchayat in Mydolalu village in Bhadravati taluk of Shimoga district. All the members had been elected for the first time and have had no such previous experience. But the village was considered as a model village.

Constitutional provisions, government policies, social action and awareness of rural women together should be able to provide women with necessary skills to enjoy equal opportunity. The Panchayati Raj has provided a common forum for social, economic, political and legal advancement of rural women. Now women are more than nominal in the political bodies and this is an epoch-making step in the women's empowerment and political participation. The Panchayati Raj Institutions have not only provided space for women to articulate and influence decision making but also in involving in the planning, implementing and administering of the programmes of development as a natural corollary to the decentralized planning. Besides this, these institutions have an important role in ensuring community participation and awareness generation which are very vital for the successful implementation of development programmes.

It is a promising trend that women are more visible in local government today than they were in the past. The policy of reservation is a necessary step to motivate participation. But women will not get equal participation in politics without undertaking major efforts themselves. There are many activities, which can aid women in reaching equal participation in local government and decision-making. In addition to obtaining better education and building networks to increase access to information and reducing isolation they should influence further those holding high positions in parties or government and should openly support women and men who are sensitive and responsive to women's problems. Women should improve their image by monitoring books and media portrayals. Within political party structure they should work for women candidates.

Now women are involved in the local political process and are confronted with complex situations while carrying out their tasks as local leaders. One of the important issues plaguing the country is widespread corruption and grass-roots level is no exception to corruption, nepotism and malpractices[4]. Studies reveal that during elections there were many malpractices. The political parties do not follow any standard nor do they maintain records. Money and muscle still rule the elections. This is an extremely difficult situation for women to enter politics. To crub this, local electoral system has to be further reformed so that money and muscle power is eradicated. Ombudsmanic institution could be introduced so that the role of the middlemen is reduced and there is direct link between citizens and the local body.

As the decisions of the local government have a profound effect on the problems that concern women, effective participation in decision making is the direct implication. Effective participation demands skill knowledge and attitude which is to a large extent conspicuously absent in women. The need for systematic training and orientation is, therefore, necessary to empower the women members to exercise their authority and to access the resources available to transform the existing conditions of existence to a better one. The political parties have to take a major responsibility in facilitating women's participation. Deliberate efforts should be made to place women members within and outside party organization. More women's organizations must take up issues of securing them rightful place in the local government. Electoral system, which is based on money power, should be changed. Electoral reforms is the major key. State funding of elections by creation of a separate election fund is a possibility. Last, but not the least, is the role of mass media in building awareness.

Simplifying the working of the Panchayats and providing easy access to information can effect participation. Mention may be made of a village called Bellandur (a village 30 minutes away from Bangalore) where the Grama Panchayat has dispensed with sloppy operations and inducted computers for administration. It has been done on the Panchayat's own initiative. Two computers at the Panchayat office display data on land holdings of each family, taxes due from them, beneficiaries covered under various housing and employment schemes. Pleas for Power and water connections can also be accessed. Such details of five villages, which fall within Ballandur, are available. This is important not only from the view of streamlining administration but also in empowering women as details of the Grama Panchayat are available within their reach at the click of a mouse.

## Gramsat

Satellite programmes for villages—an ambitious programme launched by the Government of Karnataka on an experimental basis was the first of its kind in the State and the second in the country after Gujarat. Using a "one-way video and two-way audio" satellite broadcasting technology developed by ISRO (Indian Space Research Organisations), programmes were beamed from the Main earth Station at Vijayanagar, Bangalore to seventeen districts of Karnataka.

The Department of Women and Child Welfare used their slot to beam programmes for the elected women representatives of the Grama Pancahayats. The Government of Karnataka has embarked on a programme that can converge modern and traditional media forms through satellite technology to facilitate women Panchayat members.

It is too early to assess the impact of the Constitutional status given to PRIs and the policy of reservation. However, it cannot be denied that it is a major landmark in the history of administrative reforms, a milestone in the history of rural local government and participation of women. What is needed in the given situation is capacity building for effective performance and participation. Developing human resources for managing this complex task of sustainable development should be the priority of NGOs, Voluntary Organizations, People's Organizations and Women's Groups.

It is the efficiency of the local institutions which matters most to the major part of the people and which directly touches the daily needs and interests of popular life. Besides, it is the best school of political training of the masses and a school of social service. The Grama Sabha is regarded as an instrument of direct democracy rather than representative democracy, because the Panchayat statutes provide that the activities of the village Panchayats shall be reviewed by meetings of all the adult residents of the villages falling within the jurisdiction of a village Panchayat. The Grama Panchayat offers possibilities for the training of women in social participation and leadership. Thus PRIs alone are the agencies to revolutionise the rural society by mobilising and channelising in the right direction the abundant enthusiasm and energy in the rural areas.

The process of development of women in modern India has shown that the country has sought to give women equal status in the Constitution. The 73rd Amendment and the establishment of PRIs has given expression to this democratic process. However, the statutory representation for women is only a step forward in promoting women's participation in national life. Local governments are the best means of promoting participation and efficiency. They can be much more open to public scrutiny and more accountable. Being closer to people they can be more responsive to local needs and make better use of resources. PRIs have provided an important channel for women's involvement in their own development through participation in the representative structures of the local government. Representation aims at involving women in decision making. Their roles should be recognised and strengthened so that they get full access to resources and services.

The special feature of the electoral system to reserve seats in the local bodies automatically has provided opportunities for the less privileged women. The latest election to the Gram Panchayat have shown increased number of women in the total membership. This reflects a leap forward in the political status of women. Improving the political status of women is an integral aspect of social, economic and political development and change. It will increase women's participation and motivate them to shoulder political responsibilities and will broaden the base of women's representation in political institutions.

The recent years has thus seen marked improvement in people's opportunities to take part in governance. Decentralisation has become one of the best means of promoting participation. Devolution has proved to have offered more opportunities for political participation of women. The growing women's movement in many countries and the Feminist emphasis on empowerment has resulted in gender-sensitive and women focused governance. The reservation policy can be used to advance women's agenda so that human development is engendered.

Though evolution of gender concerns in development dates back to 1960s and the seventies, it is only in the 90s that gender concerns were strengthened by the Constitutional Amendment paving the way for political participation of women. This can be considered as an achievement of the feminist movement that seeks to change the traditional role, image and status of women and to gain equal rights with men within the existing social structure.

## NOTES

1. Chris Beasley, *What is Feminism*, Sage Publications, New Delhi, 1999.
2. The Committee consisted of other members namely Dr. B.S. Bhargava, Smt. Srilata Batliwala, Prof. V.K. Natraj, Sri S.S. Meenakshisundaram, Sri M.R. Srinivasmurthy and one Member-Secretary Dr. K.B. Basappa.
3. These observations are based on the first author's visit to villages in Karnataka and interviews with women members of Gram Panchayats.
4. K Subha, "Panchayati Raj Institutions and Women", editors N. Narayanaswamy, M.P. Boraian and M.A. Jeyaraju, Concept Publishing Company 2000, pp. 163.

## REFERENCES


Bhargava, B.S. and K. Subha, "Developing Women at Grass-roots", *Kurukshetra*, February 1991, New Delhi, pp. 40-42.

Bhargava, B.S. and K. Subha, "*Women in Panchayati Raj*: Some reflections on Karnataka's experience", *Kurukshetra*, June 1994, pp.42-44

Bhargava, B.S. and S. Rama Rao, 1978, *Indian Local Government*: A Study, Minerva Associates, Calcutta.

Government of India, *Report of the Committee on the Status of Women in India*, Towards Equality, Department of Social Welfare, New Delhi.

Government of Karnataka, *The Karnataka Panchayati Raj Act* 1993, Government Press, Bangalore.

Government of Karnataka, *The Karnataka Zilla Parishads, Taluk Panchayat Samithis, Mandal Panchayats and Nyaya Panchayats Act* 1985, Government Press, Bangalore.

Government of Karnataka, '*Power to the People': Panchayati Raj Institutions in Karnataka*, Department of Rural Development and Panchayati Raj, Bangalore, 1999. (ed.)

Government of Karnataka, *Report of the Expert Committee in Karnataka Panchayat Raj Act, 1993*, Bangalore, March 1996.

Institute of Social Sciences, '*Social Background of Zilla Parishad Members in Karnataka*, 1989', ISS Occasional Paper Series 6, New Delhi, 1989.

Institute of Social Sciences, '*Karnataka Mandala Panchayat Members' Social Background*, 1990,' ISS Occasional Paper Series 7, New Delhi, 1990.

Issues of *Panchayati Raj Update* (English and Kannada), Institute of Social Sciences, New Delhi.

Issues of *Uma Prachar*, Institute of Social Studies Trust, Bangalore.

Issues of *Search Bulletin*, Search, Bangalore.

Mathew, George *Panchayati Raj in Karnataka Today: Its National Dimensions*, Concept Publishing Company, New Delh, 1986.

Subha, K. 'Training: An Aid to Empower Rural Women Leaders', *Kurukshetra*, April 1995.

Subha, K. '*Karnataka Panchayat Elections* 1995', Concept Publishing Company, New Delhi, 1997.

# ANNEXURE I

## RESERVATION IN GRAM PANCHAYATS

| Sl. No. | Districts | No. GP | Reserved Seats | | | | | Reserved Seats |
|---|---|---|---|---|---|---|---|---|
| | | | SC | ST | BCM | BCM (A) | BCM (B) | |
| 1 | 2 | 3 | 4 | 5 | 6 | 7 | 8 | 9 |
| 1. | Bangalore (U) | 112(41) | 21(7) | 6(3) | 38(14) | 31(11) | 7(3) | 47(17) |
| 2. | Bangalore (R) | 228(90) | 42(17) | 12(8) | 77(29) | 62(21) | 15(8) | 97(36) |
| 3. | Chitraduraga | 185(70) | 34 (13) | 11(6) | 62(23) | 50(18) | 12(5) | 78(28) |
| 4. | Davanagere | 230 (85) | 42(16) | 11(16) | 76(28) | 61(22) | 15(6) | 101(35) |
| 5. | Kolar | 307(120) | 56(24) | 15(10) | 100(36) | 81(26) | 19(10) | 135(50) |
| 6. | Shimoga | 260(98) | 47(19) | 14(7) | 87(32) | 69(25) | 18(7) | 112(40) |
| 7. | Tumkur | 321(121) | 59(24) | 16(10) | 108(38) | 86(28) | 22(10) | 138(49) |
| 8. | Chikkamagalur | 226(85) | 42(16) | 11(6) | 76(28) | 61(23) | 15(5) | 97(35) |
| 9. | D. Kannada | 206(75) | 38(14) | 10(5) | 68(24) | 55(19) | 13(5) | 90(32) |
| 10. | Udupi | 146(52) | 26(10) | 8(3) | 49(18) | 39(15) | 10(3) | 63(21) |
| 11. | Hassan | 258(97) | 47(19) | 13(8) | 86(31) | 68(24) | 18(7) | 112(39) |
| 12. | Kodagu | 99(38) | 18(8) | 5(3) | 33(12) | 27(9) | 6(3) | 43(15) |
| 13 | Mandya | 232(87) | 42(17) | 11(7) | 77(28) | 61(21) | 16(7) | 101(35) |

*Contd....*

*Annexure I (Contd.)*

| 1 | 2 | 3 | 4 | 5 | 6 | 7 | 8 | 9 |
|---|---|---|---|---|---|---|---|---|
| 14. | Mysore | 236(87) | 43(16) | 13(7) | 79(28) | 64(21) | 15(7) | 101(36) |
| 15. | Chamarajanagar | 121(48) | 22(9) | 7(4) | 41(16) | 32(13) | 9(3) | 51(19) |
| 16. | Belgaum | 485(172) | 87(30) | 27(10) | 162(57) | 132(46) | 30(11) | 209(75) |
| 17. | Bijapur | 199(74) | 36(14) | 10(5) | 66(24) | 52(19) | 14(5) | 87(31) |
| 18. | Bagalkote | 163(65) | 30(12) | 9(6) | 54(21) | 44(15) | 10(6) | 70(26) |
| 19. | Dharwad | 127(51) | 23(10) | 6(5) | 41(15) | 34(11) | 7(4) | 57(21) |
| 20. | Gadag | 106(44) | 19(8) | 6(5) | 35(14) | 27(11) | 8(3) | 46(17) |
| 21. | Haveri | 206(81) | 39(16) | 11(7) | 68(26) | 55(19) | 13(7) | 88(32) |
| 22. | U. Kannada | 207(86) | 38(16) | 11(11) | 69(27) | 56(22) | 13(5) | 89(32) |
| 23. | Bellary | 189(76) | 34(15) | 9(7) | 63(24) | 50(17) | 13(7) | 83(30) |
| 24. | Bidar | 175(64) | 32(12) | 10(5) | 59(21) | 48(16) | 11(5) | 74(26) |
| 25. | Gulbarga | 337(168) | 62(25) | 18(10) | 113(41) | 91(31) | 22(10) | 144(51) |
| 26. | Raichur | 164(60) | 30(11) | 9(5) | 54(19) | 44(14) | 10(5) | 71(25) |
| 27. | Koppal | 134(5) | 24(9) | 7(4) | 45(16) | 36(12) | 9(4) | 58(21) |
| | **Total** | **5659(2144)** | **1033(407)** | **296(173)** | **1886(690)** | **1516(529)** | **370(161)** | **2444(874)** |

*Source*: RDPR, Government of Karnataka

## ANNEXURE II

### DATA RELATED TO GRAM PANCHAYAT ELECTIONS CONDUCTED DURING 2000-2001

| Sl. No. | Dist-ricts | GP No. | Total No of Members | | | Reserved Category | | | | | | | | | | | | | | |
|---|---|---|---|---|---|---|---|---|---|---|---|---|---|---|---|---|---|---|---|---|
| | | | | | | SC | | | ST | | | BC(A) | | | BC(B) | | | General | | |
| | | | G | W | T | G | W | T | G | W | T | G | W | T | G | W | T | G | W | T |
| 1 | 2 | 3 | 4 | 5 | 6 | 7 | 8 | 9 | 10 | 11 | 12 | 13 | 14 | 15 | 16 | 17 | 18 | 19 | 20 | 21 |
| 1. | Banga-lore (U) | 112 | 958 | 749 | 1707 | 263 | 181 | 444 | 4 | 112 | 116 | 244 | 213 | 457 | 104 | 10 | 114 | 343 | 233 | 576 |
| 2 | Banga-lore (R) | 216 | 1864 | 1440 | 3304 | 394 | 298 | 692 | 19 | 218 | 237 | 469 | 419 | 888 | 207 | 10 | 217 | 775 | 495 | 1270 |
| 3. | Chitra-duraga | 182 | 1609 | 1175 | 2784 | 369 | 281 | 650 | 274 | 255 | 529 | 375 | 346 | 721 | 171 | 8 | 179 | 420 | 285 | 705 |
| 4. | Dava-nagere | 222 | 1539 | 1255 | 2794 | 351 | 290 | 641 | 145 | 243 | 388 | 354 | 366 | 720 | 198 | 7 | 205 | 492 | 349 | 841 |
| 5 | Kolar | 302 | 2396 | 1915 | 4311 | 673 | 482 | 1155 | 133 | 289 | 422 | 529 | 600 | 1129 | 296 | 5 | 301 | 764 | 539 | 1303 |
| 6. | Shim-oga | 253 | 1244 | 1175 | 2419 | 195 | 291 | 486 | 9 | 248 | 257 | 282 | 329 | 611 | 197 | 1 | 198 | 561 | 306 | 867 |
| 7. | Tumkur | 320 | 2809 | 2099 | 4908 | 515 | 420 | 935 | 156 | 323 | 479 | 682 | 631 | 1313 | 310 | 13 | 323 | 1146 | 712 | 1858 |
| 8 | Chikka-magalur | 220 | 1041 | 1057 | 2098 | 211 | 240 | 451 | 8 | 220 | 228 | 247 | 284 | 531 | 160 | 4 | 164 | 415 | 309 | 724 |

*Contd.....*

*Annexure II (Contd.)*

| 1 | 2 | 3 | 4 | 5 | 6 | 7 | 8 | 9 | 10 | 11 | 12 | 13 | 14 | 15 | 16 | 17 | 18 | 19 | 20 | 21 |
|---|---|---|---|---|---|---|---|---|---|---|---|---|---|---|---|---|---|---|---|---|
| 9. | D. Kannada | 202 | 1511 | 1320 | 2831 | 63 | 205 | 268 | 39 | 205 | 244 | 386 | 355 | 741 | 172 | 23 | 195 | 851 | 532 | 1383 |
| 10. | Udupi | 143 | 1171 | 994 | 2165 | 20 | 144 | 164 | 27 | 145 | 172 | 301 | 267 | 568 | 131 | 20 | 151 | 692 | 418 | 1110 |
| 11. | Hassan | 247 | 1772 | 1526 | 3298 | 328 | 302 | 630 | 4 | 247 | 251 | 421 | 442 | 863 | 232 | 6 | 238 | 787 | 529 | 1316 |
| 12. | Kodagu | 96 | 564 | 527 | 1091 | 48 | 99 | 147 | 38 | 101 | 139 | 128 | 148 | 276 | 91 | 1 | 92 | 259 | 178 | 437 |
| 13. | Mandya | 227 | 1974 | 1562 | 3536 | 245 | 249 | 494 | - | 227 | 227 | 508 | 444 | 952 | 205 | 22 | 237 | 1016 | 620 | 1636 |
| 14. | Mysore | 235 | 2170 | 1619 | 3789 | 436 | 341 | 777 | 53 | 244 | 297 | 565 | 462 | 1027 | 220 | 17 | 237 | 896 | 555 | 1451 |
| 15. | Chamarajanagar | 121 | 1088 | 834 | 1922 | 272 | 196 | 468 | 29 | 128 | 157 | 284 | 237 | 521 | 104 | 18 | 132 | 399 | 255 | 654 |
| 16. | Belgaum | 476 | 3920 | 3229 | 7149 | 360 | 537 | 897 | 64 | 489 | 553 | 1018 | 861 | 1879 | 414 | 94 | 508 | 2064 | 1248 | 3312 |
| 17. | Bijapur | 199 | 1778 | 1387 | 3165 | 366 | 275 | 641 | 8 | 201 | 209 | 444 | 396 | 840 | 191 | 22 | 213 | 769 | 493 | 1262 |
| 18. | Bagalkote | 161 | 1368 | 1095 | 2463 | 227 | 191 | 418 | 6 | 162 | 168 | 336 | 322 | 658 | 152 | 16 | 168 | 647 | 404 | 1051 |
| 19. | Dharwad | 122 | 814 | 756 | 1570 | 26 | 123 | 149 | 2 | 122 | 124 | 201 | 205 | 406 | 110 | 11 | 121 | 475 | 295 | 770 |
| 20. | Gadag | 102 | 762 | 639 | 1401 | 105 | 120 | 225 | 3 | 102 | 105 | 187 | 177 | 364 | 94 | 7 | 101 | 373 | 233 | 606 |
| 21 | Haveri | 190 | 1301 | 1152 | 2453 | 147 | 209 | 356 | 36 | 190 | 226 | 299 | 327 | 626 | 179 | 12 | 191 | 640 | 414 | 1054 |

*Contd......*

*Annexure II (Contd.)*

| 1 | 2 | 3 | 4 | 5 | 6 | 7 | 8 | 9 | 10 | 11 | 12 | 13 | 14 | 15 | 16 | 17 | 18 | 19 | 20 | 21 |
|---|---|---|---|---|---|---|---|---|---|---|---|---|---|---|---|---|---|---|---|---|
| 22. | U. Ka-nnada | 203 | 1170 | 1158 | 2328 | 46 | 210 | 256 | 8 | 204 | 212 | 290 | 310 | 600 | 168 | 1 | 179 | 658 | 423 | 1081 |
| 23. | Bellary | 185 | 1560 | 1197 | 2757 | 322 | 247 | 569 | 152 | 228 | 380 | 366 | 349 | 715 | 174 | 15 | 189 | 546 | 358 | 904 |
| 24. | Bidar | 170 | 1397 | 1094 | 2491 | 330 | 238 | 568 | 100 | 180 | 280 | 323 | 337 | 660 | 159 | 13 | 132 | 485 | 326 | 811 |
| 25. | Gul-barga | 333 | 2781 | 2206 | 4987 | 738 | 531 | 1269 | 86 | 346 | 432 | 673 | 655 | 1328 | 322 | 16 | 338 | 962 | 658 | 1620 |
| 26. | Rai-chur | 164 | 1545 | 1128 | 2673 | 297 | 224 | 521 | 153 | 194 | 347 | 380 | 331 | 711 | 153 | 24 | 177 | 562 | 355 | 917 |
| 27. | Koppal | 132 | 1167 | 899 | 2066 | 174 | 159 | 333 | 53 | 136 | 189 | 289 | 265 | 554 | 126 | 12 | 158 | 525 | 327 | 852 |
| | **Total** | **5535** | **43273** | **35187** | **78460** | **7521** | **7083** | **14604** | **1609** | **5759** | **7368** | **10581** | **10078** | **20659** | **5040** | **418** | **5458** | **18522** | **11849** | **30371** |

G– General, W – Women, T – Total
*Source*: RDPR, Government of Karnataka.

# ANNEXURE III

## RESULTS OF ZP AND TP POLLS

| | Zilla Panchayats | | | | | | | | | Taluk Panchayats | | | | | | | | |
|---|---|---|---|---|---|---|---|---|---|---|---|---|---|---|---|---|---|---|
| Districts | Constituencies | Results Declared | INC | BJP | JD (S) | JD (U) | CPI (M) | BSP | IND | Constituencies | Results Declared | INC | BJP | JD (S) | JD (U) | CPI (M) | BSP | IND |
| 1 | 2 | 3 | 4 | 5 | 6 | 7 | 8 | 9 | 10 | 11 | 12 | 13 | 14 | 15 | 16 | 17 | 18 | 19 |
| Bangalore (U) | 17 | 17 | 15 | 1 | — | 1 | — | — | — | 68 | 68 | 51 | 8 | 2 | 3 | — | — | 4 |
| Bangalore (R) | 38 | 38 | 23 | 1 | 6 | 8 | — | — | — | 139 | 139 | 86 | 6 | 21 | 25 | — | — | 1 |
| Kolar | 47 | 47 | 29 | — | — | 9 | 3 | — | 6 | 181 | 181 | 118 | — | 31 | — | 5 | — | 27 |
| Tumkur | 52 | 52 | 36 | 4 | 7 | 2 | — | — | 3 | 195 | 195 | 113 | 16 | 44 | 6 | — | — | 16 |
| Chitradurga | 31 | 31 | 24 | 2 | 1 | 3 | — | — | 1 | 115 | 115 | 68 | 12 | 10 | 16 | — | — | 9 |
| Davangere | 31 | 31 | 24 | 2 | 2 | 3 | — | — | — | 115 | 115 | 68 | 9 | 2 | 21 | — | 1 | 14 |
| Shimoga | 27 | 27 | 18 | 5 | — | 1 | — | — | 3 | 99 | 99 | 73 | 13 | 2 | 3 | — | — | 8 |
| Mysore | 41 | 41 | 18 | 2 | 20 | — | — | — | 1 | 152 | 152 | 72 | 7 | 57 | 5 | — | — | 11 |
| Chamarajanagar | 21 | 21 | 16 | — | 1 | 3 | — | — | 1 | 81 | 81 | 53 | 4 | 2 | 17 | — | — | 5 |

*Contd......*

*Annexure III (Contd.)*

| 1 | 2 | 3 | 4 | 5 | 6 | 7 | 8 | 9 | 10 | 11 | 12 | 13 | 14 | 15 | 16 | 17 | 18 | 19 |
|---|---|---|---|---|---|---|---|---|---|---|---|---|---|---|---|---|---|---|
| Hassan | 37 | 37 | 20 | — | 16 | — | — | — | 1 | 139 | 139 | 81 | 23 | 33 | 1 | — | — | 1 |
| Kodagu | 26 | 26 | 22 | 1 | 1 | — | 1 | — | 1 | 46 | 46 | 40 | 4 | — | — | — | — | 2 |
| Mandya | 39 | 39 | 21 | 1 | 12 | 1 | — | — | 4 | 144 | 144 | 63 | 4 | 50 | 13 | — | — | 14 |
| Chikka-magalur | 30 | 30 | 20 | 2 | 5 | 2 | — | — | 1 | 103 | 103 | 64 | 5 | 12 | 11 | — | — | 11 |
| Udupi | 24 | 24 | 24 | — | — | — | — | — | — | 88 | 88 | 83 | 4 | — | 1 | — | — | — |
| D Kan-nada | 31 | 31 | 30 | 1 | — | — | — | — | — | 115 | 115 | 87 | 22 | 4 | 2 | — | — | — |
| Bel-gaum | 76 | 76 | 53 | — | — | 12 | — | — | 11 | 287 | 287 | 174 | 3 | 1 | 54 | — | — | 55 |
| Bijapur | 32 | 32 | 30 | 1 | — | — | — | — | 1 | 124 | 124 | 83 | 18 | — | 17 | — | — | 6 |
| Bagal-kote | 26 | 25 | 19 | — | 1 | 4 | — | — | 1 | 99 | 99 | 61 | 4 | — | 29 | — | — | 5 |
| Dharwad | 18 | 18 | 15 | 2 | 1 | — | — | — | — | 66 | 66 | 36 | 16 | 3 | 3 | — | — | 8 |
| Gadag | 17 | 17 | 15 | — | — | 2 | — | — | — | 66 | 66 | 53 | — | 4 | 8 | — | — | 1 |
| U Kan-nada | 35 | 35 | 27 | 3 | 4 | — | — | — | 1 | 123 | 122 | 99 | 15 | 6 | 1 | — | — | 1 |
| Bidar | 26 | 26 | 22 | 3 | — | — | — | 1 | — | 101 | 101 | 76 | 18 | 1 | 3 | — | — | 3 |
| Bellary | 32 | 32 | 23 | 4 | — | 5 | — | — | — | 112 | 112 | 60 | 15 | 2 | 28 | — | — | 7 |

*Contd.....*

*Annexure III (Contd.)*

| 1 | 2 | 3 | 4 | 5 | 6 | 7 | 8 | 9 | 10 | 11 | 12 | 13 | 14 | 15 | 16 | 17 | 18 | 19 |
|---|---|---|---|---|---|---|---|---|---|---|---|---|---|---|---|---|---|---|
| Raichur | 29 | 29 | 21 | 2 | — | 6 | — | — | — | 107 | 107 | 66 | 8 | 2 | 20 | 1 | — | 10 |
| Gulbarga | 55 | 55 | 45 | 3 | 1 | 4 | — | — | 2 | 198 | 196 | 139 | 10 | 8 | 29 | 1 | 1 | 8 |
| Koppal | 23 | 23 | 16 | — | — | 4 | — | — | 3 | 83 | 83 | 53 | — | 1 | 24 | — | — | 5 |
| **Total 5586443** | **890** | **889** | **649** | **41** | **80** | **73** | **4** | **1** | **41** | **3255** | **3252** | **2099** | **249** | **300** | **357** | **7** | **2** | **238** |

*Source* : Deccan Herald News Paper, 10-06-2000.

ANNEXURE IV

## STATUS PROFILE

**Women Representatives in PRIs in Karnataka**
**(Under the PR Act, 1993)**

1. Below 30 years of age at the Grama Panchayat level, the share of the female members is 28 per cent; at the Taluk level and Zilla level their percentage works out respectively as 37 and 34. This clearly shows that younger generation women are showing interest in the PRIs.
2. In all, 17.7 per cent of the women members are illiterate. Illiteracy among female members is higher at the Grama Panchayat level. However, it is promising to observe that 17.4 per cent of the members at the Zilla Panchayat level are graduates.
3. Data show domination of the Backward castes among representation (35.3% at GP level, 34.6% at TP level and 46.4% at ZP level).
4. Women members have low exposure to mass media. This is particularly true in the case of newspaper reading at the GP level (38%).
5. Participation of female members in other organisations/ associations, such as youth associations, Mahila Mandals, co-operative societies, is very low (26% only) .
6. 94 per cent of the female members do not have any previous political experience. There are more freshers at the Grama and Taluk Panchayat levels than at the ZP level.
7. Family members, village community and self, appear to be the major motivational forces for the women representatives entry in PRIs.
8. Among other shades, social justice is the ideology of the majority of female members at all the three levels (49.3%, 68.4% and 61% respectively at GP, TP and ZP levels).
9. Data show that most women members have political party affiliations; only 6.3 per cent were independents.

*Source:* Subha, K. *Karnataka Panchayat Elections 1995: Process, Issues and Membership Profile*, Concept, New Delhi, 1997.

5

# WOMEN IN LOCAL GOVERNANCE Field Experience from Karnataka

ABDUL AZIZ

## Introduction

Reservation of seats and authority positions for women have brought a large number of women to Panchayats as members and presidents. The enhanced quota for women (compared to the previous regime) and the category-wise reservation also brought into Panchayats a large proportion of first generation elected representatives. Though this should be construed as a welcome development, in some quarters doubts are being expressed about the ability of women members to actually deliver the goods in the political space which is considered alien to them. A good deal of literature has emerged decrying "the larger than the life-size role" assigned to women in local governance. Indeed, bashing women members and presidents on this point has become fashionable in many circles even to the point of creating some myths about women's participation in the local governance system. The purpose of this note is to objectively evaluate the real imaginary positions taken on the issue of women's representation in local governance.

### The Problem of Proxy

There is a view that since the number of positions in Panchayats for women far exceeds the number of women who are competent and willing, the Panchayats get packed with inexperienced, illiterate and incompetent women members. And since the seats for women are reserved and rotated there is no chance for the sitting member to contest election next time; hence, every election brings in a new woman member who may not have previous experience. To top it all, it is also stated that since many of them are sponsored candidates they actually tend to be proxies for relatives and local leaders. By and large, this is true. Generally speaking, women members, when compared with their male counterparts, are less literate and less experienced. In such cases, relatives, especially husbands, and local leaders, especially the big land holders and contractors, serve as proxies to women members and women presidents. A recent study (*Search*, April-June 1999) shows that the women members serve as a proxy to husbands, other relatives and local leaders, and that the proxy rate among them rises as one moves from membership of the Panchayat to presidentship—for the presidentship the rate of proxy being much higher.

While admitting that the problem of proxy rule by relatives and local leaders is a fact of life, it may be desirable to note the following points: Our experience is that the proxy phenomenon is not confined to women alone; male members are also subject to this charge especially those coming from the reserved category. A majority of the males in this category are illiterate, inexperienced and incompetent. In their case also, sponsorship has been a common practice in so far as the number of reserved positions are in excess of those who are competent and willing to contest. Under the circumstance, it is strange that so much noise is made about the proxy problem only in respect of women when it exists extensively among males also. This strange phenomenon needs to be understood.

In our formal as well as informal discussions when we confronted the male members on the above issue, a point that emerged was that they were not against women becoming members of the Panchayats; their objection was to women being offered the authority position of presidentship. The objection was based on their perception that women, especially, when brought through the reservation channel, would not deliver the goods. The point that this possibility is highly probable even in respect of the male members coming through the same channel is glossed over! In order to get some insights into this contradiction in the position taken, it may be worth referring to some incidents observed by the present writer: Under the previous Panchayat regime (the 1983 PR Act), out of over two thousand Mandal Panchayats only two Panchayats were headed by women. In one such Mandal Panchayat (Honganur of Channapattana Taluk) a Hindu minority caste woman was elected as Pradhan by a quirk of circumstances. But within a couple of months, a no-confidence motion was contemplated by the male members. What is surprising is that her own party members joined hands with the opposition to dislodge her. The lady, whom this writer interviewed, in so many words gave the reason that the male members were not willing to work "under" a woman. Though one has to be cautious before generalizing from this single instance, the fact that a mindset of this nature among male members was visible on many occasions cannot be ignored. Thus, an evaluation study of the SIRD training programme for the Gram Panchayats (B.Vijaya Kumar *et al.*, June 1997) refers to an incident where the organizers make the women members sit on the floor while the male members were accommodated on chairs. When this writer organized a training programme for the Zilla Panchayat members at ISEC, Bangalore he was amused at seeing the male members always choosing to sit closer to the resource person leaving no choice to women but to sit in the back rows, and blaming the non-performance of Panchayats on the large presence of women in the Panchayat bodies.

These incidents, minor as they appear, reflect the inbuilt prejudice about the status of women in our society. This mind-set of the whole set applies equally to the sub set of the panchayats and creates an exaggerated version of the so-called incompetence of women members. It may be of interest here to digress a bit and examine why at all the proxy phenomena obtain in the Panchayats. Since women tend to be proxies largely for their family members and relatives, we interviewed some husbands and relatives to get a feel of why they shadowed the women members and presidents. The main point that emerged was the following: since the women are illiterate, elected for the first time and by reason of which are inexperienced they needed help and support from the close confidants. Husbands and close relatives come in handy to fill the bill. Husbands and relatives also feel compelled to be always on the side of the women members especially with the woman president because if the latter made a mistake or conspired to make a mistake it will be a reflection on the family honour. Hence the relatives of the woman president in particular keep company just in case she needs any help. In the opinion of this writer this is quite legitimate and there should not be any objection to the women members and presidents taking the advice of close relatives or even be guided by them. In fact, when women members came to our training programme, they came with their husbands/relatives who even sat behind them in the session taking down notes on their behalf and even prompting them to answer a question and seek a clarification. If this is the role they play even back at home in the Panchayat one should not have any objection to it.

### Awareness, Perception and Participation

One of the factors undoubtedly that is the base of better performance of the Panchayats is the higher level of awareness, and perceptions of, and participation in decision-making by, the members. A study of this aspect carried out in Chitradurga district (N. Sivanna, 1998) brings out some interesting results pertaining to male and female members. According to this study, women consistently obtained lower scores in regard to all the three parameters. However, the difference between males and females was slightly larger in regard to awareness (about 14 percentage points). But in respect of perceptions and participation this difference was lower—being 7 and 8.5 percentage points respectively. The slightly wider gap in awareness between male and female members is understandable considering that the former have a better chance of exposure to the goings on in the polity than the latter. However, lack of equal amount of exposure of female members has not deterred them from forming more or less equal perception levels and participating equally well in the decision-making process. Therefore, if the levels of awareness, perception and participation are an index of performance, then the performance levels of males does not appear to be too high to warrant creation of a myth that men can do better than women.

The above statement of facts is a quantified versions of the performance potential of males and females. Let us now examine its qualitative aspect. In his informal and unstructured discussions with some Grama Panchayat members, this writer asked them to state in order of priority three development projects they would choose if funds were made available. The male members preferred a link road to the nearest town, a bus shelter and a community hall in that order. The women members' preference on a priority basis was drinking water, toilets and street lights. A Harijan woman added "*Rudrabhoomi*"—a burial ground as her caste people were not allowed to bury their dead in the village burial ground! This gives a clue to the nature of felt needs of the people at the grass roots levels. May be the intensity of the needs felt by the male and the female members is the same and may be the needs of male and females differ. But the point that cannot be over-looked is that women members are much closer to home—to the immediate needs of the family. In so far as local governments are expected to meet the immediate needs of the family, the quality of women's perceptions appears to be a shade better.

Consider another incident in support of this point. A Panchayat in Kolar district was debating a question as to how it can utilize a grant received from an organization. The male members of the Panchayat proposed that an additional dairy building may be constructed using those funds as the present one was congested. Two women members who were present stood up and made an alternative proposal. They urged that the building where the Anganwadi children are housed presently was dilapidated and as such it may collapse any time causing death of the young children. Hence, there was an urgent need to put up an Anganwadi building. That the final decision went in favour of the dairy building is a different story. But the fact is that the concern of the women members to the safety of children cannot escape the attention of the readers.

Another case may be quite revealing. A Grama Panchayat did not have a Panchayat building. So, the Panchayat took a decision to put up a building for the purpose on a two *gunta* private plot belonging to a Panchayat member who offered it for a price of Rs. 20,000. A woman member intervened to make a suggestion. She said that it was atrocious to squander the precious Panchayat funds on purchase of land. She suggested that an announcement may be made to the effect that whichever village comes forward to donate two *guntas* of land, the Panchayat will decide to locate the Panchayat building in that village. If land is thus obtained free of cost, the amount that would have gone by way of price to be paid for land could be used for construction of the building or providing amenities to the villagers. Though the decision taken obviously went against her suggestion, the logic involved in her argument cannot be missed.

**Training Needs**

From the above discussion, it appears that though the awareness levels of women are lower, the levels of their perceptions and participation are not far below those of male members. Moreover, qualitatively women capture the felt needs that are nearer home and the needs identified by them are of immediate nature. However, women members seem to be constrained from having their say in the decision-making process. As a result, they tend to lose out to the male members. This result may be due to their inability to lobby with other members and officials, their low levels of articulation skills, and perhaps to lack of information. Therefore, it appears that asymmetry of information, inability to lobby and to be articulate act as constraints on them to get the decisions in their favour. If these constraints are released by providing them with full information about the Panchayat system, and training them in the art of articulation and lobbying, they possibly will effectively influence decision-making. This makes out a case for organizing special training programmes for women to provide them with relevant information and to impart skills of articulation and lobbying.

Realising the needs as also the importance of training, the Government of Karnataka sponsored several training programmes for the benefit of members, presidents and vice-presidents of all levels of Panchayats. The SIRD, DTI's academic institutions and NGOs organized such programmes in the State. In some cases, training programmes were targetted exclusively to women members perceiving that they needed special attention. In many cases, the programmes were targetted both for male and female members. The inputs given to the trainees were (a) basic information about the PR system with special emphasis on the legal, administrative and developmental aspects, and (b) skills of speaking in the

Panchayat meetings, seeking information, raising issues and debating on the proposals brought before the meetings, and (c) leadership skills of handling people–citizens, officials and other elected members. Some institutions also placed emphasis on changing the attitudes of members on the question of reservation, equal opportunity for weaker sections especially women and depressed classes, on corruption, class and caste harmony and such other sensitive social problems.

It is difficult to capture the exact impact of training programmes on the trainees. However, field experience seems to suggest that members benefited from such programmes though a need was felt that the training duration could have been extended, and repeat and follow up programmes organized to update knowledge and to keep members' interest alive. On women members particularly, the training programmes appear to have left a good impact. This point may be illustrated by sharing our own experience in respect of a programme organized in ISEC for the members, vice presidents and presidents of Zilla Panchayats.

The fact that out of 700 persons who attended the programme about 36 per cent were women suggests that response from them was encouraging especially when viewed from their general reluctance to come out of their homes. On the first day we found them to be overwhelmed by the new environment and strange people. But our lady colleagues did their best to put the women trainees at ease. The women members did not speak much on the first day but gradually as they went through the sessions, they picked up courage and participated in the discussions. By the end of the programme we hardly found any difference between the participatory levels of male and female members. A remark made by Dr. P.V. Shenoi, the then Director of ISEC, in regard to the participation of women members on the valedictory function of one of the programmes in the presence of the Minister of Panchayat Raj and Rural Development may be of interest to note here. He said, "on the first day they would not speak at all in the sessions. But, on the second day they would open up, they would speak on the third day and roar on the fourth day". This is a dramatized assessment of the participation of women members in the discussion. As a matter of fact, this writer who was the course coordinator, had the pleasant experience of getting congratulatory calls from the relatives of the women trainees after they went back from the course. A typical example is a call from the husband of a member who after congratulations his congratulations exclaimed: "My wife had never spoken in the Panchayat meeting until recently. After she returned from ISEC, she made a speech". We also on and off received reports that our women members had become assertive, even quoted from the Panchayat Act and referred to various Union and State government programmes and schemes funded by external agencies whenever occasions demanded. What a tribute to the role of training programmes in empowering women members! All of this underlines the importance as also the usefulness of training for Panchayats functionaries.

## Concluding Remarks

It is admitted that the women Panchayat members and presidents do have limitations arising on account of their low literacy level and lack of experience and exposure to the world outside home. This is compounded by a spurt in demand for women to assume charge of local governance due mainly to reservation of seats and authority positions. Under the circumstances, in many cases they work as proxies to relatives and local leaders. But the phenomenon of proxy rule in Panchayats is not the exclusively preserve of the female members alone; male members are also subjected to the same charge.

The levels of awareness, perception and participation among women members are, no doubt, lower compared with men but the resultant gap between the two does not appear to be wide enough to warrant such a severe criticism of women for their non-performance or low performance. Besides, the qualitative aspect of their levels of those parameters suggest that women members are nearer home and focus on the immediate needs of the family when compared with the male members.

Though women members do put across their views and appear to be logical in their arguments, they tend to lose the battle mainly because they are not articulative enough, not assertive and not equipped with adequate information. It is in this context, a need is felt to equipping them with knowledge, and skills of articulation and lobbying by organizing training programmes. Whenever training programmes have been organized, women have responded better, shown immense interest and demonstrated their ability for quick learning. Therefore, it is suggested that training for women is a must and that repeat programmes should be organized to update and keep their interest alive.

## REFERENCES

"Impact of Reservation: The Status and Power of Women Representatives in Gram Panchayats", *Search Bulletin*, Vol.XIV, No. 2. (April-June 1999)

Sivanna. N. (1998), "Process and Performance of Panchayats" in Abdul Aziz *et al.*, *Decentralised Governance and Planning: A Comparative Study in Three South Indian States* (Mimeo), ISEC, Bangalore.

Vijya Kumar, B. *et al.*, (June 1997), *Training Programme for Grama Panchayat Members: A Process Evaluation* (Mimeo), ISEC, Bangalore.

6

# DECENTRALIZED GOVERNANCE AND WOMEN EMPOWERMENT INITIATIVES

## Lessons from Kerala's People's Plan

B. MOHANAN AND P.V. MARY MATILDA

Kerala the southernmost State of India has many reasons to be proud of. In the human development and related indices it occupies prime position among the Indian States. Kerala is the only State in India with a positive sex ratio. According to 2001 estimates, in respect of education and health and population control the State occupies foremost position in the country. This is even comparable with the developed countries of the world. In other statistical indices like vaccination rates, maternal mortality, child labour, nutritional status, access to medical care, availability of roads, schools and other public facilities, Kerala has the substantial leads over the rest of the country.

But there are some paradoxes existing in the State. Kerala's achievements in the social sector did not go hand in hand in material production sectors. Stating more clearly, Kerala presents indicators of high social development in a low productive economy, setting it apart from the rest of India (K.N. Nair :2001).

The paradox exists in the case of women also. The improved physical quality of life among women is not reflected in their greater participation in politics or in gainful economic activities which are two strong indicators for empowerment.

**Some Female Status Indicators of Kerala**

| Indices | India | Kerala |
|---|---|---|
| Annual Per Capita Income | Rs. 6750 | Rs. 6000 |
| Average No. of children | 4 | 1.9 |
| Infant Mortality Rate | 80/1000 | 13/1000 |
| Life expectancy | 59 | 74 |
| Female literacy | 39.29% | 87% |
| Couple who adopted family planning method | 43% | 80% |
| Average age at marriage | 14-15 | 21 |
| Sex ratio | 927/1000 males | 1058/1000 males |

*Source :* State Planning Board.

K. Saradamani (1999) has conducted a study on status of women in Kerala in her book in Malayalam entitled *Sthree*, *Sthreevadam*, *Sthree Vimochanam*. There are some interesting and valuable findings in her book, which put women into the subordinate position, of which some are discussed below.

Kerala women are well educated compared to women in other States. There are many women who have acquired more than two degrees and the number of women acquiring expertise in specialized fields have been increasing year by year.

But the type of education women get does not help them to enhance their status. Very few women are placed in positions, which suit their educational qualifications. Women executives do not get promotion opportunities as their male counterparts. Sometimes they have to give up promotion because of transfer to different places. Majority of women consider their employment as a mere income generating activity. They are satisfied with a secondary role in the working place. They do not give any priority to their professional role over other gender roles.

Monica Erwer (1998) observes that the girls in Kerala are very brilliant at secondary school and graduate level. All the high marks go to girls. But they are not seen after that in any place either as eminent scientists or engineers. The problem is that education does not seem to give the women any confidence as is the case with men.

The many different barriers that exclude women from public

political activity seem to be as great in Kerala as elsewhere in India. Just 28 women contested in the 1987 elections to the 140 seats in the State Legislative Assembly and only 8 won. This makes the setting of the State Legislative Assembly from a gender perspective skewed with 5.7 per cent women and 94.3 per cent men. In comparison with Lok Sabha India as a nation is doing better than Kerala with 7.9 per cent women in 1984, and none of these from Kerala.

The election in 1996 to the Kerala Assembly does not present much improvement in women's participation in the political process. Of the total 1,201 candidates 55 were women and 13 of them got elected to represent the 20.67 million electorates of which 1,063 million were women. The 13 elected female representatives constituted 9.2 per cent and the 127 elected male representatives constituted 90.8 per cent of the 140 seats in the State Assembly. This made a slight improvement in the gender balance as compared with the 1987 elections.

In the 1996 elections to the Lok Sabha, 10 women were candidates for the 20 seats belonging to the State. None of the candidates got elected. All these statistics indicate the low political participation of women in the State.

The decision making committees mostly consist of men. The male dominated committees are reluctant to accept females as candidates. Whenever political parties are compelled to give party tickets to women candidates they allot the seats where the party influence is less. This is one of the reasons why women candidates get lost in the elections.

Kerala Ministries are always male dominated. Even though there are women who are performing better than their male counterparts ministership is always forbidden to them. The above facts and figures reiterate that the high status of women in Kerala is not reflected in political participation of women. This implies women have less opportunity to participate in the decision making process in the State policy matters.

In the book *Politics, Women and Well-being — How Kerala became a Model,* Robin Jeffry (1992) made a study on Kerala women. Based on his studies he says "Kerala by the 1970s was becoming an object of fascination for scholars and policy makers concerned with development. Kerala's people had the highest life expectancy in India, the lowest infant mortality rate and birth rate that seemed to be falling. In short their quality of life appeared better than that of people in India's other States". But this quality does not sustain in the case of women. As early as 1944, a Kerala scholar declared that the dissolution of mortality and the spread of male dominated monogamous households a 'retrograde' change from the feminist stand point. Among Ezhavas, a major lower caste groups, women in Kerala has not expanded steadily since 1920, nor has the influence of women in politics and domestic affairs constantly increased. Women's roles have changed but we need to consider evidence before attempting to decide whether the lot of women has improved. Women in Kerala did not enter into public politics and when they did they paid a price".

Women's organizations in Kerala are also fragmented. Most political parties have women's wings and local women's groups are common. Kerala has more hostels for working women than any State in India. But women are dissuaded from taking part in elections or other forms of public politics. Nor is there a powerful feminist organization.

Even though the above discussed subordinate position of women was existing in the State for many years, an organized effort to bring changes in the situation took place only recently especially during People's Campaign for Development Planning (PCDP) programme during the Ninth Five Year Plan. It was a campaign for decentralized planning with people's participation through the Local Self Government Institutions (LSGIs).

People's Campaign for Development Planning (PCDP) was an attempt to conceptualize, operationalise and institutionalize a system of multilevel people centered planning process suitable to the regional specifications of Kerala. Objective of PCDP was to ensure people's involvement especially women's participation in decision making process, project formulation, sharing of ideas, implementing programmes, monitoring the progress of implementation, sharing the benefits of development and their involvement in efforts to maintain sustainability of the programmes.

As Sen committee observes "even when a general enabling environment exists for people's participation, it is possible that certain groups get excluded due to their backwardness and powerlessness. In order to achieve constitutional objectives of social justice it is necessary to empower such established groups. In Kerala SC/ST and women belong to this category. (Sen Committee Report, 1998). So ensuring participation of women by empowering them became an objective in the people's planning programme.

A women component plan was constituted as the part of people's planning campaign to ensure the participation of women in the process.

**An Overview of Activities under Women Component Plan (WCP)**

***Gram Sabha***

Gram Sabhas are considered as a form of direct democracy where the people are given a chance not only in electing their representatives but also in discussing, deciding and participating in the developmental activities of the Panchayat. The 73rd Constitutional Amendment Act (1992) made the Gram Sabhas an integral part of the Panchayati Raj set-up and made constitution of Gram Sabhas a mandatory provision by the respective State governments. The Kerala Panchayat Raj Act, 1994 constituted Gram Sabhas for each ward of the Gram Panchayat due to the high density of population in the State. The meetings, which were two times in a year originally were increased to four times subsequently.

The first phase of the people's campaign was the identification of the felt needs of the people in the Gram Sabha meetings. Instead of having a general body meeting. The meetings of the Gram Sabhas were held in smaller subject groups in order to ensure participation by all its member. Special emphasis was given to ensure women's participation in Gram Sabhas. For discussing women and gender related issues, a subject group on women and development was made mandatory. In these group meetings women were given opportunity to discuss the problems facing them and make suggestions for solutions to the problems identified.

***Financial Devolution for WCP***

Under the people's planning process, the government for the first time decided to devolve 35-40 per cent of the Plan outlay to the local bodies in the form of grant-in-aid. The grant in aid had three components. General plan fund, funds for scheduled castes known as Special Component Plan (SCP) and funds of scheduled tribes known as Tribal Sub Plan (TSP). The local bodies were asked to set apart 10 per cent of the overall grant-in-aid to the Women Component Plan. But during the first year allocation by the Panchayats for the WCP fell far short of the suggested minimum of 10 per cent of the grant-in-aid. During the subsequent years, the suggestion to set apart 10 per cent of the Plan fund was made mandatory. The Panchayats were asked to hike the allocation to WCP beyond 10 per cent if there were shortfall in the proceeding years.

The money allotted for WCP was to be utilized by preparing projects that directly benefit women and only those that are organized and managed by women were to be included in the women component plan. During second year, the guidelines for designing women's projects were distributed to every Panchayat in the women and development handbook. Some examples of the suggested projects are: counselling centres, women's transport cooperative society, women masons, fertilizer production, cane work training, computer skill education and auto rickshaw driving.

### *Training and Capacity Building*

Training and Capacity Building is an essential aspect in the process of empowerment. An important component of the people's campaign was the elaborate capacity building exercises undertaken through the training programmes. The campaign was one of the largest campaigns the country has ever witnessed. The State planning board had organized systematic training for a large number of resource persons. In the seventh rounds of training, at State, district and local level, 15,000 elected representatives, 25,000 officials and around 75,000 volunteers were given training.

For effective implementation of women component plan, government has taken earnest efforts in capacity building of elected women representatives, women task forces, officials as well as non-officials. Five exclusive books on women development have been prepared in simple language for shedding light on WCP projects. Training programmes were designed as a part of the annual plan.

They were:

1. A State level training programme of relatively longer duration.
2. One day orientation programme for all women elected representatives at district level.
3. Block level project clinics/workshops to help the preparation of women development projects. A separate handbook on women and development has been prepared and distributed in training programmes. The trainng module includes street play which has been a dramatic of experience sharing exercise of elected representatives.

The course material included:

1. Handbook on women and development,
2. People's planning and women empowerment,
3. Equality in development,
4. Status of women studies, and
5. People's planning, advancement of women.

***Achievements of WCP***

The WCP has many achievements to its credit. They are:

1. For the first time, through WCP, the development of women was brought to the agenda of each of the local bodies, women were treated not as mere beneficiaries but partners in the development process. This was made possible by the decentralized planning process.
2. For the first time in the history of the LSGIs these bodies were asked to set apart 10 per cent of the grant-in-aid for projects that directly benefited women. Unlike earlier programmes which were from above, in WCP, the local bodies formulated projects based on the felt needs of the people that were put forth in the Gram Sabha. This statutory requirement of setting apart funds for WCP helped the women to occupy space to intervene in the development process.

3. The gender dimensions were brought into the planning process. During the second phase of planning strategic gender needs addressing issues of violence, gender division of labour in terms of equal wages for equal work, etc., atrocities against women came up in various local bodies.

4. With WCP, there was a quantum increase in the benefits given to women. Within this broad context the disadvantaged like windows, separated women and families with unmarried girls were given more weightage while selecting the beneficiaries for various projects.

5. The 10 per cent outlay was set apart by the local bodies uniformly without taking into account the percentage or integrate it with its own funds while preparing projects. They also had the freedom to increase the percentage or integrate with its own funds while preparing projects. Though instructions were given to the local bodies on the use of WCP funds, the local bodies had the freedom to prepare location specific projects based on the felt needs of the people.

6. Under WCP, participation of women was ensured in all sphere of activities including expressing opinions, taking part in discussions, formulating project proposals, monitoring and implementation. Nearly one-third of the participants in the development seminars were women and they were active in the subject group which discussed the women development reports.

7. New forms of women organizations such as neighbourhood groups and self help groups were successfully promoted in Panchayats under WCP. One positive outcome of this was the increased women participation in Panchayats which have promoted self help groups.

8. There has been an improvement in the conceptualization of WCP over the years. During the first year, there was no clarity regarding what all could be brought under WCP and this was reflected in the nature of projects prepared by the Panchayats. Houses, roads, sanitation etc. which in the strict sense should

have been part of the general projects, were prepared under WCP during the first year. But there was a marked improvement in the nature of projects prepared during the subsequent phases. There as a reallocation of resources from agriculture to industry, perceptible fall in infrastructure projects and a shift from service sector to employment and other social welfare programmes.

9. There has been a qualitative change in the nature of projects over the years. A few Panchayats have formulated projects that have gone beyond the stereotyped gender projects. Projects like auto-rickshaw driving technology etc. have been prepared that aim at breaking the monopoly of men in these fields. Welfare oriented programmes have been changed into empowerment oriented programmes in some Panchayats. These Panchayats have exemplary models which need to be replicated in other Panchayats.

10. Capacity building was given due importance under WCP. The elected women members and women task force members were given training in matters related to women issues and preparation of women related projects.

11. Due to the efforts at capacity building, a positive impact has been created in women empowerment such as leadership development, communication skills, group dynamics and enhancement of their decision making powers. This was reflected in the recent elections to the local bodies where women came forward to contest elections on their own instead of being forced as was the case earlier.

12. There was considerable enhancement in confidence and decision making capacity of women participants in Gram Sabhas, who were mere spectators in early stages, have turned into active participants in subsequent phases. This was made possible by the emphasis on group discussion (Oommen John and Leelakumari 2001).

### *WCP and Women Empowerment*

In this context a study on contribution of WCP towards the empowerment of Kerala women seems to be meaningful.

Empowerment is a word widely used but seldom defined. It is a process and, therefore, not something that can be given to people. Women's empowerment can be viewed as a continuum of several interrelated and reinforcing components as awareness building about women's discrimination and opportunities as a step towards gender equality. Collective awareness building provides a sense of group identity and the power of working as a group. Empowerment also consists of capacity building and skills development especially the ability to plan, make decisions, organize, manage and carry out activity to deal with people and institution in the world around them (Sushma Sahay 1998).

In the book titled *Empowering the Indian Women,* empowerment has been defined by different authors. According to K.D.Gangrade, empowerment may mean equal status to women, opportunity and to develop herself. According to Kiren Devendra, empowerment of women would mean equipping women to be economically independent, self reliant, have a positive self esteem to enable them to face any difficult situation and they should be able to participate in developmental activities. The empowered women should be able to participate in the decision making process.

The following can be considered as qualitative measures for empowerment process:

*Awareness*

Awareness about women's situation,

Awareness about discrimination,

Awareness that gender is socially constructed,

Awareness about women's right's—one's own rights,

Awareness about their opportunities, and

Awareness about the need for equality at all levels.

*Capacity Building and Skills Development*

Ability to specify problems and issues,

Ability to plan problems and issues into projects,

Capacity to utilize decision-making opportunity,

Capacity to execute power in decision making,

Capacity to organize a group,

Capacity to manage a group,

Capacity to carry out activities,

Capacity to maintain public relations,

Capacity to communicate matters, and

Capacity to carry out activities with clear perspective.

*Participation in Development Progress/Governance*

Participation in decision making in the family,

Participation in the group—outside home, community and society,

Participation in economic activities,

Participation in controlling resources like money, land and property,

Participation in women's burden of work within the home,

Creation and strengthening of women's group and organizations,

Promoting qualities of nurturing, caring, gentleness not only in women but also in men, and

Enhancement of human potential at individual and social level of expression.

*Autonomy*

Women can define their attitudes, values and behaviour in relation to their own real interests,

Women can maintain equal mindedness rather than act out roles that confront and challenge male dominance,

Women can respond as equals and cooperate towards that common end, and

Women can use their talents for fulfilling their real life and maintain their strength.

If we take the above qualitative indicators for empowerment into consideration we can understand that Women Component Plan had an impact in empowering women. Gram Sabhas helped women to have increase in self esteem and also participation in the decision making process.

The capacity building programmes for women representatives in the local bodies equipped with communication and other leadership skills. The improvement in the quality of women representatives in the local bodies is an outcome of the training programmes.

The self-help groups of women under the women component plan helped women to be financially self reliant which is an important aspect of empowerment. Several projects were implemented whose primary beneficiaries were women.

But when we look into the quantitative aspect of empowerment, the number of women benefited out of the women component plan was not enough to make an improvement in the empowerment level of Kerala women. The reports about women in Kerala reveal that Kerala women are not empowered as per the indicators of empowerment.

Atrocities against women are on the increase in Kerala, which is called God's own country. The Kerala Women's Commission has received more than 38,000 complaints from women over a variety of crimes meted out to them till 2001.

The volume of cases also shows that Kerala is still an unsafe place for women. In 2001 alone there were around 7,000 police cases on crimes against women of which 1,800 related to rape, molestation and kidnap. Studies show 250 per cent increase in the number of cases of rapes of girls below 10 years or aged between 10 and 16.

According to statistics with crime records bureau at Trivandrum, there is three fold increase in crimes against women during the course of ten years. Total registered cases increased from 1,967 in 1991 to 8,120 in 2001.

The latest report of the UN sponsored National Family Health Survey India, conducted by the International Institute for Population Sciences reveals the alarming statistics of domestic violence in Kerala. Sexual harassment at the work place is on the increase (*Mean Time* : July 2002).

Apart from the increase in number of atrocities against women, Kerala is registering an increase in the number of women reported missing and women committing suicide. During the past year, 971 women and 336 children have gone missing in the State. Since last

May, 2131 people have been reported missing of which 60 per cent were women and children. About 50 per cent of the missing women were young—between 19 and 30 years.

The number of harassment cases filed at various police stations in the State exceeded 5,250. They include dowry harassment and domestic violence. More than 500 rape charges have been registered by May 2001 and 2002.

Politics and governance have been male domain ever since the beginning of the recorded history. The emergence of women leaders was a twentieth century phenomenon and several countries in Asia and Europe elected women leaders during the later half of the country. However at the dawn of the twenty first century, main remain at the periphery of main stream politics and all the initiatives for the empowerment of women are focused on education, employment, health care, violence against women and so on. Women's lack of involvement in the political field has not been adequately explored and little effort has been made to understand the structural constraints that prevent from seeking and attaining political power. Kerala is no exception to the above situation.

Kerala women are still in the grip of gender roles attributed by the society. It was quite evident during the process of implementation of women component plan. As observed by Thomas Issac, "The women development projects were constrained not only by technical and financial factors but also in terms of ideological perspective. The projects in general did not attempt to challenge the existing gender based division of labour either by starting industries in the male dominated areas or upgrading the skill of women in increase their occupational mobility into new sectors. They were only a few projects that attempted to address the cultural and ideological issues related to women status".

Kerala needs a rethinking about empowering of women. One of the major issues is lack of proper strategies for empowerment. To identify proper strategies for empowerment a study on present level of empowerment of Kerala women becomes a prerequisite.

## REFERENCES

*Census of India* 2001.

Erwer Monica, (1998), *Development Beyond the Status of Women—The Kerala Model from a Gender Perspective*, South India Licentia thesis Getesberg University.

John Oommen & Leelakumari (2001): *Report of the Study of Women Component Plan in Kerala*, Unicef, Chennai (2001).

Jeffrey, Robert (1992), *Politics, Women and Well being—How Kerala became a Model*, Oxford University Press.

Kapur, Promilla (ed), *Empowering the Indian Women*, Publications Division Ministry of Information and Broadcasting, Government of India.

Mohanan, B. (2003), *Women and Law: The Case of Kerala*, ISDA, Trivandrum.

Nair, K.N. (2001), *Kerala Research Programme on Local Development*, Centre for Development Studies, Trivandrum.

Roy Mathew (2002): Atrocities against Women on the Rise, the *Hindu*, April 13, 2002.

Sarada Mani, K. (1999): *Sthree, Sthreevadam, Sthree Vimochanam* (Malayalam), DC Books, Kottayam.

Sahay, Sushama (1998): *Women and Empowerment*, Discovery Publishing House, New Delhi.

7

# POLITICAL EMPOWERMENT OF WOMEN THROUGH DECENTRALIZED INSTITUTIONS (PRIs) IN KARNATAKA

K. SUBHA AND B.S. BHARGAVA

One theme on which Gandhiji wrote repeatedly was the need to improve the status of women. Pandit Nehru also believed in improving the status of women and involving them in the process of development. He was the chairman of a special sub-committee in the National Planning Committee to report on the role of women in the planned economy. He want the sub-committee to examine the question of women's role from all angles—social, political, legal and economic. Gandhiji's repeated exhortations and Nehru's commitment led to equality of sexes being included as a Fundamental Right in the Karachi Congress in 1931.

The dawn of India's Political Independence in August 1947, and the establishment of a republican form of state in 1950, brought to women the promise of adult franchise and equality of opportunity in all spheres which included social, economic and political activities. The assumption underlying these provisions was that every adult women, irrespective of her social status, would function as a citizen and as an individual in the task of nation building. The constitutional rights were to serve as instruments for achieving equality of status and opportunities in all spheres. Equality in all spheres is inseparable from active political participation. This means not only using the right to vote but also power-sharing, profit sharing, co-decision making and co-policy making at all levels of government. The highest law of the land, i.e., the Constitution of India pledges equality of status and opportunity, justice—social, economic and political—and dignity of the individual, to men and women equally.

The globe also was generating awareness about the problems of women in all spheres of life. The charter of the United Nations dedicated that organization should work for "promoting and encouraging respect for human rights and for fundamental freedoms for all without distinction as to race, sex, language or religion", while the preamble to the Charter spoke of "the equal rights of men and women".

The seventies changed the scenario and brought women to the forefront of development concerns. During the International Women's Decade in India, there was unprecedented efforts from various sectors to reassess the role of women and direct policies and programmes towards women's need. The first-half of the decade was a period of research, review and rethinking to make women's issues visible to planners. As the decade advanced, new issues came to be identified making women's equality a complex goal.

The 1960s and 1970s policy-makers and practioners, particularly in southern countries, focused on women on account of their disadvantages and development needs. The Northern aid system prioritized support to projects that met women's needs and consequently, NGOs formulated development projects for women. Thus, in the development approach, women found organizational expression in the form of separate departments or units that concentrated exclusively on their issues and needs. This resulted in mainstream structures sidelining women's issues to the periphery.

However, since the mid-1980s, the women's movement and feminist scholarship have been exposing the unequal division of labour, power and resources between women and men and the different ways they are affected by policies and programmes which claim to offer equal benefits to everyone in the community. The women's movement has thus put gender relations at the centre in the analysis of social relations which has led to the inclusion of gender in the development approach. The gender approach recognizes women's subordinate position and inequalities in power distribution and aims at restructuring power in favour of gender justice and equity.

The Government appointed a committee on the status of women in India (CSWI) in 1977 to undertake a "comprehensive examination of all the questions relating to the rights and status of women". It had commented on the failure of an earlier policy to induct women into local government bodies through reservation of a few seats, as a form of tokenism, and recommended the establishment of statutory women's Panchayats at the village level to ensure greater participation in the political process.

The publications of the report of the committee on the status of women the observance of International Women's year in 1975, the formulation of a National Plan of Action for Women, setting up of a National Committee with the Prime Minister as the head proved the concern for women. Since then scholars and policy-makers diverted their attention to the issues of women which culminated in establishing a National Commission for Women in 1992 and the National Perspective Plan for Women (1988-2000).

National development will be more effective, citizen irrespective of being a man or woman has an active share in all its activities. However, previous experiences show that women have rarely occupied leading positions and have not made, much progress in spite of the laws that guarantee opportunity. There is thus a need for empowering women. Empowerment has different dimensions — political, social and economic. It is a process of redistribution of resources in the society in such a way that women get equal access and control over the resources.

It is at the grassroots level that women should participate more because, the decision of the local government have profound effect on the problems that concern women about the quality of life. This is more so during the period of child-bearing and motherhood when women are the major consumers of local government services either directly for themselves or indirectly for their children. These issues are among the major concerns of the local governments. Therefore, the awareness in women and their experiences in dealing with local concerns especially qualities them to participate in local government. So, the inclusion of women concerns and their representation in public life might lead to a profound redefinition of public life itself. Thus, successful participation of women in a large segment of local government is possible only by a woman to woman contact. Woman members should be present in the local bodies who can come in direct contact with the women, bring about mobilization, understand the special problems first-hand, seek effective solutions and channelize the welfare activities towards the felt needs of the deprived and the discriminated.

Since the rural local body is the most important channel for popular participation in the process of development and as it deals with the day-to-day affairs of the rural folk it should keep close contact with the people and draw up ways and means to serve them. By doing so, it can emerge as a model in incorporating women's talents in the light of the special nexus between women's concern and local issues and thereby enhance the status of women through political empowerment.

Empowerment gives women the capacity to influence decision-making process, planning, implementation and evaluation by integrating them into the political system. This implies political participation which includes right to vote, contest, campaign, party membership and representation in political offices at all levels and effectively influence decisions thereby leading to political empowerment.

The Gender Empowerment Measure (GEM) concentrates on economic, political and professional participation. One of the important indicators for women political participation would be her share of representation in local bodies. Reservation is one of the instruments of political empowerment as it guarantees representation. The passing of the Seventy Third and Seventy Fourth Constitutional Amendment can be considered as the greatest event for women's empowerment as one-third of the seats are reserved for women in the local bodies. The Constitution (Seventy Third Amendment) Act of 1993 which was brought into force from April 24, 1993, established India's Panchayati Raj Institutions on a sound footing. The Amendment gave the much needed impetus to the concept of local self-government which till then suffered from lack of Constitution protection. It envisages a polity where more powers are decentralized to the third level of government.

## LOOKING BACK

Indian environment is predominantly rural and the rural sector occupies an important place in Indian economy. Even today, more than 70 per cent people live in rural areas. The focus on rural development started with the realization of the fact that the rural sector was underdeveloped economically, socially and politically and needed special attention of the government. The Community Development Programme was launched in 1952 covering the entire nation. Later on, the institutional arrangement that was assigned the major task of uplifting the weaker sections which included women. But when the system was introduced, very few women contested or got elected. It was the publication of the Report Committee on the status of women that there was a demand for representation of women in Panchayati Raj Institutions by reservation. Having set the ball rolling, it is necessary to sketch the position of women in grass roots organisation as it is the most approachable unit.

The Community Development Programme was started in 1952 to improve the living conditions of the rural poor. Unfortunately it could not deliver much. The Balwant Rai Mehta Committee observed that the main factor that caused the failure of the Community Development Programme was the absence of people's participation.

The Committee recommended the creation of three-tier system as the institutional arrangement to make people's participation meaningful and effective. Necessary legislation was to be enacted by every State to implement the Panchayati Raj system as a form of local self-government to perform developmental, administrative and political tasks. Rajasthan and Andhra Pradesh were the first States to adopt this system in 1959, followed by Karnataka and Orissa. Since then Karnataka has been at the forefront of decentralisation.

A National Committee on Panchayati Raj Institutions, headed by Ashok Mehta was appointed in 1977 by the Janata Government which was in power at the Centre. The report submitted in 1978 recommended a two-tier system in the rural local government and emphasized the need for constitutional sanction to the Panchayati Raj Institutions.

Most of the principles enunciated in this Report became the basis of the Karnataka Zilla Parishads, Taluk Panchayat Samitis, Mandal Panchayat and Nyaya Panchayat Act 1985. This was a radical change brought about by the Janata Party which formed the government in Karnataka in 1983 under the Chief Minister - ship of Ramakrishna Hegde. It was implemented to give the highest priority to rural development to eradicate poverty and to improve the rural economy through people's participation.

In addition to the Zilla Parishad at the District level followed by the Mandal Panchayat comprising of a group of villages, the Act also provided for two other statutory bodies — the Taluk Panchayat Samiti at the Taluk/Block level, which was an advisor and co-ordinating body with no executive function and the Gram Sabha (Village Assembly) below the Mandal Panchayat. The Mandal Panchayat was the first elected tier located between the village and the Taluk while the Zilla Parishad which was the second directly elected tier was a powerful body which administered schemes and programmes evolved by it and transferred to it. Cadres were maintained for manning the Zilla Parishad and the Mandal. Elections were held in January 1987. For the first time the elections were conducted on party lines.

Another significant feature of this act was that, it realized women were inadequately represented in politics and an effort was made to do justice to them. Reservation upto 25 per cent was provided in the local bodies. Women's participation in the political process took a different turn in the history of Karnataka. Earlier when the Panchayat Raj system was introduced, very few women contested or got elected. The committees which recommended the creation of Panchayati Raj Institutions (PRIs) did not say much about the role of women in these bodies. Balwantrai Mehta Committee recommended that in the constitution of Panchayats, provision may be made for the cooption of two women members, "who are interested in work among women and children". The Ashok Mehta Committee had mentioned that two women securing the highest number of votes among the women candidates in the election could take the seats reserved for them, a method of co-option by election. Though PRIs were established in almost all the States, women's representation did not exceed two or three.

Consequent to the 1987 elections women occupied twenty five per cent of the seats in all the districts. Table 7.1 and Table 7.2 show the number of women and Scheduled Caste and Scheduled Tribe women elected to the Zilla Parishads and Mandal Panchayats.

It became evident that women had made an entry into the political arena which was till then left untouched to a great extent. Earlier only one or two women members were co-opted or nominated into these institutions.

**Table 7.1**: Distribution of Elected Members according to Status of Constituency

| Sl. No. | District | General | SC/ST Male | Women | SC/ST Female | Total |
|---|---|---|---|---|---|---|
| 1. | Bidar | 12 | 5 | 6 | 0 | 23 |
| 2. | Gulbarga | 27 | 8 | 13 | 1 | 49 |
| 3. | Raichur | 25 | 9 | 10 | 1 | 45 |
| 4. | Bijapur | 29 | 12 | 14 | 1 | 56 |
| 5. | Belgaum | 38 | 14 | 17 | 1 | 70 |
| 6. | Dharwad | 34 | 3 | 16 | 1 | 64 |
| 7. | Bellary | 17 | 5 | 7 | 1 | 30 |
| 8. | Chitradurga | 22 | 7 | 10 | 1 | 40 |
| 9. | Tumkur | 27 | 11 | 13 | 1 | 52 |
| 10. | Bangalore | 21 | 8 | 9 | 1 | 39 |
| 11. | Kolar | 22 | 13 | 12 | 1 | 48 |
| 12. | Mandya | 21 | 8 | 8 | 1 | 38 |
| 13. | Mysore | 33 | 13 | 15 | 1 | 62 |
| 14. | Shimoga | 22 | 8 | 10 | 1 | 41 |
| 15. | Kodagu | 13 | 6 | 7 | 1 | 26 |
| 16. | Hassan | 19 | 7 | 9 | 1 | 36 |
| 17. | Chikmagalur | 9 | 5 | 5 | 1 | 20 |
| 18. | Uttara Kannada | 13 | 5 | 7 | 1 | 26 |
| 19. | Dakshina Kannada | 30 | 1 | 13 | 1 | 55 |
| | Total | 434 | 168 | 200 | 18 | 821 |
| | Percentage | 52.81 | 20.54 | 24.45 | 2.20 | 100 |

*Source:* Department of Rural Development & Panchayati Raj, Government of Karnataka, Bangalore, 1987.

**Table 7.2:** Total Number of Mandal Panchayats, Number of Members Elected, Number of Members in General Category and Number of Scheduled Caste/Scheduled Tribe Members and Scheduled Caste/Scheduled Tribe Women

| Sl. No. | Name of the District | No. of Mandal Pancha-yats | No. of elected Members | No. of members in General | No. of SC/ST Members | No. of Women inclusive SC/ST | No. of SC/ST women |
|---|---|---|---|---|---|---|---|
| 1. | Gulbarga | 166 | 3615 | 1950 | 748 | 917 | 166 |
| 2. | Bellary | 89 | 2017 | 1061 | 447 | 509 | 89 |
| 3. | Bidar | 73 | 1782 | 958 | 367 | 457 | 73 |
| 4. | Raichur | 139 | 3099 | 1711 | 614 | 774 | 139 |
| 5. | Bangalore(R) | 103 | 2805 | 1516 | 611 | 680 | 102 |
| 6. | Shimoga | 165 | 2540 | 1254 | 647 | 639 | 165 |
| 7. | Kolar | 125 | 3067 | 1517 | 770 | 782 | 125 |
| 8. | Chitradurga | 116 | 2838 | 1437 | 671 | 730 | 116 |
| 9. | Tumkur | 145 | 3650 | 1926 | 792 | 932 | 145 |
| 10. | Belgaum | 200 | 4868 | 2630 | 998 | 1240 | 200 |
| 11. | Bijapur | 166 | 3986 | 2164 | 802 | 1020 | 166 |
| 12. | Uttar Kannada | 123 | 1673 | 879 | 359 | 435 | 123 |
| 13. | Dharwad | 163 | 3985 | 2176 | 800 | 1009 | 163 |
| 14. | Mysore | 160 | 3937 | 2010 | 920 | 1007 | 160 |
| 15. | Mandya | 99 | 2523 | 1363 | 513 | 647 | 99 |
| 16. | Dakshina Kannada | 167 | 3913 | 2115 | 803 | 995 | 167 |
| 17. | Kodagu | 60 | 853 | 436 | 198 | 219 | 60 |
| 18. | Hassan | 04 | 2424 | 1280 | 526 | 618 | 104 |
| 19. | Chikmagalur | 107 | 1604 | 807 | 382 | 415 | 107 |
| | Total | 2469 | 55188 | 29197 | 11968 | 14025 | 2469 |

*Source :* Department of Rural Development and Panchayati Raj, Government of Karnataka, Bangalore, 1987.

Almost half the population, which was excluded from the development process was given a chance to participate in making decisions to determine their needs and priorities. However, a review of the working of the system gained from field experiences revealed some thought provoking problems. Recruitment of women was a problem in the absence of motivation and mobilization.

Political parties found it difficult to locate women who could contest for the two tiers. The numbers were so huge and the parties who are the recruiting centres, were not prepared for a work of this magnitude. Only major parties, Janata and Congress, could succeed to some extent. Moreover, women rarely came on their own. Voluntarily Organisations could not come up to the situation to educate of sensitize women or make them understand the suitable aspects of Panchayati Raj functioning. As a natural corollary to this, the people who were locally influential and belonged to the dominant castes inducted their women into the Panchayats.

There is no comprehensive study on the basis of which it could be concluded as to how Panchayati Raj members especially women members performed their role in Panchayati Raj Institutions, in the sub committees, in decision making and formulation of rural development schemes. It is only on the basis of some reports published in the newspapers it can be inferred that in each Panchayati Raj Institution some women proved very assertive and active in decision making and to some extent for the cause of women.

## THE PRESENT SCENARIO

The first five year term of the Panchayats ended on January 1, 1992. Instead of holding elections, the Congress (I) government appointed administrators to Zilla Parishads and Mandal Panchayats. The 1985 act was superseded by a new Act of the State — The Karnataka Panchayati Raj Act 1993, when the Congress (I) came to power after the 1989 Assembly elections. This Act incorporated the essential features of the 73rd Constitutional Amendment and established elected bodies at three tiers — the village, Taluks and district levels so that there is "greater participation of the people."

Among the salient features of the Act, it is worth noting that the Act established a three-tier Panchayati Raj system in the State based on the population as ascertained at the last preceding census of which the figures have been published. It envisages elected bodies at all the three levels, it provides for reservation of seats in favour of scheduled castes and scheduled tribes in proportion of their population and for reservation of one-third of the seats for women at all levels, it also provides for reservation of seats and offices of chairpersons at all levels for the persons belonging to backward classes, scheduled castes, scheduled tribes and women.

The historic bill was introduced by the Karnataka Government in the Legislative Assembly on April 1, 1993 to replace the existing enhancement. it was passed on April 7. The Legislative Council unanimously passed the bill on April 13 and it came into force from May 18, 1993. There is now an elected three-tier structure of rural local government. The tiers are the Gram Panchayat, Taluk Panchayat and Zilla Panchayat. The Act also provides for a Gram Sabha.

**Gram Panchayats**

A Gram Panchayat is constituted for a population not less than 5,000 and not more than 7,000 area or group of villages will be considered as a Panchayat's area and there will be one member for every 400.

Elections to 5,640 Gram Panchayats were held in December 1993. They consist of elected members each representing about 400 people. The average population of each Gram Panchayat is 5,300 according to 1991 census. Of the total number of 80,627 members in all the Grama Panchayats, 35,305 (43.8%) are women. The category-wise reservation of seats is shown in Table 7.3.

**Table 7.3:** Reservation of Seats in Grama Panchayat

| | | |
|---|---|---|
| S.C | 17918 (22.2%) of which 7373 are women | (41%) |
| S.T. | 7575 (9.4%) of which 5933 are women | (78%) |
| B.C. | 26828 (35%) of which 11325 are women | (40%) |
| General | 28306 (35%) of which 11278 are women | (40%) |
| Total | 80627 of which 35,305 are women | (43.8%) |

*Source :* Department of Rural Development and Panchayati Raj, Bangalore.

The offices of Adhyaksha and Upadhyaksha of Gram Panchayats have also been reserved for various categories. The breakup of reservations is shown in Table 7.4.

**Table 7.4 :** Reservation of Presidents in Grama Panchayat

| | | |
|---|---|---|
| S.C | 1025 of which 342 are women | 33.36% |
| S.T. | 295 of which 99 are women | 33.56% |
| B.C. | 1880 of which 626 are women | 33.30% |
| General | 2440 of which 813 are women | 33.32% |
| Total | 5640 of which 813 are women | 33.33% |

*Source :* Department of Rural Development and Panchayati Raj, Bangalore.

**Gram Sabha**

It is a body consisting of persons registered in the electoral rolls relating to a village comprised within the area of Gram Panchayat. It meets twice in a year. The Gram Sabha is a very important forum in which the annual statement of accounts, report of administration and the development works undertaken by the Gram Panchayats are reviewed. It also considers the development programmes proposed by the Gram Panchayats for the current year. It is responsible for identifying beneficiaries under different poverty alleviation and development programmes.

**Taluk Panchayat**

A Taluk Panchayat has been constituted for every revenue Taluk as the intermediate level in the Panchayats system. It consists of elected members at the rate of one member for every 10,000 population or part thereof. However, Taluks having a population of not exceeding 1.00 lakh have 11 elected members. Elections to all the 175 Taluk Panchayats in the State were held during 13th to 18th March, 1995 on party basis. The number of seats reserved for different categories of elected members is shown in Table 7.5.

**Table 7.5:** Reservation of Seats in Taluk Panchayat

| | | | |
|---|---|---|---|
| 18% | S.C | 601 of which 261 are women | (43.4%) |
| 5% | S.T. | 169 of which 104 are women | (61.5%) |
| 26.75% | B.C-A | 894 of which 389 are women | (43.5%) |
| 6.68% | B.C-B | 223 of which 52 are women | (23.3%) |
| 43.5% | General | 1453 of which 537 are women | (36.95%) |
| | Total | 3340 of which 1343 are women | (40.2%) |

*Source :* Department of Rural Development and Panchayati Raj, Bangalore

The offices of Adhyaksha and Upadhyaksha of Taluk Panchayats have also been reserved for different categories as shown in Table 7.6.

**Table 7.6 :** Reservation of Presidents in Taluk Panchayat

| | |
|---|---|
| S.C | 32 of which 11 are women |
| S.T | 9 of which 3 are women |
| B.C.-A | 46 of which 15 are women |
| B.C.-B | 12 of which 4 are women |
| General | 76 of which 26 are women |
| Total | 175 of which 59 are women |

*Source :* Department of Rural Development and Panchayati Raj. Bangalore.

## Zilla Panchayats

There were 20 Zilla Panchayats in the State (presently 27) consisting of elected members at the rate of one member for every 40,000 population and part thereof (one member for every 30,000 population in Chickmagalur and Uttar Kannada Districts and one member for every 18,000 population in Kodagu District). Elections to all the Zilla Panchayats were held during March 1995 on party basis. The category - wise reservation of elected members is as shown in Table 7.7.

**Table 7.7** : Reservation of Seats in Zilla Panchayat

| | | |
|---|---|---|
| S.C | 165 of which 63 are women | 38% |
| S.T | 47 of which 22 are women | 46.8% |
| B.C.-A | 243 of which 89 are women | 36.6% |
| B.C.-B | 63 of which 19 are women | 30% |
| General | 401 of which 142 are women | 35.4% |
| Total | 919 of which 335 are women | 36.5% |

*Source :* Department of Rural Development and Panchayati Raj, Bangalore.

The first set of elections to the offices of Adhyaksha and Upadhyaksha were held during 3rd to 10th April, 1995. The category-wise reservation of these offices is indicated in Table 7.8.

**Table 7.8** : Reservation of Presidents in Zilla Panchayat

| | | |
|---|---|---|
| S.C | 4 of which | 2 are women |
| S.T | 1 | |
| B.C.-A | 6 of which | 2 are women |
| B.C.-B | 1 | |
| General | 8 of which | 3 are women |
| Total | 20 of which | 7 are women |

*Source :* Department of Rural Development and Panchayati Raj, Bangalore.

In all local government institutions the following reservation is mandatory.

| | |
|---|---|
| Scheduled Castes and Scheduled Tribes | In proportionate to their population |
| Other Backward Classes and Women | One-third of the total number of each category for women respectively |

Election occupies the most central place in any modern system. The State Election Commission was appointed in May 1993. Elections to all the three tiers were to be conducted in December 1993 on separate dates. The dates of elections to the Gram Panchayats was fixed on December 29th, 1993 and Taluk Panchayat and Zilla Panchayats on 23rd January, 1993. But only the elections to the Gram Panchayat were conducted and the other had been postponed indefinitely. Delimitations had to be done afresh as the previous Mandal Panchayats were to be delimited to form Gram Panchayats. Out of a total electorates of 2,06,36,782 there were 1,01,93,188 women.

Karnataka thus became the first State to bring the Panchayati Raj Legislation in line with the Central Act and to hold elections to the Panchayats under the new Act.

At the Gram Panchayats level, the elections are fought on a non-party basis with the intention of maintaining a better atmosphere in the village, to minimise conflicts and to assure full participation of the people. However, the Gram Panchayats elections were held in Karnataka in December 1993, there were no takers for the 1,239 seats mostly reserved for the backward classes, SC and ST women.

The State recorded many strange incidents. In Kalloli Gram Panchayats seats were auctioned for the welfare of the village. The Janata Dal had threatened to boycott the election if the twelve amendments proposed are not incorporated. A writ petition was submitted in the High Court questioning the 73rd Amendment pertaining to the reservation of women, Scheduled Caste, Scheduled Tribe and Backward Classes. In Sirichand Gram Panchayat, election was unopposed because the rivals were kept out of the fray at gun point.

It is interesting to note that this time (unlike under 1985 Act) election to Gram Panchayat in 20 districts were conducted on a non-party basis. In many polling booths women outnumbered men. For example in Dharwar, Shimoga and Bidar there were large number of women. This could be attributed to the 33 per cent reservation. But it is sad that most were vacant due to lack of women candidates. Of the 200 seats reserved for women in North Canara, 162 seats were vacant.

The elections to the office of the Adyaksha was conducted in the first meeting of the Gram Panchayats on March 5th, 7th and 9th of 1994. Incidents of violent clashes, kidnapping of members including women and few deaths were reported. This law and order situation was shown as one of the basis for postponing elections to the other tiers as it is not conducive to conduct free and fair election.

There are 175 Taluk Panchayats (TP) and 20 Zilla Panchayats (ZP) comprising 3,340 TP members and 919 ZP members. A total of 1,343 (40%) seats in TP and 335 (36%) seats in ZP were reserved for women. The elections were held in three phases on March 13,15 and 18, 1995.

Elections were held for 914 ZP seats and 3,340 TP seats spread over 20 districts. Over 2.16 crore voters including 1.06 crore women were eligible to exercise their franchise in the elections.

The Panchayat elections in the State were thus completed in two phases — 1993 and 1995. The 1993 Gram Panchayat elections were held under the 1993 Act as passed by the Assembly. The 1995 elections to the other two tiers (Taluk and Zilla Panchayats) were also held under the 1993 Act but just with one amendment relating to the backward classes reservations. The amendment introduced two categories of Backward Classes – 'A' and 'B'. 'A' category was considered most backward and 'B' category more backward. The former was given reservation to the extent of 26.6 per cent and the latter 6.4 per cent. Under category 'A' 190 castes were listed and nine castes under category 'B'.

When the Panchayat elections were held in Karnataka in December 1993, there were no takers for the 1,239 seats mostly reserved for the backward classes, SC and ST women. Out of 80,631 Gram Panchayat members, 35,160 (43.6%) are women members and of the total 5,640 Gram Panchayats, 1,878 (33%) are headed by women presidents and vice-presidents. An important outcome of the election process was, although the Act provides for 33 per cent reservation to women, the actual reservation for them became 43.6 per cent in the Gram Panchayats. It is disheartening to note that the elections for Village Panchayats due to the end of March 1999 had been postponed in the ground of non-viability of many small Village Panchayats and that the government to make them bigger and viable ones. It is reported that the number of Village

Panchayats will be reduced by around fifty per cent (nearing Mandal Panchayats under the Act of 1985) of the existing Panchayats. The government also gave reason of parliamentary and Assembly elections. Assurance has been given that Panchayat will be conducted after these elections. This has blocked the entrance of fresh women members of Village Panchayat, and at the same time postponement of election has given a big jolt to the growth and sustainability of these grass root institutions.

In 1995 the State Government appointed an Expert Committee to suggest amendments to the Karnataka Panchayati Raj Act, 1993. The Committee worked under the Chairmanship of P.R. Nayak, IAS (Retd), former Additional Chief Secretary to State Government*. The Expert Committee reviewed the 1993 Act and finalised its report in March 1996. Among other significant recommendations are that the Adyaksha should be designated the Executive Head of the Taluk/Zilla Panchayat and the Executive/Chief Executive Officer should function subject to the Adhyaksha's overall supervision. The term of the office of Adhyakshas and Upadhyakshas should be in the range of 36 months. Women members of PRIs should represent on all standing committees at one-third of the total committee membership.

Keeping in view the recommendations of the P.R. Nayak committee and impressed by the need to make Panchayati Raj legislations blend with changing requirements the 1993 Act was substantially amended in 1997.

The preamble to the Act expresses its basic tenet by declaring that PRIs should function as units of local self-government. Among other changes achieving universal enrollment in primary schools, providing sanitary latrines, improving water supply, establish health and maternity centres and social forestry are to be among the priorities at each level.

---

* The Committee consisted of other members namely Dr. B.S. Bhargava, Smt. Srilata Batiwala, Prof. V. K. Natraj, Sri S.S. Meenakshisundaram, Sri M.R. Srinivasamoorthy and one Member-Secretary Dr. K.B. Basappa.

## SOME OBSERVATIONS AND REFLECTIONS

Karnataka can very well take pride in the fact that before the 73rd Amendment to the Constitution, reservation of seats in favour of women under the 1985 Act was 25 per cent in Mandal Panchayats and Zilla Parishads. Now, reservation is also applicable to the offices of Adhyaksha (chairperson) and Upadhyaksha (vice chairman) at all levels. And it is in the same proportion as in the case of seats. Reservation for these offices is on the basis of rotation among different categories.

The Panchayats have thus been formed and for the first time women made an entry in large numbers. But impressions from the field, revealed that mostly illiterate women with no political background and having no knowledge of the functioning of the Panchayats have become Panchayat members (see Annexure). During the elections, incidence of women being kidnapped and being forced to withdraw their nominations were plenty. However there are exceptions where women have fought these forces which tried to nip a woman's potential in the beginning itself.

Many of the Panchayat members were accompanied by a male member of the family. There are instances where the male escorts participate in the deliberations. Some women members admit that they feel uncomfortable to sit on the chair along with their male counterpart. Sometimes women were told not to sit with the men who are elders of the village as a sign of respect. In one village, a lady was elected as the vice president of that Panchayat. But some men got together and managed to get the reservation cancelled. Accordingly, a male member became the vice president*.

It cannot be undermined that all talks on empowerment and equality becomes meaningless if it is not backed by access to political power and decision making. This implies a need to develop gender aware political perspective. Women being half the population should participate in more number to bring about this perspective. The reservation has provided the basis as for the first time a large number of women were elected to the rural local bodies. At the

---

* These observations are based on the first author's visit to villages in Karnataka and interviews with women members of Gram Panchayats.

national level, a total of 9,88,106 (35.9%) women have got elected as Gram Panchayat representatives; 59,688 women (40%) have been elected as Zilla Panchayat members. however, Karnataka has the distinction of having the highest number of women elected at all levels — 37,689 (46.7%) for Gram Panchayat, 1,343 (40.2%) for Taluk level, and 335 (36.45%) for the Zilla Panchayat (see Annexure). Karnataka also has an all-woman panchayat in Mydolalu village in Bhadravati taluk of Shimoga district. All the members have been elected for the first time and have had no such previous experience. This village is now considered as a model village and the locals admit that the work of this Panchayat is better than that of the mixed Panchayats.

Constitutional provision, government policies, social action and awareness of rural women together should be able to provide women with necessary skills to enjoy equal opportunity. The Panchayati Raj has provided a common forum for social, economic, political and legal advancement of rural women. Now women are more than nominal in the political bodies and this is an epoch-making step in the women's empowerment and political participation.

Women members can effectively participate in the various sectors of rural development. For instance, in India, the question of health was addressed through various documents like National Perspective Plan for Women 1988, National Commission for Self-employed Women in India 1988, examination of Maternal Mortality and Morbidity in India 1987, the chapter on women and development for India's Eighth Five Year Plan and the National debate on women's health and family planning issues in 1994 in preparation for ICPD, Cairo. This International Conference on Population and Development (ICPD) formulated a growing international consensus that improving reproduction health and family is essential to human welfare development.

According to the Karntaka Panchayati Raj Act of 1993, Zilla Panchayats are to look after the management of hospitals and dispensaries excluding district hospitals under direct government management (those with more than 50 beds) and the implementation of maternity and child health, family welfare and immunisation and vaccination programmes. Apart from operating the district sector budget, Zilla Panchayats also implement State sector schemes entrusted to them by the government. Taluka Panchayats look after health and family welfare programmes and promote immunisation and vaccination programmes; they also supervise health and sanitation facilities at village fairs and festivals. Gram Panchayats deal with family welfare programmes, preventive measures against epidemics, regulation of the sale of food articles, participation in immunisation programmes, licensing of eating establishments and the regulation of offensive and dangerous trades.

The Panchayati Raj Institutions have provided space for women to articulate, influence decision making and to work towards improving this neglected field. Women should mobilise themselves and the community to demand this basic health need. The women representatives should act as motivators and spread awareness in this regard as their presence will ease communication with neither to unexposed women in the villages. Formation of women's groups will improve access to services and increase the sensitivity of programmes to women's needs.

One of the functions of the Panchayats is the management of local environment which include agriculture, social and farm forestry, minor irrigation, water management and watershed development maintenance of Common Property Resources in the village, village sanitation, optimum land use of natural fertilizers. women have to be made aware of their role as environment resource managers in the light of sustainable development. They should be encouraged to participate in the Joint Forest Resource Management Committees. the Panchayats have provided a forum for planning and management of these issues and thereby protect their environment.

Panchayati Raj Institutions not only can play a very role in the integration of programmes but also ensure that the benefits of the area. The involvement of the Panchayati Raj Institutions in the planning, implementing and administering of the programmes of women and child development is a natural corollary to the decentralised planning. Besides this, these institutions have an important role in ensuring community participation and awareness generation which are very vital for the successful implementation of development programmes.

Community participation is a pre-requisite for the successful implementation of the programmes of welfare and development. Unless the community needs are properly identified, participation cannot be achieved. No government programme can be relevant unless it addresses to the needs and the aspirations of the community. Panchayati Raj Institutions can enable participation in the planning, managing and supervising the programmes related to women and children and integration of various departmental programmes and their functionaries. The women members can play an important catalyst role in these bodies. They can ensure that the programmes of women and child development get proper attention in the agenda of these bodies. They should also make efforts to organise local women groups such as Mahila Mandals, other local voluntary organisations so that the community becomes receptive to these programmes.

Women are more visible in local governments today than they were in the past. This trend is promising for women. However, their share as office holders is still quite low; naturally more women should be drawn into local government. Men and women cannot change their opinion about women much unless women are given new options, achieve high positions, succeed financially and gain political power. And with each occupational or political improvement, opinions and ideologies about women are likely to become more favourable to womenfolk. The policy of reservation is a necessary step to motivate participation. But women will not get equal participation in politics without undertaking major efforts themselves. There are many activities which can aid women in reaching equal participation in local government and decision-making. In addition to obtaining better education and building networks to increase access to information and reducing isolation they should influence those holding high positions in parties or government and should openly support women and men who are sensitive and responsive to women's problems. Women should improve their image by monitoring books and media portrayals. Within political party structure they should work for women candidates.

Women are getting involved in the local political process and are confronted in carrying out their tasks with all facts of communal services, amenities and administration which are complex. One of the important issues plaguing the country is widespread corruption. It is in politics and administration that corruption is most prevalent. This could be attributed to the compulsions of democracy. Elections involve huge sums of money. The money to invest in elections is very huge. The candidate requires money to invest and later on expects substantial returns on this investment. Corruption is the answer and the status provides the scope.

Grass roots level is no exception to corruption, nepotism and malpractice. It has also become a 'culture'. PRIs are not above corruption. Studies reveal that during elections there were many malpractices. Money and muscle still rule the elections. This is an extremely difficult situation for women to enter politics. To curb this, local electoral system has to be further reformed so that money and muscle power is eradicated. Ombudsman institution could be introduced so that the role of the middlemen is reduced and there is direct link between citizens and the local body.

The decisions of the local government have a profound effect on the problems that concern women. In the absence of awareness it is illogical to except the leaders to articulate their demands. Effective participation demands skill, knowledge and attitude. The need for systematic training and orientation is necessary to empower the women members to exercise their authority. The political parties have a major responsibility in facilitating women's participation. Deliberate efforts should be made to place women members within and outside party organisation. Women's organisations must take up issues of securing them rightful place in the local government. Electoral system which is based on money power should be changed. Electoral reforms is the major key. State funding of elections by creation of a separate election fund is a possibility. Last, but not the least is the role of mass media in building awareness.

Simplifying the working of the Panchayats and providing easy access to information can effect participation. Mention may be made of a village called Bellandur (a village 30 minutes away from Bangalore) where the Gram Panchayat has dispensed done on the Panchayats own initiative. Two computers at the Panchayat office display data on land holdings of each family, taxes due from them, beneficiaries covered under various housing and employment schemes. Plea for power and water connections can also be accessed. Such details of five villages which fall within Ballandur are available. This is important not only from the view of streamlining administration but also in empowering women as details of the Gram Panchayat are available within their reach at the click of a mouse.

GRAMSAT — Satellite programmes for villages — an ambitious programme launched by the Government of Karnataka on an experimental basis was the first of its kind in the State and the second in the country after Gujarat. Using a "one-way video and two-way audio" satellite broadcasting technology developed by ISRP (Indian Space Research Organisation), programmes were beamed from the main earth at Vijayanagar, Bangalore to seventeen districts of Karnataka.

The Department of Women and Child Welfare used their slot to beam of programmes for the elected women representatives of the Grama Panchayats. The Government of Karnataka has embarked on a programme that çan cover modern and traditional media forms through satellite technology to facilitate women Panchayat members.

It is too early to assess the impact of the Constitutional status given to PRIs and the policy of reservation. However, it cannot be denied that it is a major landmark in the history of administrative reforms, a milestone in the history of rural local government and participation of women. What is needed in the given situation is capacity building for effective performance and participation. Developing human resources for managing this complex task of sustainable development should be the priority of NGOs, voluntary organisations, people's organisation and women's groups.

It is the efficiency of the local institutions which matters most to the major part of the people and which directly touches the daily and the interests of popular life. Besides, it is the best school of political training of the masses and a school of social service. The Gram is regarded as an instrument of direct democracy rather than representative democracy, because the Panchayat statutes provide that the activities of the Village Panchayats shall be reviewed by meetings of all the adult residents of the villages falling within the jurisdiction of a Village Panchayat. The Gram Panchayat offers possibilities for the training of women in social participation and leadership. Thus PRIs alone are the agencies to revolutionise the rural society by mobilising and channelising in the right direction the abundant enthusiasm and energy in the rural areas.

The process of development of women in India has shown that the country has sought to give status to women in the Constitution. The 73rd Amendment and the establishment of PRIs has given expression to this democratic process. However, the statutory representation for women is only a step forward in promoting women's participation in national life. Local governments are the best means of promoting participation and efficiency. They can be much more open to public scrutiny and more accountable. Being closer to people they can be more responsive to local needs and make better use of resources. PRIs have provided an important channel for women's involvement structures of the local government. Representation aims at involving structures of the local government. Representation aims at involving women in decision making. Their roles should be recognised and strengthened so that they get full access to resources and services.

## REFERENCES


Bhargava, B.S. and K. Subha, "Developing women at grass-roots", *Kurukshetra*. February 1991, New Delhi, pp. 40-42.

Bhargava , B.S. and K. Subha, "Women in Panchayati Raj: Some reflections on Kranataka's experience', *Kurukshetra*, June 1994, pp. 42-44.

Bhargava, B.S. and S. Rama Rao, 1978, *Indian Local Government: A Study*, Minerva Associates, Calcutta.

Government of India, *Report of the Committee on the Status of Women in India, Towards Equality*, Department of Social Welfare, New Delhi.

Government of Karnataka, The Karnataka Panchayati Raj Act. 1993. Government Press, Bangalore.

Government of Karnataka, The Karnataka Zilla Parishads, Taluk Panchayat Samitis, Mandal Panchayats and Nyaya Panchayats Act 1985, Government Press, Bangalore.

Government of Karnataka, *'Power to the People'*. Panchayati Raj Institutions in Karnataka, Department of Rural Development and Panchayati Raj, Bangalore.

Government of Karnataka, *Karnataka State Gazetteer II*, Karnataka Gazetteer Department, 1983.

Government of Karnataka, *Report of the Expert Committee in Karnataka Panchayat Raj Act, 1993*, Bangalore, March 1996.

Institute of Social Sciences, Social Background of Zilla Parishad Members in Karnataka, 1989, ISS Occasional Paper Series 6, New Delhi, 1989.

Institute of Social Sciences, 'Karnataka Mandala Panchayat Members' Social Background, 1990; *ISS Occasional Series* 7, New Delhi, 1990.

*Issues of Panchayati Raj Update* (English and Kanada), Institute of Social Sciences, New Delhi.

Issues of *Search Bulletin*, *Search*, Bangalore.

Issues of *Uma Prachar*, Institute of Social Studies Trust, Bangalore.

Mathew, George (Ed.), *Panchayati Raj in Karnataka Today: Its National Dimensions*, Concept Publishing Company, New Delhi, 1986.

Subha, K. 'Training : an Aid to Empower Rural Women Leaders', *Kurukshetra*, April 1995.

Subha, K. *Karnataka Panchayat Elections 1995*, Concept Publishing Company, New Delhi, 1997.

*ANNEXURE*

## STATUS PROFILE OF WOMEN REPRESENTATIVES IN PRIs IN KARNATAKA

(Under the PR Act, 1993)

1. Below 30 years of age at the Grama Panchayat level, the share of the female members is 28 per cent; at the taluk level their percentage works out respectively as 37 and 34. This clearly shows that younger generation women are showing interest in the PRIs.

2. Overwhelming majority (88%) of the women members covering all the 3 spatial levels of the PR system, are married. However, single women like widows, divorcees and *devadasis* also attained power positions. This is a promising start.

3. In all, 17.7 per cent of the women members are illiterate, Illiteracy among female members is higher at the Gram Panchayat level. However, it is promising to observe that 17.4 per cent of the members at the Zilla Panchayat level are graduates.

4. Data show domination of the Backward Castes among women representation (35.3% at GP level, 34.6% at TP level and 46.4% at ZP level).

5. Women members have low exposure to mass-media. This is particularly true in the case of newspapers reading at the GP level (38% only).

6. Participation of female members in other organisations/ associations, such as youth associations, Mahila Mandals, cooperative societies, is very low (26% only).

7. 94 per cent of the female members do not have any precious political experience. There are more freshers at the Gram and Taluk levels than at the ZP level.

8. Family members, village community and self, appear to be the

major motivational forces for the women representatives entry in PRIs.

9. Among other shades, social justice is the ideology of the majority of female members at all the three levels (49.3%, 68.4% and 61% respectively at GP, TP and ZP levels).

10. Data show that most women members have political party affiliations; only 6.3 per cent were independents.

---

*Source* : Subha, K., *Karnataka Panchayat Elections 1995: Process, Issues and Membership Profile*, Concept, New Delhi, 1997.

8

# DECENTRALIZATION OF CHILD CARE SERVICES

M.S. SWAMINATHAN FOUNDATION

## INTRODUCTION

The Panchayati Raj system has long been a part of the Indian tradition, and there is no doubt that the country is now committed to the concept of local self-government. The concept of decentralization, which is a broader term of reference, includes, but it is not confined to the term "Panchayati Raj". The highly dispersed nature of the population and the immense diversity of our country makes decentralisation imperative. Yet governance cannot be handed over to unprepared communities. The concept has to be understood realistically, since many hurdles, real and imagined continue to be a threat in the actual devolution of power to the local bodies. Tamil Nadu is a "late comer" in the actual implementation of the Panchayat elections, and in fact, has been the last State to actually conduct the local bodies elections. (The elections were held in October 1996 and the elected representatives took office in November1996).

Ms. Lakshmi Pranesh, Secretary for Social Welfare, Government of Tamil Nadu, opened the proceedings with an account of the history and current status of child welfare services in Tamil Nadu. The earliest child welfare programme which involved the community was the Applied Nutrition Programme (ANP), started in the sixties and intended for children below five years. Some of the nutritional needs of the children like eggs and vegetables, were met through a common poultry farm and kitchen garden, and often, the space for the Balwadis was provided by the community — panchayat. During the early days the community considered the programme as a blessing and, therefore, there was a great deal of community involvement. Later the attitude changed as the community was sidelined and the programme became more centralised in its implementation. Though the programme later became defunct in the country, in Tamil Nadu, it was responsible for the establishment of an astonishingly large number of Balwadis in rural areas.

The Directorate of Women Welfare decided to maintain the Balwadis started during this period and subsequently, nearly 100 to 200 Balwadis were started every year. By the year 1974-76, i.e., even before the ICDS was initiated, there were nearly 4,344 State-run Balwadis in Tamil Nadu, while in the rest of the country there were more child care centres run by the voluntary sector than by the government. The ICDS programme in Tamil Nadu began in only 3 Blocks (two rural and one urban). Later, in July 1982 the State-wide Noon Meal Programme was started almost overnight by the then Chief Minister, Dr. M.G. Ramachandran, bringing the total number of child care centres, including the Balwadis and ICDS to nearly 28,000.

The administration of this programme was under the BDO. The only element of local participation in it, was the appointment of the child care worker who was to be either a resident of the village, or residing within 1 km radius (later increased to 3 km) from the centre. The Tamil Nadu Integrated Programme (TINP) children for below 3 years was later started with the assistance of the World Bank. 12.5 lakh children (3-5 years) and 13/14 lakh children (under 3 years) were covered under both the programmes in the State.

Some of the States that have rich experience in the administration and conduct of Panchayati Raj Institutions, in Kerala, West Bengal, Karnataka and Gujarat can provide important inputs in the process of decentralisation in Tamil Nadu. The experiences of West Bengal and Tamil Nadu for example, are different. The West Bengal experience is of a well-developed Panchayati Raj system, while Tamil Nadu on the other hand, is still in its very infant stage. But, the child care centres are very advanced in Tamil Nadu as compared to West Bengal. Tamil Nadu has also achieved a degree of decentralisation already with regard to the appointment of Anganwadi workers.

At the outset, it is necessary to clarify terms like community participation, decentralisation and empowerment, as these have various connotations. For the people of this report these terms have been defined as follows:

- *Decentralisation* – The process of redesigning the decision-making and administrative powers in a hierarchical system so that policy implementation moves down to the level of the lowest administrative body.
- *Empowerment* – Achieving equality and equity among all social groups, including women and men, through the recognition and removal of all subordinating structures which restrict participation in political, social, economic and environmental policies, programmes and structures.
- *Community Participation* – The involvement of all sections of the local people at different levels in policy evolution, resource mobilisation, programme planning and implementation, monitoring and evolution.

**Whose Responsibility?**

Whose responsibility is child care? Does it only concern the immediate beneficiaries? Recognising that the welfare of children is in the best interest of the community as a whole, a holistic perspective is essential and child care services must become a part of the community's agenda and not merely the women's agenda. This perspective should find a top priority in any agenda for sensitization of local bodies, especially in the light of the reservation of seats for women in these bodies.

**Child Care today is not a priority because**

- it is considered as women's responsibility,
- its impact is not measurable,
- its importance is not well-known, and
- it brings no financial gains.

## FINANCIAL AND ADMINISTRATIVE ISSUES

The first stage of the decentralisation process, no doubt, is the conduct of the elections, but it is the next stage, that of letting go the reins which is more important, so that the local bodies could take care of their area programmes. In view of the lapse of nearly twenty years since the last bodies elections, what is the time-frame required for the process? Especially, what should the community, the bureaucracy, the government and local bodies themselves now do to ensure the smooth transfer of power into the hands of the people? Massive changes are needed in terms of policy formulation, legislation, programme planning and implementation and most of all, attitudinal changes among all partners in the change process, though change may be unpopular among the bureaucrats who have been orchestrating programmes so far.

### Planning and Programme

A major expectation from decentralisation is of a qualitative improvement of services, and bridging the existing gap between people's needs and available resources. In the top-down approach in programme implementation adopted so far, there has been a gap between policy formulation and programme implementation. Over the years and after eight Five-Year Plans and many short-term plans, it is obvious that most of the anti-poverty programmes and welfare schemes have not managed to reach the people for whom they were intended. Yet centralised programme planning has received the support of all sectors, since it is less threatening for all concerned. Simple, time-tested, involving implementation in a remote or detached manner, and accounting in financial terms, it fulfils bureaucratic needs.

The existing policies and programmes have to be critiqued to ascertain of they really meet the needs of people as a whole. The vast majority of programmes are top-heavy and bureaucratically governed and realistic evaluations can help to trim down expenditure. The bulk of the allocations for most programmes go towards infrastructure and salaries, and little really shifts down to the grass roots. The more localised the planning and control over the implementation, the more effective will be the services. Ensuring transparency in delivery services, which is lacking at present, is vital in bridging the gap between demand and services. A shift in approach from a bureaucratic service delivery pattern to a more people-oriented approach is part of the decentralisation process.

Demand assessment which proceeds planning and implementation must also get decentralised if the entire process is to be completed. A process has to be evolved to assess the quantity and quality of services available in the community, and to match needs assessment with services in the community.

The social and political structures required and the legal aspects also need to be considered. There is need to give the legislation sufficient teeth so that delays and postponements can be offset.

**Sources of Funding**

There are four sources of funding that the Panchayat can draw on

- Finances from the State or Central government,
- Finances generated and available with the local bodies through their own tax base,
- Finances raised from the community through non-revenue sources including donation, and
- User contribution.

The State should provide the basic funds through its tax base, part of which should be devolved to the local Panchayats. The memorandum submitted to the State Finance Commission (by TN-Forces) suggest that while devolution of financial powers to the village and Block level continue, there should be sufficient allocation of resources for the local bodies to run the child care centres. It is not the best strategy to mandate from the State or Central level the allocation of resources available for each programme. There is bound to be a close call regarding which aspect of the welfare programme. There is bound to be a close call regarding which aspect of the welfare programmes (health, nutrition or literacy) will be prioritised. The long-term strategy should be basically to orient and sensitise the community as a whole on the priorities with regard to their own needs. In Tamil Nadu there is an expenditure of about 3,000 per village per month (36,000 to 40,000 per annum) and the government has the largest commitment financially at present with regard to health and nutrition. In the devolving process, there should be an effort to push a portion of this allocation towards child care centres. There is the possibility of legislating that a fixed percentage of the funds available to the Panchayats be devolved into a core fund for child care services.

**User Contribution**

Should the beneficiaries to any welfare service be asked to pay for the service? There are two opinions regarding this. One school of thought spearheaded with active pressure from some international funding agencies, is that the user must pay, while others believe the contribution must be voluntary, and that the user as a member of the community should be involved with the decision-making process in the programme implementation. The user fee/contribution is still an ambitious subject since very often it is the people from lower economic groups who already contribute through their labour or taxes, and so to tax the same group is both unfortunate and unnecessary. Further they need the services most, so the user fee may be both unethical and counter-productive.

The argument in favour of charging the user is the belief that there is a positive correlation between the right to question and paid services. If a person contributes to the service, there will be an associated rage that would follow in case of non-contribution. It is this attitude of "Claiming your rights" that is likely to influence or effect any improvement to the quality of service. In terms of overall expenses, the contribution may not be much, in fact, it would be only a minuscule amount. Nevertheless, this would shake the community out of its customary state of apathy, towards a free service.

Some others believe that up to a level, services should be free, after which, on a conditional basis, these services could be expanded, if there is a matching contribution from the community. Contributions from the community need not be in monetary terms alone. They could be in kind, through provision of space, services or materials.

Contributions in terms of user fee etc., should not be at the cost of the poor. If the burden on the poor is not reduced, with the structural adjustments in various programmes that are being evolved, the poor are going to be even more marginalised than at present. Capacity to contribute should be the criterion and should exclude the poorest of poor. How much can the community of people living below the poverty line raise in terms of resources for programmes which are targetted to benefit them? Alternatives have to found to be bridge the gap.

**Raising Funds**

A fear expressed is of the scope for misuse if Panchayats are allowed to raise their own resources without any form of accountability. At present, as per the provisions of the Tamil Nadu Act, there is limited scope for the local bodies to raise their own resources. It is unrealistic to expect the community to follow through on their own without statutory powers. Beyond the basic funding given to the Panchayats, the rest of it should be raised locally and the State should provide guidelines in these areas to streamline the process. The system need not be uniform throughout the country, but the exact modalities for raising resources locally have to be indicated. An in-built system of accountability should follow, with transparency in the income generation and expenses of any local body.

It is not feasible to reject contributions from individual donors who automatically become stakeholders in the programme, but care should be taken to ensure that such dynamics do not work against the best interests of the community. Income generation programmes should be developed, may be through certain Common Property Resources (CPR) which could be attached to child care centres for this purpose. Rural self-help groups (comprising of rural poor, especially the landless classes) may contribute to a common fund.

Some programmes which depend on user contributions have been successful, e.g., self help groups, so the community may be willing for other activities that are effective. Clarity in communicating the needs of women and children is needed. Once the community understands the rationale and the financial implications involved in other words the cost-effectiveness of the programme, they are more likely to contribute.

Contributions from the community, however small, are basic towards ensuring the rights approach in service delivery, and better quality, which will benefit all welfare programmes.

**Political Support**

Although today, politics may be driven by dividing factors like caste, class and gender, the need for child care services should cut across party lines. Often the ultimate objective of candidates is to climb the political ladder, the exercise of joining Panchayats being merely considered as stepping stones or training ground for future political aspirants. The voting public by and large are cued to party politics and not to individual personalities — with a few exceptions. The legitimacy of political parties in Panchayat elections is, therefore, very obvious.

Hence, there is need to generate the interest of the political parties and local MLAs and MPs on such issues. Getting child care on the agenda of political parties should be one of the goals of decentralisation. Even in the case of bureaucracy, these are topics of low priority, being non-revenue-based. Political parties will respond once the demand for the service arises. The left parties are probably the only ones who are conscious enough to create the necessary impetus at the grass root level, especially in relation to women's issues.

**Policy Strategies**

- Government should have a planned withdrawal policy from schemes to be decentralised, and different government schemes should be integrated.
- Job responsibilities of CDPOs and supervisors should be redefined to build the capacity of community.
- Minimum standards of child care services should be prescribed by the local body.
- State level fund for child care should be created – allocation of funds on per child basis.
- Mechanism for a revolving fund for each Anganwadi centre should be evolved.
- *Anganwadi* workers should be locally selected.
- Community should have the liberty to control and manage the centres.
- Local communities should select the target children.
- A majority entitlements package should be evolved including wage protection for six months, worker's contribution for maternity insurance, and a State-level maternity fund.

## COMMUNITY PARTICIPATION AND GENDER ISSUES

Decentralisation itself has a connotation of community participation. Government bureaucracy and people must have the confidence that the system will work, but this sense of preparedness must not be seen as a prerequisite for the process to begin or the wait will be indefinite. Yet one cannot, from a practical point, rush or force the pace. This implies that the government does not merely invite the community to participate, through forcible involvement, but recognises community initiative and works to sustain it.

Capability building exercises within a community should create an awareness among the people to accessing their rights without waiting for others to confer it on them. Groups may not come together for a cause on their own — there is a need to create within the group an exhibition of their strength, to overcome the inherent fear about political processes which are visualised as working against them. People can have a direct influence more at the Panchayat level than at the district or State levels. Interest in the programme will automatically follow resources and power, once demands and needs are prioritised.

### Gram Sabha

The people's collective is the Gram Sabha and it is this organ of the decentralised set-up which should be built up. The 73rd Amendment has down played the role of the Gram Sabha emphasising only its constitution, but saying little about its powers. Ideally, the people collective (Gram Sabha) should be the forum for individual members to express ideas that could lead to change. But for this, Gram Sabhas needs to be strengthened through statutory powers.

It has been assumed that the Gram Sabha can become an instrument of change in the community. In the existing social milieu, it is fár fetched and naive to presume that the entire population will be identical in its view or opinions. The community as it exists in India today divided by caste, class, religion, politics, etc. These divisions do not aid in promoting the formation of common objectives or goals. There is no doubt that the Gram Sabha can be influenced, but this change should and come from within the community.

If the village elders, who have the respect and confidence of the community, can be influenced then social change can be made with the least possible resistance from the rest of the community.

To take a common example, often many of the services are duplicated because of the lack of solidarity in the community. Cooking food, serving and distributing it, is usually done by a non-Harijan person at all child care centres in Chamoli area, and there is evidence of a similar pattern in many parts of the country. Often the ideological beliefs of NGOs are quite contrary to actual practice. It is known that often NGOs as well as the government prefer to have a programme duplicated in both the Harijan and non-Harijan areas rather than risk alienating the entire community. The emphasis on having a local person as the Anganwadi worker too can create a similar situation, since such persons can rarely go against the social mores of the group. Since such persons can rarely go against the social mores of the group. Negative situations get reinforced and programme which is supposed to bring about change actually perpetuates social practices.

To expect the Gram Sabha as a whole to be the agent of change in the light of such facts may sound unrealistic at present. To expect traditional structures to provide progressive policy changes is highly unlikely but not impossible, if the motivation is there. Yet the Gram Sabha has to play this role since it has both backing of the community and the legal mandate, and outsiders cannot perform this role indefinitely. So along with strengthening the powers of the Gram Sabhas there must be techniques for integrating the needs of the community into policy initiatives, and initiating legislative support. The experience of empowering the Gram Sabha is new to Tamil Nadu, but in Kerala there are over 1,000 Gram Sabhas formed which have started actively planning for the Ninth Five Year Plan.

**Women's Empowerment**

The major recent change in the local bodies has been in the number and concentration of elected women representatives to the Panchayats, more than 12,000 at all levels, but their role is still not clear. Most of the earlier nominated members were *benami*, but a recent study found that only about 50 per cent of the elected women could be said to *benamis*. Keeping in mind the low profile role played by nominated women members earlier, it may be difficult for either the Panchayat, the women, the community of the administration to envisage a more active role for women. In view of the patriarchal nature of society as a whole and the tradition-bound rural scenario, the socialisation process ensures that very often women may be as patriarchal in outlook as men. They have to be made politically aware and emboldened to act.

Child Care services can be in itself a road to women's empowerment. A quality child care centre should give women an avenue to realise their own potential by reducing the effort and time spent on child care. The responsibility that women feel with regard to child care will not be voluntarily given up unless there is an dependable substitute service that will give her the time and space for participation in community activities. This service traditionally has been provided by the immediate family, especially the larger family network. With urbanisation and the associated migration there has been a breakdown of the joint family network. With urbanisation and the associated migration there has been a breakdown of the joint family spirit even in the rural household. Today the Balwadi is resorted to mainly to meet nutritional needs, and the community essentially remains alien from the woman's needs. But of change agents enter the community with militant feminist ideas the process of sensitisation may be much more difficult. Understanding has to be created of how women's lives are structured and why such service, are needed. Who else needs gender sensitisation beyond women, parents and the larger community? It should be an integral part of training of the bureaucracy, and NGOs, not merely at the conceptual level, but also in the managerial and technical aspects of programmes. When imparting such training there is also need distinguish between the practical needs of women (timing, seasonality, location, health, sanitation) versus strategic concerns, or looking at gender relations as a whole (issues of female infanticide and foeticide, registration of births and deaths, alternative value formation among children to offset caste/class divides, male responsibility for child care, documentation of indigenous knowledge of women on child care etc).

The experiences of various States like Kerala, West Bengal and Maharashtra could provide the stimulus for new initiatives. The control political parties exert over the candidates in West Bengal is far different from the rest of the country. The relative success of land reforms in West Bengal, which was responsible for empowering the people economically, may have made the difference, since sometimes factors can overcome divisive forces like religion and caste. In Kerala, one strategy used successfully was wide scale publicity on child care. The need for equitable, non-profit good quality child care supported by the State, was brought into the common man's conversation through a widely publicised pre-election opinion poll. The success of this strategy may be related to the higher literacy levels in the State.

## THE NGO CONTRIBUTION

Of late, there has been a tendency on the part of government to farm out child care services to the NGOs. Throughout the country, except in Tamil Nadu, a number of ICDS centres have been handed over to the NGOs. This experience has evoked mixed responses, and difficulties have been expressed by all the concerned parties. On the one hand, the community has not been happy with the outcome in many instances, while in other cases the workers have not been satisfied with the working conditions and supervision. In yet other cases, the NGOs themselves have not had a positive experience with the government in relation to the style of the supervisions, red tapism and bureaucratic functioning involved.

The State may use the NGOs to abandon its commitment to the social service sector, but the NGO sector cannot substitute for the government. The volume of the problem is so massive and widespread that NGOs cannot make a deep dent in terms of numbers or uniform spread. There are not enough NGOs to cover the half million villages in India. While NGOs cannot and should not restrict themselves to operating just like a developmental department or merely executing governmental programmes, the government should not hand over its responsibilities to the NGOs.

The government itself has not expressed sufficient confidence in the NGOs to deliver the service. In many instances the NGOs bring to the very term. Approximately, one-third of the NGOs are bound to be questionable. There is a need to consider legitimacy of NGOs, besides their track record with regard to the community. The elected bodies have the required social legitimacy to initiate action for the community, which NGOs do not.

In Tamil Nadu, the type of NGOs that function are the bilaterally funded NGOs are present and many of the externally-funded NGOs are slowly withdrawing from Tamil Nadu. Some of these NGOs are as patriarchal in structure as any government departments. As long as vested interests play a role in programme implementation it will be next to impossible to do away with NGOs who are fraudulent but still supported by the State machinery.

**Role for NGOs**

There are a wide range of issues related to gender and child care that have been the tradition focus attention of NGOs, and they have a big role to play, but this role cannot be the same as that of the local bodies or the community itself. NGOs and NGO-initiated bodies can be roped in through women's groups and Sanghams, for example the training of child care functionaries also could become a part of the NGO agenda, as well as articulation of the existing governmental programmes and dissemination of information to the especially success stories.

The major role for NGOs is to develop the community's skills, capabilities and awareness especially regarding their rights and their capacity to manage their own affairs, meaningfully participate and develop programmes through their own initiative. There is a widespread belief that NGO participation should be based genuine volunteerism not commercialism.

At an earlier seminar jointly organised by MSSRF and ICCW on the theme of partnership in child care services between government and NGOs, the discussions led to the insight that two more pillars were needed to make the partnership strong—that is, grass roots-level community organisations and local bodies. There is need to distinguish clearly between the two merely handing over powers to the local bodies is inadequate since the local bodies are anyway post of the administration. The involvement of organisations that spring from within the community is necessary to complete the picture.

**Demand Creation**

There is no mechanism to articulate demand from within the community at present. The community often has to be made aware of the need for a programme, or the value of a change. This is the first step in the process, perhaps the most difficult one. For the demand to arise, there must be effective leadership which will facilitate community participation and leadership from within. This is where NGOs can rightly come in — to create the demand, as well as the capability among the people to manage their own resources. Today there is an expectation that either the government of the NGO sector will step in to do the ground work. Rightly the process of decentralisation should not be initiated by the government, although there have been instances of the government filling this role. One such governmental initiative, which was conveniently confused with community participation, was a recent G.O that all nutritious meal centres should be monitored by the Village Panchayat and the District Panchayat (each tier in Tamil Nadu is an independent body with no linkages between the Village Level Panchayat and the District Panchayat Union). Such a step alone, without a series of other measures, cannot be productive. The initiative of running the programme should be left to the people following which there may be a need for a change in management style. Yet the government also cannot be sidelined entirely as an agent of change. The Mahila Samakhya experience should be considered as an example of a governmental programme which did bring about change.

## ALTERNATIVE STRUCTURES FOR MANAGEMENT

Developing alternative local structures for managing child care services and styles of management which would give members of the community an opportunity to participate in a meaningful manner, are two issues for consideration.

## Group Formation in the Community

Community based groups at the village level, such as, working groups for partnership, child care committees or councils, with representation from all sections of the community should be set up for monitoring, outside the Panchayat structure. In Maharashtra there is the Village Education Committee (VEC) which monitors the education system. Nari Vikas Samitis of West Bengal and the Mahila Samakya groups in Gujarat have also experience in handling, monitoring and helping to create a demand for child care. In Rajasthan there is the village and district level Balasevika Samiti. If such structures exists, this will limit the various players to the roles they are intended to perform. These groups organised need not necessarily be formal groups or single-purpose ones. They could be groups organised for other reasons, such as local self-help groups (used at present by banks for channelling loans), political parties, industrial establishment etc., with additional roles to play. If there are multiple committees formed it may in fact inhibit the performance or delivery of services. On the other hand, to expect the infrastructural development committee to oversee the functioning of the child care services is also farfetched. Women-exclusive committees should not be the end result when such specialised committees are formed. It should include all sections of the population, otherwise it will be self defeating. Maharashtra has women on all committees irrespective whether it is service-related or not (70-30 combination).

The existence of women groups and catalytic change agents like NGOs should not be assumed. Nearly 90 per cent of the villages in India do not have women's groups.

Caste-based groups have been used for political purposes and cannot be ignored at the Panchayat level. There is need to promote non-religious, non-caste based organisations which have development as their ideology. Child care can be a common area since it will appeal to the sentiment of most sections of the population. Government policy directives e.g. start a women's group in six months, time are far too stringent. These kind of reforms cannot have a fixed time frame. The input should be consistent and gradual. It is not possible to build community spirit on a government based time frame.

## Group Functioning

Role allocation for individuals and groups should be clear, so there is no overlapping of areas. Rivalry among different groups and political interference must be considered. Who decides in the group, who attends meetings, inter-village visits, practical solutions to problems must be discussed. The approach should help the community develop its own resource base, priorities develop their own programme, tailor-made to their local needs, and arrive at their own solutions.

## Programme Design

Programme design must be evolved by the groups. There should be an identification and prioritising of needs and resources. The general ideology may be the same but, the parameters for running the centres will be different for each village. mapping the community, especially the clusters within the community with special reference to marginalised groups, is the first step. Caste, gender, religion and deprived indiv.iduals within the community must be taken into considerations.

Ensuring availability of resources, and deciding what are the parameters of quality follow. Rigid norms based on population should be avoided, Anganwadi centres should work in shifts with flexible timings. Alternative home-based child care models should be developed. Availability of materials, physical space, and time, the strengths, weakness and resources of the community have to be included in this planning, exercise. There must be integration with other schemes and flexibility of planning, promoting linkage and avoiding duplication, while the services should be extended to cover the maximum possible clientele. There is presently a tendency to adopt a frugal approach with regard to the actual amount spent per child. The bulk of the expenses go towards salaries and other infrastructural requirements. Resources should be more equitably distributed.

Building the capability of the community to access available services and facilitating leadership at the local level is an ongoing process. Balancing the agenda will become a key role of the leaders. Implementation of the programme will include regulating interaction between the grass roots level workers, the people and the planners.

Review of programmes is essential, along with monitoring the delivery of services. Mainstreaming gender in the overall agenda as well as in training programmes will be needed to maintain the momentum.

Decentralisation does not mean only devolution of powers. The latter can take place without a corresponding community involvement, in which case participation will be limited to the Panchayat members and only the services prioritised by them will receive attention. In such a scenario, child care can easily get sidelined. Thus the alternative structures which give scope for grass roots organisations from a much needed counter balance to the powers of the Panchayat.

## CHILD CARE WORKERS AND DECENTRALISATION

Child care workers, from a major group to be convinced on the need for decentralisation. At present, the top down approach is definitely preferred by the child care workers. The preference for the State government as the employers as against the local bodies, is based on the expectation that no extra demands are made on the employees time. An employer who is remote (State or Central) preferable to one that is more immediate (Panchayat). They also anticipate that service conditions may deteriorate. The workers have to be motivated to understand the value of the move towards decentralisation, and not feel that the transfer of power to the local level will intact be a threat to them, or merely an attempt to control their functioning. Accountability if the child care workers should be to the Panchayat, but this must be ensured without trampling on their elementary rights.

### Past Experience

The apprehension that the services of the local level/village level workers will be misused by the elected members at the village level is another fear, with some basis in past experience. This has to be given recognition and importance since such apprehensions are very real, In some instances, the employees have been asked to assist in domestic work by the local elected representatives, or the families of the elected leaders have assumed that the powers vested in the leader also can extended to them. The employees often end up in situations which they cannot handle except to yield to the pressure tactics of local politicians. Avenues available for them for redressal of their grievances are too remote to help overcome their immediate problems. Nepotism at the local level has resulted in the closure of the channels available to workers for redressal of their problems. The power networks after an election create barriers for healthy feedback, and workers are sucked into the quagmire of such relationships. These patterns of corruption often end up tightening the hold of the local leaders on the employees, though they are not the one who pay their salaries.

**Supervision**

Duplication of supervision is major hurdle in gaining acceptance for decentralization. The supervisors appointed under the scheme at present visit the Balwadi only periodically – not daily, while the most available resource for supervision is the Panchayat, which has no real powers to supervise. If the local bodies are entrusted with supervisory powers and the services are found to be inadequate, do they have the right to impose corrective measures? At present, disciplinary powers do not rest with the Panchayats, and there have been instances in the past, when the representatives of local administrative bodies have misused their powers. Yet It would be both impractical and counterproductive to have both the Gram Panchayat and the government-appointed supervisors trying the programme implementation.

The staff are not likely to take lightly the Panchayats control of the centres. Protests at the grass roots level are inevitable. A shift in the whole administration with emphasis on sustained motivation of the workers over a period of time is needed, and this may be difficult. The short term motivation of the literacy campaign workers provide a classic example of the success of campaign strategies which may be harder to achieve in the long run. Nevertheless it is possible to bring about such changes with the right incentives. Attitudinal changes must start with the recognition that the local level bodies, as organs of the government elected through a democratic process, are the rightful authorities.

**The Worker's Role**

At present the role of the Anganwadi worker is far too ambitious. It is topian to imagine that the low-paid *Anganwadi* worker can influence the community in the manner expected in the ICDS programme. The worker is often from the same village, and her exposure to larger social issues may be limited. The NGOs equally suffer from the weakness of expecting too much from the grass root level worker. While the chief functionary may have a progressive outlook, these aspirations cannot be expected from all those operating at different levels in the organization. Without adequate motivation (both monetary and non-monetary) the grass roots level workers cannot be expected to function as agents of change and progress. To sustain a group and keep it together is difficult, when red tapism and paper work eats up a major part of their time.

### Training

Training of child workers should aim to bring about a consensus regarding the issue of decentralisation. There are Block level training centres in the State — In the three specialities related to child care (health, nutrition and family welfare), staffed by Block Level Extension Trainers. In the new context, the training programmes must be revised to accommodate new areas of thinking and thrash out problems especially with regard to decentralisation. In Rajasthan and a few other States also there is an effort to shift the responsibility for training to the Block level, which can spearhead the new approach.

## MANAGEMENT OF SERVICES

The issues under this broad title include training of elected members and functionaries, supervision of services, and monitoring and evaluation of child care services.

Not only the motivation and commitment to child care services, but the capability of elected members to supervise them, is essential for success. This stage will only be reached when people become aware of the worth of the their contribution, and if there is a system for the development of skills necessary for such participation. The planning phase itself should use a bottom-up approach, for only then will there be true community involvement. Taking responsibility is different from making financial contributions. If elected leaders have to accept and fulfil responsibilities then communities must have with sensitive people sitting on them, with powers and adequate staff to oversee. Decentralisation in fact, requires a more sophisticated level of management, becoming ever more complex, which government may find increasingly difficult to achieve.

## Need For Training

Since child care as such is not an issue, nor is it included in any of the core functions at Panchayat or district level, it is unlikely that the elected representatives wil! be very concerned with such intangible issues. Other issues like street lights, roads, earth works etc., are not only more obvious, but require extensive contracting, with appeal to the local vested interests. So Panchayat members need orientation on issues of gender and children, and experience on how to handle issues hitherto considered unimportant. Training in such areas may be needed till the representation to elected bodies become more representative of the group.

Linking such issues to rights or to vote-catching mechanisms in the region may be a practical approach. Popular schemes of most governments have this basic concept in them (e.g. Mid-day Meal Programme of late Dr. M.G. Ramachandran). The outcome should be a shift from mere service provision by the government to response to a demand by the people. NGOs can play a significant role in training. There should be a wide dissemination of information regarding the 73rd and 74th Amendments and the 11th and 12th Schedules which is lacking not only among the people but even in the NGO sector. Empowerment should be seen as process of changing the existing balance in the power structure, and facilitating the formation of a structure in which people now without power will gain the power needed to function effectively. The training module should provide for stimulated situations to clarify how it can help them in every day life. The content must include legal awareness as well as information on public services like the Public Distribution System. Officials can be manipulative and created situations where the villagers both men and women, are victimized, but there are instances as in Rajasthan when women have become more strident as in Rajasthan as a result of the training methods adopted.

Officials who have the upper hand may often manoeuvre to undermine the authority of the elected representatives. Information about their roles and responsibilities, as well as rights and powers, may not come to them from official channels, and disinterested third parties must help impart such information. Youth and women must be given the support not to be cowed down by older or more experienced members. Empowerment includes all these aspects and does not refer to mere information transfer.

## Evaluation and Monitoring

The need for structures for monitoring and building the capability of groups has already been mentioned. Identification and training of key functionaries to facilitate leadership at local level is required. The training must enable the leadership to identify groups, their strengths and resources for partnership, understand the dynamic within groups and within the community, identify individuals within them, and facilitate democratic leadership.

Monitoring of service delivery includes ensuring accessibility and coverage of various groups, physical space and materials, regular visits and timely interventions. Ongoing evaluation through regular interaction, and access to records and documentation has to be ensured. Decentralisation may require a more sophisticated level of management which is becoming ever more complex. But there is little the Panchayat as a whole or individual members can do if monitoring and evaluation is done on a programme over which there is little or no control. Control over the finances must go hand in hand with supervision.

The dangers and pitfalls of monitoring and evaluation by local leaders are of two kinds, on the one hand, there are external factors like clash of interests, leadership clashes, financial constraints, lack of co-operation from other departments, rivalry among groups and political interference. On the other, at the programme level, the lack of linkages, a top-down approach, a focus on quantity not quality, and the poor feedback system could lead to problems.

## Accountability and Transparency

For the families who benefit from the service, there must be a form to represent their cause at the village level. The more localised the procedure for redressal of grievances, the better would be the quality of service. This can be that the procedural delays are minimised and the quality of service is maintained.

Transparency is needed at all stages of programme implementation, as the tendency to cover up political and bureaucratic meddling and mudling creates a feeling of alienation. Accountability can be established not so much by disciplinary proceedings from a remote place as by the individual immediately conscious of his negligence. Panchayati Raj is still the best alternative since with an elected body, accountability is more definite and immediate, in case of misappropriation or deficiencies in services, making the system more desirable than a rigid and unresponsive bureaucracy.

### Communication

The literacy mission succeeded to a large extent by the use of the Jatha as a technique for the spread of the message. Skits, street plays and puppetry can equally be used to convey the importance of child care. Undoubtedly the message is easier with regard to literacy, since there is no dispute about its essential role in development. In the case of child care services, the message is not so obvious nor does it carry the same weight, since there is still a widespread belief that child is not so obvious nor does it carry the same weight, since there is a still widespread belief that child care is now a part of the woman's domain. But ignoring the child leads to spending crores later on adult literacy programme, instead of the other way round. There is no alternative to an Intensive campaign of political education to educate the masters at the local level.

## STRATEGIES FOR ACTION

Action could be initiated at following levels to proceed towards decentralisation. The various levels offer opportunities for initiating different types of activities to move towards the goal.

### Gram Sabha

- Clarify role of Gram Sabhas with regard to powers and functions, going to the courts, if necessary;

- Ensure transparency, once established;
- Identify priorities for the community;
- Grass roots planning;
- Mobilisation of resources;
- Set a time frame;
- Make demands on State government, hold government accountable;
- Create political awareness; and
- Make Gram Sabha an agent of change.

**Gram Panchayats**

- Initiate demands for decentralisation of child care;
- Promote education of the girl child;
- Develop standing committees — modelled on A.P./Maharashtra experience;
- Insist on representation of women on committees — minimum quorum for making decisions;
- Training and sensitisation of Panchayat members; and
- Set up village education council — to supervise and monitor.

**NGOs/Research and Academic Institutions**

- Set up a collective of women's organisations to review the T.N. Panchayat Act from a gender perspective and child care perspective;
- Develop training manuals on child care;
- Develop gender-sensitive resource and training materials; and
- Compile available material for dissemination.

**Political Parties**

- Educate MLAs and members of political parties;
- Tap influential members for mass awareness programmes; and
- Work with leaders and opposition parties for acceptability of new approaches.

**Bureaucracy and Government Functionaries**

- Sensitise middle-level functionaries on issues;
- Promote a perspective in which all schemes are seen as parts of a whole;

- Promote inter-sectoral coordination;
- Take up gender sensitisation of different departments, such as roads, water supply, electricity etc., all of which may have a significant role;
- Key departments like SIRD to develop curriculum and course content for government personnel;
- Develop alternative and multiple solutions; and
- Reduce gap between functionaries and people.

Some of the following groups can also find important roles in working towards decentralisation:

- Unions — irrespective of political affiliation;
- Service clubs and organisations;
- Associations of child care workers;
- Professional associations;
- Women's groups and organisations;
- Student groups and unions;
- School-teachers, children, P.T. As;
- Media;
- Medical Profession; and
- Business and corporate sector.

For a long time to come the State will continue to be the major contributor towards child care services in Tamil Nadu in both urban and rural areas. How then, and from where, can the process of decentralization be initiated? Obviously, all the major players must simultaneously initiate actions at different levels, nibbling away at the rug, as it were, from different corners. The following may be crucial starting points for action:

**Ten Starting Points for Action**

- Strengthen village groups and initiate need-based planning;
- Clarify roles and responsibility of the various sectors by wide-ranging inter-sectoral discussions;
- Develop mechanisms for communication between sectors;
- Initiate monthly review for feedback and planning at community level;

- Build perspective of government functionaries, from the highest to lowest levels;
- Widely disseminate minimum specifications for ECCD;
- Develop indicators and checklists for monitoring child care services and qualitative reporting;
- Set up inter-departmental co-ordination committee at official levels;
- Make district authority answerable for progress review on decentralisation; and
- Develop mechanisms for supportive supervision.

9

# EMERGING PATTERN OF RURAL WOMEN LEADERSHIP IN PANCHAYATI RAJ INSTITUTIONS IN TAMIL NADU

A.Celine Rani

## STATEMENT OF THE PROBLEM

Leadership plays an important role in shaping the socio-economic and political structure of any society.[1] Emergence and development of leadership is the result of social interaction among the members of the community. Establishment of leadership pattern is fully determined by the individual's power and influence over the society.[2] In any developing society, where the process of modernisation of political structure is going on at a rapid pace, the study of the emerging pattern of leadership is of crucial importance. The leadership pattern appears to be changing from the traditional-oriented system to the modern institutional system.[3]

In rural India, traditionally, leadership positions were secured by persons belonging to higher castes with better economic conditions.[4] The zamindars, village headmen and the village priests acquired their leadership as hereditary right. All the community issues pertaining to social action, resolution of all types of issues and rural development activities were under the control of the traditional institutions.

The tradition of the Indian rural society is that man is superior to woman. Keeping in line with this tradition, the leadership in villages seemed to be male dominated.[5] After the dawn of Independence, with the introduction of Village Panchayats, Land Reforms, the Co-operative Movement and the Community Development Programme, a new type of leadership has emerged gradually in rural India, replacing the traditional leadership. Replacement of the tradition-oriented power group by a progress-oriented power group may indicate a process of far-reaching changes in the community. The establishment of the Indian Republic in 1950 brought to women the promise of adult franchise, equality of opportunity and equal rights on par with men in all spheres of life.

As women represent an important sector of human resource affecting national development and also form half of the population,[6] women's participation in grass roots democracy has widely been recognised. To provide enhanced representation to rural women in Panchayati Raj Institutions (PRIs), specific provisions have been incorporated in the Constitution of India through the Seventy-third Constitution (Amendment) Act 1992. The significant provision of the new Panchayati Raj Act is the reservation of one-third of the seats for women in all positions in local bodies.

Against this backdrop, the present study aims at examining the emerging pattern of rural women leadership in PRIs with reference to the Village Panchayats in Dindigul District in the State of Tamil Nadu. The main questions addressed in this study are: (1) has the socio-economic status of rural women helped in the process of their emergence as leaders?; (2) has the political background of rural women leaders and their families enabled them to so emerge?; (3) can the positions held by the rural women and their family heads in various socio-political organisations influence their emergence?; (4) can the reputation of rural women and their families promote the process of achieving leadership?; (5) can the participation of rural women and their family heads in the decision-making process on the local community issues enable rural women to secure leadership?; and, (6) will the syntheses of different bases of power facilitate the emergence of rural women leadership?

## A FRAMEWORK FOR ANALYSIS

There has been so much empirical research in the field of leadership and group dynamics in the past five or six decades. The leadership of the Village Panchayats has been researched more extensively than that of the two higher tiers, namely Panchayat Samiti (middle tier) and Zilla Parishad (top tier), which have come into being since the late fifties.[7] Leadership is the outcome of the complex integration of individuals and social functions closely related to formal and informal group life.[8] To have a clear understanding of this research problem, it will be helpful to investigate the problem against the backdrop of a theory.

M.G. Ross and C.E. Henry[9] have presented three theories of leadership (1) trait or "Great Man" theory, (2) leadership as a function of the group, and (3) leadership as a function of the situation[10] in which the group is placed. The three types of leadership have to be taken into consideration for a clear understanding of the concept of leadership. A group is the combination of various individual members and, hence, individual personality traits cause variations in the contribution made by each member of the group.[11] In order to exhibit one's leadership quality one has to expose some qualities which are significantly different from those of the other members of the group. Leadership regarded as an activity of influencing people to co-operate towards some goal is found desirable.[12] Leadership is also understood as a relation between an individual and a group established around some common interest and behaviour as directed or determined by the leader.[13] The modern trend is to view the concept of leadership based on the functional aspect. Leadership is thus a function of a group. The dimensions of leadership are leadership behaviour, leadership action and integration between leaders and non-leaders.[14] Interpersonal leadership is largely determined by the structure of the group rather than by the personality of the individual.[15]

The leadership concept in the changing group system may be viewed on traditional-modern dimensions. Max Weber considers traditionalism as one of the bases of authority, the others being charisma and law.[16] The theories of leadership are not mutually exclusive and they have their own shortcomings. In this sense no theory has been fully formulated so far to cater to the need of the present study. However, a syntheses of all the available theories may be useful for this study.

The following approaches, which may help in tracing the emerging pattern of rural women leadership, are ramifications of the theoretical discussions presented above.

## APPROACHES TO IDENTIFY THE PATTERNS OF RURAL LEADERSHIP

A number of studies have been undertaken in India and abroad on leadership patterns of communities. Most of these studies have employed either the positional approach, the reputational approach, the decisional approach, or, a synthesis of these three approaches to locate the community leaders.[17] Used exclusively, none of the approach provides consistent and reliable results. However, recent comparative studies on community leadership through these three approaches seem to provide some consensus regarding the methodological problem. In the following pages, the three approaches and their syntheses are examined in order to identify the pattern of leadership emerging through them.

### Objectives

To investigate the various factors contributing to the emergence of rural women as leaders and to identify the pattern of emergence of rural women leadership, the following objectives have been deduced from the theory for this study :

1. To investigate the relevance of socio-economic states in promoting the emergence of rural women leadership.
2. To find out the relationship between the political background and the emergence of rural women leadership.
3. To analyse the contributory role of positional status towards the emergence of rural women leadership.
4. To measure the influence of family reputation on the emergence of rural women leadership.

5. To trace the link between the decision-making capacity and the emergence of rural women leadership.
6. To probe the interdependence cf the various bases of power of rural women leadership.

## Hypotheses

On the basis of the issues raised and the objectives mentioned, a battery of six hypotheses have been formulated for empirical testing:

1. The socio-economic status is a significant factor in determining rural women leadership.
2. The higher the political background of the family, the greater will be the emergence of rural women leadership.
3. The positions of the rural women and their family heads as bases of power have their own impact on the emergence of rural women as leaders.
4. The higher the reputation of the family, the greater will be the prospects for the rural women to emerge as leaders.
5. Decision-making of the rural women and their family heads plays a significant role in the process of the emergence of rural women as leaders.
6. The different types of syntheses of position, reputation and decision-making as bases of power significantly enhance the emergence of rural women leadership.

These hypotheses have to be empirically tested through the data collected from 206 rural women leaders in Dindigul District. The major findings of the analysis are to be discussed in detail in the order of the issues dealt with.

## Methodology

The study has been carried out in 107 Village Panchayats, the office of the chairpersons of which were reserved for women in the Local Body Elections held in October 1996. The elected Village Panchayat Presidents and their immediate rivals in 107 Village Panchayats were contacted as respondents by adopting census survey method.

The primary data were collected from the respondents through informal personal interviews and discussions with the help of a well structured interview schedule. The collected data were later counter-checked with the local knowledgeable and responsible informants like Village Administrative Officers, School teachers, temple priests and caste leaders. Relevant secondary data were collected from the records of Collectorate, Panchayat Union Offices, Census reports and other documents.

For the purpose of testing the hypotheses, the defeated and the elected respondents were grouped into low, medium and high groups on the basis of the composite score of each independent variable. The composite score of each independent variable was obntained by the linear sum of unweighted scores assigned to each category within each component of the variable.

Using this scheme of scoring, the indices for assessing the socio-economic status, political background, positional, reputational and decision-making profiles were prepared and used.

For the analysis of data measures of central tendencies, chi square test of significance, pearson's correlation coefficent and multivariate regression analysis were used.

*Socio-Economic Status*

A leader is a person, whose guidance and direction are supposed to be accepted by the rest of the people in the community. Leadership signifies a blend of personal traits of the leaders and the social setting in which they are placed. A leader is basically a human being and is related to other human beings through different sets of relationships.[18] Sociologists[19] have described social mobility to be highly dependent on the social circumstances of the individual. The social background of the leaders not only manifests the ascriptive status and, style of life but also the capacity of the leaders to attain and sustain power. In ascription-oriented societies, such as India, the socio-economic status of an individual is relevant in determining the nature and pattern of leadership.

*Leadership vis-a-vis Socio-Economic Status*

The emergence of rural women leadership cannot be measured on the basis of a single influencing factor. The collective impact of multiple socio-economic factors like age, caste, education, occupation, annual-income, land holdings, assets, marital status, type of family, size of family, type of house, place of residence and possession of modern facilities is vital in determining the emergence of leadership and hence it deserves an in-depth analysis.

The respondents of the study are classified into three categories according to their socio-economic status as low (status), medium (status) and high (status).[20]

**Hypothesis 1 : "The socio-economic status is a significant factor in determining rural women leadership".**

In statistical terms, the hypothesis means that there is a significant relation between socio-economic status scores and the votes polled by the respondents in the Village Panchayat elections.

**Table 9.1 :** Leadership vis-a-vis Socio-Economic Status

| Votes Polled | Socio-Economic Scores | | | |
|---|---|---|---|---|
| | Low | Medium | High | Total |
| Defeated (0-49) | 32 (32.3) | 54 (54.6) | 13 (13.1) | 99 (48.1) |
| Elected (50-100) | 16 (15.0) | 66 (61.7) | 25 (23.3) | 107 (51.9) |
| Total | 48 (23.3) | 120 (58.3) | 38 (18.4) | 206 (100) |

*Source:* Computed.

*Note:* Figures in the parentheses show percentages.

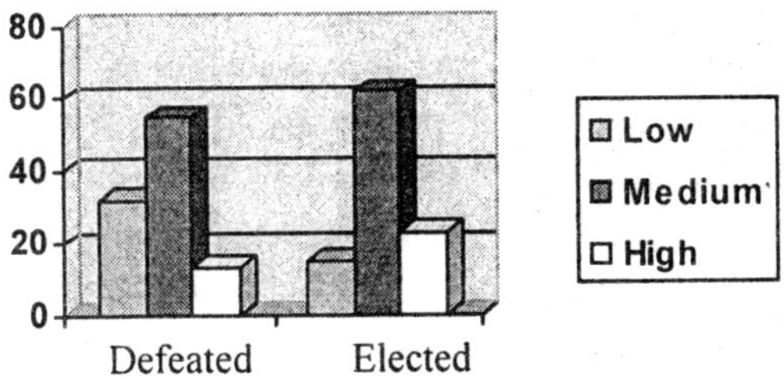


Table 9.1 shows that 85 per cent of the elected respondents belong to medium or high socio-economic status groups as against

67.7 per cent of the defeated respondents belonging to the medium and high status groups. It is also observed that 15.0 per cent of the elected respondents belong to the low socio-economic status group compared to 32.3 per cent of the defeated respondents coming under the same group.

The statistical analysis brings out the fact that the votes polled and the socio-economic status scores secured by the respondents are significantly associated with each other.

$(\chi^2 = 10.03 ; D.F. = 2; P < .01)$

This inference leads to the conclusion that the hypothesis namely, "The socio-economic status is a significant factor in determining rural women leadership", is affirmatively validated.

*Political Background*

The leaders in the village are the change agents of the society. Their understanding and perception of the political system will enhance the functioning of the rural polity.[21]

The political involvement of the citizens is a *sine qua non* for every political system and it is the principal means by which consent is granted or withdrawn in a democracy making the rulers accountable to the ruled.[22] Political participation is the extent to which individuals are involved at various levels in the political system.[23] An individual's social environment comprises diverse elements that will prevail on the nature and extent of that individual's political participation. The most important among these diverse elements are sex, age, education, occupation, income, residence, mobility, religion, race and group influence.[24] The success of democracy depends upon the levels of political awareness and political participation by the members in the society and polity.

The socio-economic variables produce only "distal" effect and as such do not automatically assure a person power and influence in proportion to his base values such as respect, status and wealth.[25] Factors like pattern of party affiliation, media of political socialisation, political links, length of active political life, etc. go a long way in determining influence and resource potential of political actors.[26] To achieve political leadership, the base values of the political actors need to be manipulated along with political participation characterised by factors like age of political awareness, age of entering politics, sources of political inspiration, pattern of party affiliation, political positions and political ambitions.

As the heads of the families are males and the deciding authorities with more exposure to the outside world, they have more political involvement compared to their womenfolk. Therefore, the analysis of the emergence of the leadership of the respondents has to be carried out taking into account the political background of their family heads.

It is, therefore, decided to analyse the integrated impact of multiple political variables, namely age of political awareness, age of entering politics, sources of inspiration for political interest, positions held in political parties, stimulant for political participation and political ambitions of the respondents together with the party affiliations, positions held in political parties, nature of involvement in political activities of the family heads on the emergence of leadership.

The elected and defeated respondents are categorised on the basis of their political background scores as low, medium and high groups.[27]

**Hypothesis 2 : "The higher the political background of the family, the greater will be the emergence of rural women leadership."**

The content of this hypothesis in statistical terms is that there is significant relation between the votes polled and the scores secured for political background by the respondents.

**Table 9.2 :** Leadership vis-a-vis Political Background

| Votes Polled | Political Background Scores | | | |
|---|---|---|---|---|
| | Low | Medium | High | Total |
| Defeated<br>(0-49) | 22<br>(22.2) | 61<br>(61.6) | 16<br>(16.2) | 99<br>(48.1) |
| Elected<br>(50-100) | 12<br>(11.2) | 57<br>(53.3) | 38<br>(35.5) | 107<br>(51.9) |
| Total | 34<br>(16.5) | 118<br>(57.3) | 54<br>(26.2) | 206<br>(100.0) |

*Source:* Computed.
*Note:* Figures in parentheses are percentages.

Table 9.2 reveals that 88.8 per cent of the elected respondents belong to medium and high political background groups as against 77.8 per cent of the defeated respondents and that 11.2 per cent of the elected respondents belong to the low political background group compared to 22.2 per cent of the defeated ones.

The statistical analysis shows that there is significant association between the votes polled and the political background scores secured by the respondents.

($\chi^2$ = 11.75; D.F.=2; P<.01)

Therefore the statistical analysis leads to the conclusion that hypothesis namely, "The higher the political background of the family, the greater will be the emergence of rural women leadership" is validated affirmatively.

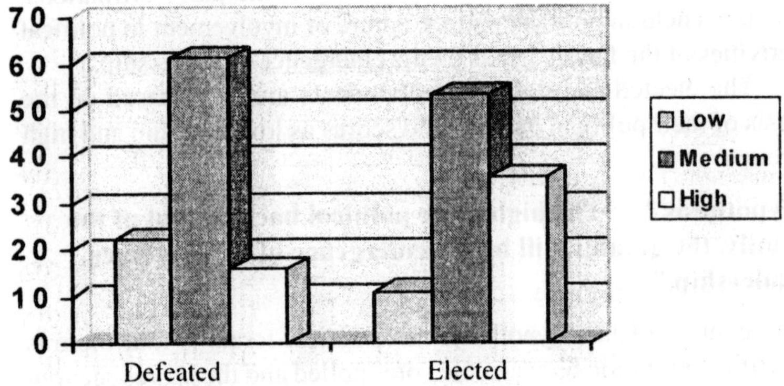


*Identification of Power Bases*

The substantive issue of the study is the identification of the pattern of rural women leadership in Dindigul District of Tamil Nadu. The elected women and their immediate rivals in the elections for the office of Village Panchayat president are presumed to have emerged as rural women leaders. For finding the pattern of their leadership, an appropriate methodology has to be employed.

A large number of studies have been undertaken on the subject of identification of community leaders in India and abroad. These studies have adopted one or another of the following three approaches to identify the community leaders: (i) Positional

Approach, (ii) Reputational Approach, and (iii) Decisional Approach.[27] Despite their wide application by researchers both in and outside India, they suffer from inadequacies and shortcomings. Vehement criticisms and counter-arguments against the acceptability of these approaches have revealed the actual weaknesses of the approaches. Consequently scholars have shifted their methodology to a combined approach for the identification of leaders in the community, at least in similar studies in the Western countries.

With the underlying assumption that the elected rural women Village Panchayat Presidents and their immediate rivals in the elections to the Village Panchayats in Dindigul District are identified as leaders in this study, the core task of this study is to categorise them under different patterns. The approaches mentioned above and their syntheses are employed in this study not for the identification of the leaders, but for the identification of the power bases through which their leadership has emerged. The identified power bases will help to assess the pattern of the rural women leadership that has emerged.

The application of different approaches by the scholars in identifying the community leaders has facilitated the location of different types of leaders.[28] A synthesis of the three approaches may give rise to yet other types of leaders. But the agreement and disagreement between these combinations and the validity and reliability of the findings can only be ascertained through a comparative analysis. Freeman *et al.*, have utilised a synthesis of the three approaches and compared the findings of each of the approaches[29] to identify different types of leaders in the community.

In the following pages, the positional approach, the reputational approach, and the decisional approach (issue participation approach or event-analysis), a combination of any two of them and a synthesis of all the three are examined in order to categorise the rural women who have emerged as leaders of the Village Panchayats in Dindigul District.

### *Leadership vis-a-vis Position*

The basic assumption behind the positional approach is that people who hold important positions in formal as well as informal organisations are leaders in a village. In order to examine the level of influence of positions as bases of power on the emergence of leadership, the multiple positions held by the respondents and their family heads in different organisations under consideration are analysed statistically.[30]

**Hypothesis 3 : "The positions of the rural women and their family heads as bases of power have their own impact on the emergence of rural women as leaders".**

The statistical version of this hypothesis implies that there is a positive relationship between the votes polled and the positional scores secured by the respondents.

**Table 9.3** : Votes Polled vis-a-vis Positional Scores

| Votes Polled | Level of Positional Profile Scores | | | |
|---|---|---|---|---|
| | Low | Medium | High | Total |
| Defeated (0-49) | 44 (44.4) | 46 (46.5) | 9 (9.1) | 99 (48.1) |
| Elected (50-100) | 31 (29.0) | 57 (53.3) | 19 (17.8) | 107 (51.9) |
| Total | 75 (36.4) | 103 (50.0) | 28 (13.6) | 206 (100) |

*Source:* Computed.

*Note:* Figures in parentheses are percentages.

Table 9.3 reveals that 71.1 per cent of the elected respondents and 55.6 per cent of the defeated respondents come under high and medium levels of positional scores whereas 44.4 per cent of the defeated respondents and 29.0 per cent of the elected respondents fall under low level of positional scores.The statistical analysis concludes that there is a positive relationship between the votes polled and the positional scores secured by the respondents.

$(\chi^2 = 6.70 \;;\; D.F.= 2 \;;\; P< .05)$

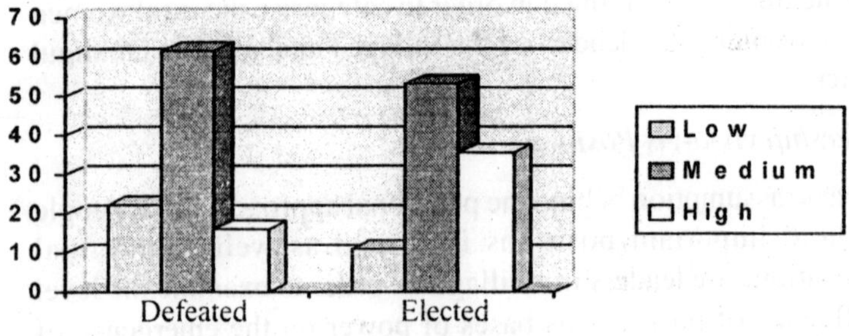

Hence the affirmative validation of the third hypothesis of the study, namely "The positions of the rural women and their family heads as bases of power have their own impact on the emergence of rural women as leaders".

## *Reputational Approach*

People acquire reputation by virtue of their social status, which mostly depends on caste, land holdings, wealth, public positions and combinations of a few or all of these. In the Indian rural scenario, age also contributes to reputation because wisdom and knowledge necessary for solving disputes are correlated with age.[31] However, the young men who are active in public affairs along with their academic credentials or new skills are not to be ignored. Besides, a person may be weighed in the light of his/her personality traits and activities as good, bad, efficient, inefficient, courageous, cowardly, cunning etc., all of which may alter the reputation of a person in a community.[32]

The inherited social position and the reputation of a family play an important role in determining its leadership position. Besides, the behaviour and the achievement of the living members also determine the status of the family and leadership of its members.[33]

The reputation flowing from one's familial lineage is termed ascribed reputation, while the reputation secured by virtue of one's personal traits and social interaction is called achieved reputation. Both these reputations have their role in determining the emergence of leadership. Those persons who have emerged as leaders by means of reputation are called reputational leaders. The correlates of both ascribed and achieved reputations possessed by the respondents are to be examined for declaring them reputational leaders.

### *Correlates of Ascribed Reputation*

The determinants of ascribed reputation are classified into four groups as: (i) Social Correlates, (ii) Economic Correlates, (iii) Political Correlates, and (iv) Community Service Correlates for the sake of simple percentage tabular analysis.

### *Correlates of Achieved Reputation*

Achieved reputation or personal reputation refers to the reverence secured by means of one's own personal traits like hospitality, honesty, helping tendency, sociability, accessibility, tolerance, courage for atriculation, intelligence, self-confidence and fighting spirit. These personal traits constitute the correlates of personal reputation for the present study.

A respondent is deemed to have achieved reputation if she possesses at least any five of the aforesaid ten correlates of personal reputation. When the respondents were asked to mention the factors responsible for their emergence as leaders, a few of the respondents replied that they emerged as leaders because of their personal reputation in addition to the influence of their family reputation.

In the present study, 11.2 per cent of the respondents have been identified as persons with personal reputation. It is encouraging to learn that at least 11.2 per cent of the respondents were able to acquire personal reputation.

*Leadership vis-a-vis Reputation*

The underlying assumption in the reputational approach is that those who possess reputation for power emerge as leaders. With a view to identifying the level of influence of reputation as a base of power on the emergence of leadership, the reputation of the respondents, both ascribed and achieved, are analysed statistically.

**Hypothesis 4: "The higher the reputation of the family, the greater will be the prospects for the rural women to emerge as leaders".**

The implication of this hypothesis in the statistical sense is that the votes polled by the respondents have positive relationship with the reputational scores of the respondents.

**Table 9.4** : Votes Polled vis-a-vis Reputational Scores

| Votes Polled | Levels of Reputational Scores | | | |
|---|---|---|---|---|
| | Low | Medium | High | Total |
| Defeated | 85 | 9 | 5 | 99 |
| (0-49) | (85.9) | (9.1) | (5.1) | (48.1) |
| Elected | 71 | 19 | 17 | 107 |
| (50-100) | (66.4) | (19.2) | (15.9) | (51.9) |
| Total | 156 | 28 | 22 | 206 |
| | (75.7) | (13.6) | (10.7) | (100) |

*Source:* Computed.

*Note:* Figures in parentheses are percentages.

Table 9.4 indicates that 35.1 per cent of the elected respondents and 14.2 per cent of the defeated respondents come under high or medium levels of reputational scores, while 85.9 per cent of the defeated respondents and 66.4 per cent of the elected respondents fall under low level of reputational scores.

The statistical analysis of the votes polled and the reputational scores secured by the respondents brings out the fact that there is a direct and positive relationship between them.

($\chi^2$ = 11.08; D.F. = 2; P < .01)

Therefore, the fourth hypothesis of the study, namely "*The higher the reputation of the family, the greater will be the prospects for the rural women to emerge as leaders*" is affirm atively validated.

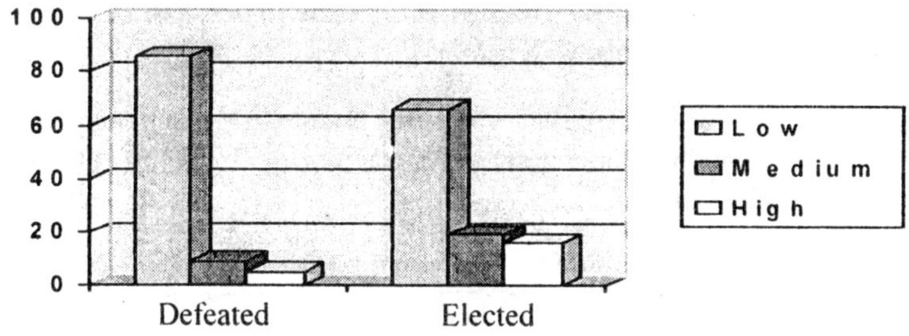


*Decisional Approach*

This approach lays emphasis on the assumption that those who actually participate in the decision-making process are the leaders as they have demonstrated their influence in real-life situation.

In order to empirically analyse the emergence of rural women leadership through this approach, certain specific determinants such as decision on their candidature, participants in various socio-political activities, the mode adopted by them in settling the issues, the promises made during the election campaign and strategy adopted by them during electioneering are conceptualised and their contributory role in the emergence of leadership is examined.

Political decision-making in villages is varied and is multidimensional. One's entry into politics itself requires deep contemplation and wise decision-making. The initial decision of one to enter the political power structure may be made on the volition of the individual concerned or by the influence of external motivating forces.

*Leadership vis-a-vis Decision-Making*

The decision-making approach rests on the assumption that those who actually participate in the decision-making process are the leaders as they have already demonstrated their influence in actual-life situations. In the light of this assumption, an attempt has been made to ascertain the level of influence of the decision-making of the respondents and their family heads on the emergence of respondents as leaders.

**Hypothesis 5: "Decision-making of the rural women and their family heads plays a significant role in the process of the emergence of rural women as leaders".**

This hypothesis, in its statistical terms, means that the votes polled and the decision-making scores secured by the respondents have a positive association.

**Table 9.5** : Votes Polled vis-a-vis Decisional Scores

| Sl. No. | Votes Polled | Levels of Decisional Scores | | | |
|---|---|---|---|---|---|
| | | Low | Medium | High | Total |
| 1. | Defeated (0 - 49) | 50 (50.5) | 42 (42.4) | 7 (7.1) | 99 (48.1) |
| 2. | Elected (50 -100) | 21 (19.6) | 63 (58.9) | 23 (21.5) | 107 (51.9) |
| | Total | 71 (34.5) | 105 (51.0) | 30 (14.6) | 206 (100) |

*Source:* Computed.

*Note:* Figures in parentheses are percentages.

Table 9.5 shows that 80.4 per cent of the elected respondents come under either the medium or the high group of decisional scores as against 49.5 per cent of the defeated respondents, while 50.5 per cent of the defeated and 19.6 per cent of the elected respondents fall under the low group of decisional scores.

The statistical analysis of the votes and the decisional scores of the respondents brings out the fact that there is a significant association between the variants.

($\chi^2 = 24.30$ ; D.F. = 2; $P < .01$ )

Hence, the fifth hypothesis of the study, namely "Decision-making of the rural women and their family heads plays a significant role in the process of the emergence of rural women as leaders" is validated empirically.

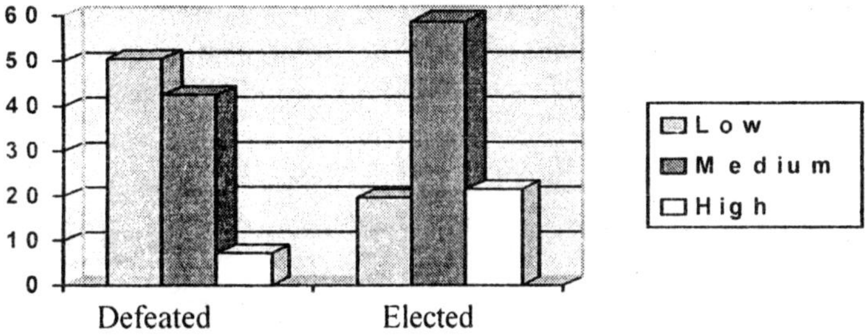


*Integrated Approach to the Identification of Power Bases*

An empirical study based on the integrated application of the Positional, the Reputational and the Decisional approaches through which the rural women have emerged as leaders provides an opportunity for measuring the combined effects of integrated approaches in the emergence of rural women leadership.

*Syntheses of Different Approaches*

The Positional, the Reputational and the Decisional approaches may be integrated in four ways by combining any two or all the three simultaneously as follows:

1. Synthesis of Position and Reputation,
2. Synthesis of Reputation and Decision,
3. Synthesis of Decision and Position, and
4. Synthesis of Position, Reputation and Decision.

**Hypothesis 6: "The different types of syntheses of position, reputation and decision-making as bases of power significantly enhance the emergence of rural women leadership".**

In statistical terms, the above hypothesis means that there is a positive relationship between the votes polled and the sum of the scores secured by the respondents for the power bases of Position, Reputation and Decision-making taken two by two and all the three simultaneously.

For the purpose of statistical analysis, the composite scores of the respondents falling under different types of syntheses are computed by adding the scores of the components in the respective synthesis.

### *Leadership vis-a-vis Position and Reputation*

**Table 9.6** : Votes Polled vis-a-vis Combined Scores on Position and Reputation

| Sl. No. | Votes Polled | Levels of Combined Scores | | | |
|---|---|---|---|---|---|
| | | Low | Medium | High | Total |
| 1. | Defeated (0-49) | 72 (72.7) | 24 (24.3) | 3 (3.0) | 99 (48.1) |
| 2. | Elected (50-100) | 54 (50.5) | 37 (34.5) | 16 (15.0) | 107 (51.9) |
| | Total | 126 (61.2) | 61 (29.6) | 19 (9.2) | 206 (100) |

*Source:* Computed.

*Note:* Figures within parentheses are percentages.

Table 9.6 reveals that 49.5 per cent of the elected respondents have secured medium or high scores for position and reputation as against 27.3 per cent of the defeated respondents and that 50.5 per cent of the elected respondents come under low composite scores of position and reputation compared to 72.7 per cent of the defeated respondents.

The statistical analysis of Table 9.6 shows that there is a positive and significant association between the votes polled and the combined scores on position and reputation of the respondents.

($\chi^2$ = 13.95 ; D.F. = 2 ; $P < .01$)

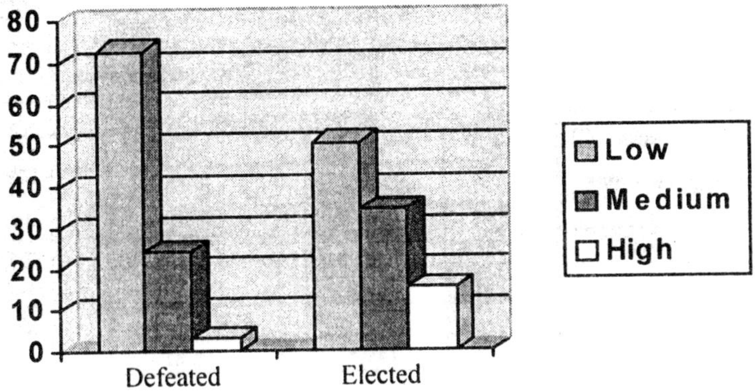


## *Leadership vis-a-vis Reputation and Decision-making*

**Table 9.7** : Votes Polled vis-a-vis Combined Scores on Reputation and Decision-making

| Sl. No. | Votes polled | Levels of Combined Scores | | | |
|---|---|---|---|---|---|
| | | Low | Medium | High | Total |
| 1. | Defeated (0-49) | 66 (66.7) | 30 (30.3) | 3 (3.0) | 99 (48.1) |
| 2. | Elected (50-100) | 35 (32.7) | 54 (50.5) | 18 (16.8) | 107 (51.9) |
| | Total | 101 (49.0) | 84 (40.8) | 21 (10.2) | 206 (100) |

*Source:* Computed.

*Note :* Figures within parentheses are percentages.

Table 9.7 makes it evident that 67.3 per cent of the elected respondents have secured medium or high levels of combined scores on reputation and decision-making whereas only 33.3 per cent of the defeated respondents have scored at medium or high levels. On the other hand, the defeated respondents numerically outnumber the elected respondents in getting low scores by 34 per cent.

The statistical inference drawn from the above finding is that the combined effect of reputational and decisional variables has significant association with the emergence of the leadership of the respondents.

($\chi^2$ = 26.82 ; D.F. = 2 ; P < .01)

### *Leadership vis-a-vis Decision-making and Position*

**Table 9.8** : Votes Polled vis-a-vis Combined Scores on Decision-making and Position

| Sl. No. | Votes Polled | Levels of Combined Scores | | | |
|---|---|---|---|---|---|
| | | Low | Medium | High | Total |
| 1. | Defeated (0-49) | 59 (59.6) | 38 (38.4) | 2 (2.0) | 99 (48.1) |
| 2. | Elected (50-100) | 28 (26.2) | 64 (59.8) | 15 (14.0) | 107 (51.9) |
| | Total | 87 (42.2) | 102 (49.5) | 17 (8.3) | 206 (100) |

*Source:* Computed.

*Note:* Figures within parentheses are percentages.

It is clear from Table 9.8 that 73.8 per cent of the elected respondents come under medium or high levels of combined scores on decision-making and position, while 40.4 per cent of the defeated respondents fall under medium or high levels. Also it is found that 59.6 per cent of the defeated respondents fall under the low group as against 26.2 per cent of the elected respondents.

The statistical inference drawn from the above findings is that the impact of decisional and positional variables taken together is significantly associated with the emergence of the leadership of the respondents.

($\chi^2 = 27.35$ ; D.F. = 2 ; $P < .01$)

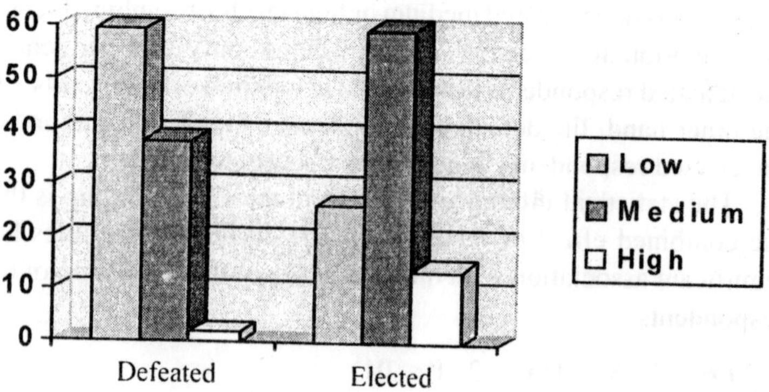

## *Leadership vis-a-vis Position, Reputation and Decision-making*

**Table 9.9** : Votes Polled vis-a-vis Combined Scores on Position, Reputation and Decision-making

| Sl. No. | Votes Polled | Levels of Combined Scores | | | |
|---|---|---|---|---|---|
| | | Low | Medium | High | Total |
| 1. | Defeated (0-49) | 72 (72.7) | 25 (25.3) | 2 (2.0) | 99 (48.1) |
| 2. | Elected (50-100) | 47 (43.9) | 41 (38.3) | 19 (17.8) | 107 (51.9) |
| | Total | 119 (57.8) | 66 (32.0) | 21 (10.2) | 206 (100) |

*Source:* Computed.
*Note:* Figures in parentheses are percentages.

Table 9.9 shows that 56.1 per cent of the elected respondents have secured medium or high levels of combined scores on position, reputation and decision-making as against 27.3 per cent of the defeated respondents on the same levels. It is also seen that 72.7 per cent of the defeated respondents fall under the low group compared to 43.9 per cent of the elected respondents.

The statistical inference drawn from the above findings is that the influence of positional, reputational and decisional variables taken together is significantly associated with the emergence of the respondents as leaders.

$(\chi^2 = 22.62 ;\ D.F. = 2 ;\ P < .01)$

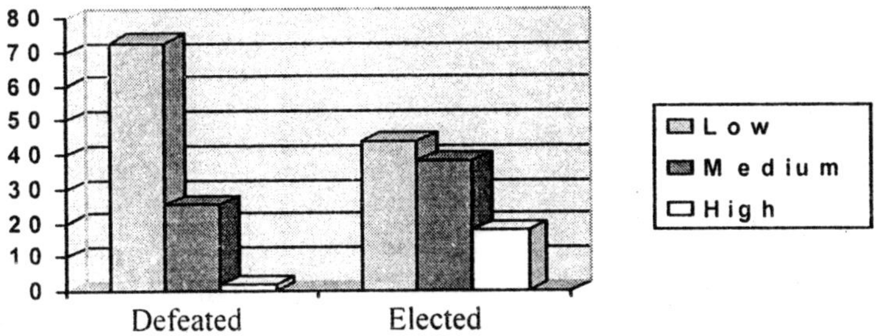


The comparative analysis of the aforesaid statistical findings reveals that the syntheses of "Reputation and Decision-making," "Decision-making and Position" and "Position, Reputation and Decision-making" influence the rural women leadership of the respondents more significantly than the combination of "Position and Reputation".

*Overall Statistical Findings of the Three Approaches*

**Table 9.10** : Leadership vis-a-vis Position and Integration of Position with other Bases of Power

| Sl. No. | Bases of Power | $\chi^2$ (Votes vis-a-vis Bases of Power) | D.F. | P* | R* | Order of Effective-ness |
|---|---|---|---|---|---|---|
| 1. | P | 6.70 | 2 | 0.05 | 0.18 | 4 |
| 2. | P+R | 13.95 | 2 | 0.01 | 0.26 | 3 |
| 3. | P+D | 27.35 | 2 | 0.01 | 0.34 | 1 |
| 4. | P+R+D | 22.62 | 2 | 0.01 | 0.34 | 2 |

*Source:* Computed.

P — Positional scores; R — Reputational scores; D — Decisional Scores.

P* — Level of Significance; R* — Pearson's Correlation

The data in Table 9.10 reveal that the combined scores on position, with those on reputation and decision, taken two by two and all the three simultaneously are more significantly associated with the votes polled by the respondents compared to the single effect of positional scores on votes polled by the respondents. Then again, among the combined scores, the combined scores on position and decision bear the most significant relationship with the votes secured by the respondents followed by the combined scores on all

**Table 9.11** : Leadership vis-a-vis Reputation and Integration of Reputation with other Bases of Power

| Sl. No. | Bases of Power | $\chi^2$ (Votes vis-a-vis Bases of Power) | D.F. | P* | R* | Order of Effective-ness |
|---|---|---|---|---|---|---|
| 1. | R | 11.08 | 2 | 0.01 | 0.25 | 4 |
| 2. | R+P | 13.95 | 2 | 0.01 | 0.26 | 3 |
| 3. | R+D | 26.82 | 2 | 0.01 | 0.36 | 1 |
| 4. | R+P+D | 22.62 | 2 | 0.01 | 0.34 | 2 |

*Source:* Computed.

R — Reputational Scores: P — Positional Scores; D - Decisional Scores.

secured by the respondents followed by the combined scores on all the three and those on position and reputation.

The data in Table 9.11 bring out that the combined scores on reputation, with those on position and decision-making, taken two by two and all the three simultaneously are significantly related with the votes secured by the respondents. Among the combined scores, the combined scores on reputation and decision bear the most significant relationship with the votes secured by the respondents followed by the combined scores on all the three and the combined scores on reputation and position.

**Table 9.12** : Leadership vis-a-vis Decision-Making and Integration of Decision-Making with other Bases of Power

| Sl. No. | Bases of Power | $\chi^2$ (Votes vis-a-vis Bases of Power) | D.F. | P* | R* | Order of Effective-ness |
|---|---|---|---|---|---|---|
| 1. | D | 24.30 | 2 | 0.01 | 0.36 | 2 |
| 2. | D + P | 27.35 | 2 | 0.01 | 0.34 | 3 |
| 3. | D + R | 26.82 | 2 | 0.01 | 0.36 | 1 |
| 4. | D + P + R | 22.62 | 2 | 0.01 | 0.34 | 4 |

*Source:* Computed.
D — Decisional Scores ; P — Positional Scores ; R — Reputational Scores.
P* — Level of Significance; R* — Pearson's Correlation

The contents of Table 9.12 reveal that the combined scores of decision-making with those on position and reputation, taken two by two and all the three simultaneously are significantly associated with the votes secured by the respondents. Among the combined scores, those on decision-making and reputation bear the most significant relationship with the votes secured by the respondents followed by the single effect of decision-making. It is observed that the significance of the decisional score on votes secured declines whenever it is combined with position.

An overview of the statistical findings drawn from Tables 9.10, 9.11 and 9.12 lead to the consolidated conclusion that the sixth hypothesis, namely "The different types of syntheses of Position, Reputation and Decision-making as bases of power significantly enhance the emergence of rural women leadership" is validated affirmatively.

*Categorisation of Leadership*

In order to categorise the rural women leadership as positional, reputational and decisional, the mean score on each power base is considered as the cut-off point.

**Table 9.13** : Distribution of Respondents by their Power Bases

| Sl. No. | Power Bases | Respondents | | | | | |
|---|---|---|---|---|---|---|---|
| | | Elected | | Defeated | | Total | |
| | | No. | % | No. | % | No. | % |
| 1. | Positional Leaders | 69 | 64.5 | 43 | 43.4 | 112 | 54.4 |
| 2. | Reputational Leaders | 58 | 54.2 | 26 | 26.3 | 84 | 40.8 |
| 3. | Decisional Leaders | 71 | 64.4 | 29 | 29.3 | 100 | 48.5 |
| 4. | Other Leaders | 8 | 7.5 | 38 | 38.4 | 46 | 22.3 |

*Source:* Computed.

Mean Score on Position = 9.23 out of the maximum of 42 scores
Mean Score on Reputation = 7.88 out of the maximum of 30 scores
Mean Score on Decision = 15.68 out of the maximum of 50 scores

It is evident from Table 9.13 that 54.4 per cent of the leaders possess position as a base of power, 48.5 per cent have decision-making as base of power and 40.8 per cent have reputation as base of power. It is also observed that 22.3 per cent of the respondents have emerged as leaders without any of the aforesaid bases of power.

It is also obvious that the elected respondents outnumber the defeated respondents in possessing the different bases of power.

*Pattern of Emergence of Respondents' Leadership*

The pattern of the emergence of the respondents as leaders is determined by taking into account the number of bases of power namely position, reputation and decision-making possessed by them. Those leaders who have all the three bases of power are classified as primary leaders, those who have only any two of the three are classified as secondary leaders and those who have only one base

**Table 9.14 :** Leadership Pattern of Respondents

| Sl. No. | Pattern of Leadership | Respondents | | | | | |
|---|---|---|---|---|---|---|---|
| | | Elected | | Defeated | | Total | |
| | | No. | % | No. | % | No. | % |
| 1. | Primary Leaders | 34 | 31.8 | 8 | 8.1 | 42 | 20.4 |
| 2. | Secondary Leaders | 31 | 28.9 | 21 | 21.2 | 52 | 25.3 |
| 3. | Tertiary Leaders | 34 | 31.8 | 32 | 32.3 | 66 | 32.0 |
| 4. | Situational Leaders | 8 | 7.5 | 38 | 38.4 | 46 | 22.3 |
| | Total | 107 | 100.0 | 99.0 | 100.0 | 206.0 | 100.0 |

*Source:* Computed.

of power are categorised as tertiary leaders. Lastly leaders with none of the three bases of power are classified as situational leaders.

It is apparent from Table 9.14 that 20.4 per cent of the respondents are primary leaders as against 25.3 per cent being secondary leaders and 32 per cent being tertiary leaders, while 22.3 per cent have emerged as situational leaders. It is important to note that the elected leaders outnumber the defeated leaders under the categories of primary, secondary and tertiary leaders.

The fact that primary leaders are minimal in number compared to secondary and tertiary leaders leads to the conclusion that there is a dispersal of power resources in the villages of Dindigul District.

Although there is overlapping of power bases among the respondents, there are 32 per cent respondents having only one source of power. Their numerical identity and the exact approach through which they have emerged as leaders is displayed in Table 9.15.

**Table 9.15** : Distribution of Respondents with Single Base of Power

| Sl. No. | Bases of Power | Respondents | | | | | |
|---|---|---|---|---|---|---|---|
| | | Elected | | Defeated | | Total | |
| | | No. | % | No. | % | No. | % |
| 1. | Position only | 11 | 10.3 | 18 | 18.2 | 29 | 14.1 |
| 2. | Reputation only | 10 | 9.3 | 8 | 8.0 | 18 | 8.7 |
| 3. | Decision-Making only | 13 | 12.2 | 6 | 6.0 | 19 | 9.2 |

*Source:* Computed.

The data in Table 9.15 indicate that 14.1 per cent of the respondents have emerged as leaders with only position as base of power, 9.2 per cent with decision-making alone as base of power, and, 8.7 per cent with only reputation as base of power. These leaders are called the tertiary leaders.

*Regression Analysis of Multi-variants*

The multi-variants considered for the statistical study of the emergence of rural women leaders are the socio-economic variable ($x_1$), political background variable ($x_2$), positional variable ($x_3$), reputational variable ($x_4$) and decisional variable ($x_5$). The votes secured by the respondents depend upon the aforesaid multi-variants. The multi-variant regression analysis of the votes polled on the independent variants is computed as

$$y = a_0 + a_1x_1 + a_2x_2 + a_3x_3 + a_4x_4 + a_5x_5$$

where

$a_0 = 24.806918$
$a_1 = .171270$
$a_2 = .167805$
$a_3 = -.022622$
$a_4 = -.007222$
$a_5 = .295164$ and $R^2 = .19738$

The value of $R^2$ shows that there are some other factors which intervene in the process of the emergence of the respondents as leaders. The leaders who have emerged through "some other factors" are called situational leaders in this study. Peculiar situations suddenly intruding upon a political system or a community may turn to be the basis for the emergence of the new type of leaders called situational leaders.

Alliance policies of political parties, sudden phenomena causing political waves, religious, communal and inter-village animosities, sudden upheavals giving rise to anomic leaders, the dormant support of unknown influentials, caste and village affinities may be some of the peculiar situations for the emergence of situational leaders.

Freed W. Fielder[34] and his associates at the University of Illinois have suggested a contingency theory of leadership. This theory holds that people become leaders not only because of attributes of their personalities, but also because of various situational factors and the interactions between leaders and group members.

## CONCLUSION

In the attempt to find answers to the questions raised, the study first arrived at the result that there is affirmative and significant relationship between the votes polled by the rural women leaders in their Village Panchayat elections and the scores on their socio-economic status variables at one per cent level of significance of Chi square test.

This result implies the positive validation of the hypothesis that "*the socio-economic status is a significant factor in determining rural women leadership*", which provides the answer to the first question.

The analysis of the study in relation to the second question showed that the association between the votes polled in the elections and the scores secured for the political background factors was validated at one per cent level of significance of chi square test.

The implication of this result positively justifies the hypothesis pertaining to the second question that "*the higher the political back ground of the family, the greater will be the emergence of rural women leadership*".

The finding of the study as to the third question revealed that there was positive relationship between the votes polled and the scores secured for the positions as per the chi square test at 5 per cent level of significance.

This finding provides the answer to the third question by positively validating the hypothesis that, "*the positions of the rural women and their family heads as bases of power have their own impact on the emergence of the rural women as leaders*".

The outcome of the study with regard to the fourth question revealed that there was significant association between the votes polled and the scores on reputation of the leaders at one per cent level of significance of chi square test.

This result of chi square test leads to the conclusion that "*the higher the reputation of the family, the greater will be the prospect for the rural women to emerge as leaders.*"

The Chi square test has further established that the dependent variable, namely the votes polled, has positive association with the scores on the decision making capabilities at one per cent level of significance.

Thus the answer to the fifth question is the affirmative validation of the corresponding hypothesis that, "*decision-making of the rural women and their family heads plays a significant role in the process of the emergence of rural women leadership*". On finding the answer to the last question, the following statistical inferences were arrived at.

The chi square values of the associations between votes polled by the leaders and the scores secured by them for their Position, Reputation and Decision-making integrated two by two and all the three simultaneously, were positively significant at one per cent level.

This inference confirms the last hypothesis of the present study that, "*the different types of syntheses of Position, Reputation and Decision-making as bases of power significantly enhance the emergence of rural women leadership*".

These conclusions of the present study explain the pattern of rural women leadership that has emerged in Dindigul District through the Village Panchayat elections held in October 1996. To sum up, the present study has identified the emerging pattern of rural women leadership as Primary, Secondary, Tertiary, Situational leaders.

The emergence of rural women leadership at the grass roots level of democracy has, as per the present study, come into being with the support base of ascribed status. Leadership will be a reality when it emerges largely through the achieved status of the leaders. With this view in mind, the family members of the rural women in particular and the society in general have to ensure women equal participation in the decision-making process, the control over resources and the mechanisms for sustaining these gains.

## NOTES

1. Udai Pareek and S.K. Reddy, "Studies in Indian Rural Leadership-A Review", *Studies on Rural Leadership* (ed.) Udai Pareek, Delhi: Behavioural Science Centre, 1966, pp.101-112. Also see Leela Dube, "Studies on Leadership in Village India", *Emerging Patterns of Rural Leadership in South Asia*, Hyderabad: National Institute of Community Development, 1965, pp.107- 134.

2. Charles P. Loomis, *Social Systems; Essays on the Persistence and Change*, New Jersey: Princeton, 1963.

3. Ferdinand Tonnies, *Community and Society*, Translated from German and edited by Charles Loomis, New York: Harper and Row, 1963.

4. Iqbal Narain, *The Rural Elite in an Indian State – A Case Study of Rajasthan*, New Delhi: Monohar Book Depot, 1976, p. 72.

5. D.C. Miglani, *Politics and Rural Power Structure*, New Delhi: Deep and Deep Publications, 1993, p.199; G.D. Bhatt, *Emerging Leadership Pattern in Rural India- An Empirical Study*, New Delhi: M D Publications Pvt. Ltd., 1994, p.131.

6. B.S.Bhargava, and K. Subha, "Women in Panchayati Raj: Some Reflections on Karnataka's Experience", *Kurukshetra*, Vol. XLII, No. 9, June, 1994, p. 42.

7. N.R. Inamdar, " Panchayati Raj Leadership: Emerging Dimensions", *Journal of Rural Development*, Vol. 10, No.5 September-October, 1991, pp. 561-573, Hyderabad: NIRD.

8. R.C. Clark, *A Review of Leadership Studies, Selected Readings and References*, in 4H Club Work, p. 85.

9. Murray G. Ross and Charless E. Hendry, *New Understanding of Leadership: A Survey and Application of Research*, New York: Association Press, 1957.

10. Cecil A. Gibb, "Leadership", in *Handbook of Social Psychology*, (Ed.), Gardner Lindzey, New York: Addison Wesley Publishing Company, Vol-II, 1954, p. 901.

11. *Ibid.*, p. 889.

12. Ordway Tead, *The Art of Leadership*, New York: McGraw Hill Book Co., 1963.

13. Richard Schmidt, "Leadership", *Encyclopedia of Social Sciences*, (ed.), R.A. Edwin Seligman, Vol. IX-X, New York: The Macmillan Company and Free Press,1972, pp. 91-113 ;S.C. Dube, "*A Framework for the Study of Rural Leadership in Transitional Societies*", in Emerging Patterns of Rural Leadership in Southern Asia, Hyderabad: National Institute of Community Development, 1965. pp. 24.

14. Murray G. Ross and Charles E. Hendry, *op.cit.* p. 22.

15. David Krech and Richard S. Crutchfield, *Theory and Problem of Social Psychology*, New York: McGraw Hill Book Co, 1948, p. 401.

16. Max Weber, "Types of Authority", *Essays in Sociology*, (ed.), H.H. Gerth and C.W. Mills, Oxford University Press,1946.

17. An Excellent review of these approaches is found in Charles M. Bonjean and David M. Olsen, "Community Leadership : Directions of Research", *Administrative Science Quarterly*, Vol. 9. No. 3, December 1964, pp. 278-300.

18. Trueman, *et al.*, "United Senator and the Class Structure", in H. Eulau, S.J. Eldesrweld and M. Janowitz, (ed.), *Political Behaviour – A Reader in Theory and Research*. Delhi: Amerind Publishers Pvt. Ltd., 1972, p. 184.

19. S.M. Lipset, and R. Bandix, *Social Mobility in Industrial Society*, Berkeley and Loss Angels: University of California Press, 1959, pp. 63-64; C.A. Anderson, "Skeptical Note on the Relation of Vertical Mobility to Education", *American Journal of Sociology*, Vol. LXVI, No. 5, March, 1961, pp. 560-70; R. "Stalcup, *Educational Sociology*, U.S.A: Mersill and Co., 1967, pp. 7-17; M.N. Srinivas, *India's Villages*, Bombay: Asia Publishing House, 1960, p. 2.

20. The grouping of the elected and the defeated leaders into different S.E.S groups is made on the basis of the composite scores assigned to the influencing factors of leadership. In order to obtain the composite socio-economic score, the seven determinants of leadership namely caste, education, occupation, Heads education and occupation, annual income and total assets are taken into consideration. The composite scores are obtained with the help of a linear unweighted sum of the ranks given to each category within each of the variables.

21. C.E. Merriam, and H.F. Cornell, *American Party System*, New York: The Mac Millan Co., 1949, p. 464.

22. Amal Kumar Mukhopadhyaya, *Political Sociology: An Introductory Analysis*, Calcutta: K.P. Bagchi and Company, 1980, p. 120.

23. Michal Rush and Philip Althoff, *An Introduction to Political Sociology*, London: Thomas Nelson & Sons Ltd, 1971, p. 75.

24. Amalkumar Mukhopadhyaya. *op.cit.*, p.126.

25. Iqbal Narain, K.C. Pande, and Mohan Lal, *Rural Elite and Elections in an Indian State — A Study of Panchayati Raj Leadership in the Context of Rajasthan Electoral Politics*, Jaipur: National Publishing House, 1976, p. 51.

26. Giovanni Sartori has forcefully made in this regard a point by way of plea to restore the autonomous character and identity of political science. See his article "From the Sociology of Politics to Political Sociology", in S.M. Lipset (ed,) *Politics and the Social Sciences*, New Delhi: Wiley Eastern, Private Ltd., 1972 , pp. 66-17.

27. The categorising of the elected and defeated rural women leaders into three group is effected on the basis of the composite scores obtained by them for their political background with the help of a linear unweighted sum of the ranks given to each category within each of the variables.

28. C.M. Bonjean, and Olsen, D.M., "Community Leadership: Directions of Research", in M. Aiken, and P.E. Mott (ed.), *Ibid.*, p. 347.

29. L.C. Freeman, *et al.*, *op.cit.*, pp. 340-347.

30. For detail see Appendix.

31. S.R. Mehta, *Emerging Pattern of Rural Leadership*, New Delhi: Wiley Eastern Private Limited, 1972, p. 80.

32. G. Narayana Reddy, *op. cit.*, p. 104.

33. M.E. Opler and R.D. Singh., "Economic, Political and Social Change in North Central India", *Human Organisation*, Vol. II, No. 2, Summer, 1952, pp. 5-12.

34. Freed E. Fielder, *A Theory of Leadership Effectiveness*, New York: McGraw Hill, 1967, p.151.

10

# WOMEN IN PANCHAYAT RAJ SYSTEM

## Empowerment Through Self Help Groups

N. Lalitha

There can never exist a true democracy in any country unless there is participation of women both in governance and in developmental programmes. If development is meant to widen opportunities for all people, then continuing exclusion of women from opportunities of life totally warps the process of development. Gender discrimination is an universal phenomenon. Both inside and outside households women face discrimination and are excluded from position of power and are denied opportunities to participate on the decision making process. There is no rationale for such discrimination and exclusion. In fact women are essential agents of political part of the sustainable human development. Human development if not engendered is endangered[1]. And continuing exclusion of women from economic and political opportunities are a continuing indictment of modern progress.

Moving towards gender equality is both political process and economic process. If the human development paradigm, which puts people at, the entire of its concerns is to be engendered, women must be considered as agents and beneficiaries of change. Empowering their choices is not only valuable in itself but it also the surest way to contribute to overall development. Rural women in developing countries are too unorganised and powerless to be individually able to better their lot in societies and hence group strategies based on self help principle are emerging as alternative mechanism to empower women.

Formation of groups by individuals for social upliftment, economic betterment, cultural efflorescence is a natural and traditional response to overcome marginalisation of weaker sections. A Self-Group denotes an institutional framework wherein the members co-operate on a continuing basis to pursue one or more objectives through joint action and self- help. The distinctive feature of a self help initiative is the substantial contribution made from the individual's or group's own resources in terms of labour, capital or land and entrepreneurial skills. In generic terms Self Help Organisations are the organisations whose members have united on the basis of common interests to improve their economic and social conditions in order to pursue their paramount long term goals[2].

Only recently has the potential of Self - Help approach been explored by the development specialists and Self Help has emerged as a new paradigm for combating poverty and inequity in developing countries. Self Help promotion has become one of the major trust areas of Non-governmental organisations (NGOs) in India.

## Shift in Development Theories: NGOs and SHGs between Concept and Reality

The focus of development administration has changed over the years, keeping pace with new development theorising. One contemporary trend in development administration theory is a shift from a 'blue print' approach to a 'learning process approach' and from 'production centered approach to a people centered approach'. Learning process approach, involves a cybernetic power by which development administration can adapt itself to changing environment and incorporate mid course correction, based on existing local conditions[3]. Problems are diagnosed and solutions implemented by people and administrators jointly via a process of mutual learning[4]. The production centered development approach emphasis production of goods and services to maximise returns on investment. This approach stresses (1) Industry over agriculture, (2) Urban development over rural development, (3) Utilisation of capital resources over human resources, (4) Exploiting the environment for short term gain over sustained harnessing of natural resources, and (5) Establishing large scale industries over small scale industries[5]. Such a developmental approach neglects the basic needs of the rural poor in Third World countries and results in socio economic inequity. The people centered approach views people not as subject but as actors who define the goals, control resources and direct the process affecting their life[6]. The central themes of people centered development are (i) empowerment of people and (ii) development of an administrative process which responds to the needs of the people[7]. Key elements in people centered development are (i) human growth and well-being, (ii) equality, (iii) self reliance, (iv) Participation, (v) Sustainability, (vi) developing people industries, (vii) self generation of resources and (viii) building support among political elites and community groups[8].

**Self-Help Organisations in Rural Development**

The new development strategy based involvement in decision making process at all levels and 'self help' and 'mutual help' at local level. The need for self help organisations that could be owned and controlled by the poor themselves was 'clearly evident'. As Krish *et al.*[9] Report in this study the World Bank as main source of finance for rural development emphasised the importance of self help groups within the field of rural development. Self-Help-Groups are generally considered as desirable project support because they encourage local populations to carry out certain tasks jointly which can be more rationally performed by a group than by individuals.

- are easily as channels for projects inputs like credit, extension etc.,
- became focal points for job opportunities, local investments and further development activities,
- motivate local population to participate actively in achieving project activities, and
- reduce project supervision of national agencies.

Most of the development specialists of 'Self Help School' hold participation of the local population as the main factor in the development strategy, although they agree that the weaker-sections in the rural areas themselves cannot achieve much without external support and assistance. All villages even the poorest have considerable potential for helping themselves and improving the conditions of their members, but to realise the potential they require initial stimulation and sustainable assistance but the right kind at the right time rendered in a way that will strengthen rather than initiate their spirit of self-reliance and self determination[10].

The Self-Help-Groups take several forms in various countries like (i) Community organisations such as hill resource management groups in India, agricultural development in Nepal and Pakistan and Water Conservation groups in France, (ii) Natural resource, management groups such as irrigation tank management in India, soil and water conservation in Kenya, Irrigation groups in the Philippines and Sri Lanka and for soil and water conservation in Australia, (iii) Farmer research groups such as in Zambia, Botswana, Ecuador, Colombia and Britain during the agricultural revolution of the eighteenth and nineteenth centuries, (iv) Farmer to farmer extension groups such as for soil regeneration in Honduras and for irrigation management in Nepal, (v) Credit Management groups such as in southern India, Bangladesh and Nepal, and (vi) Consumer groups such as women's consumer production groups in Japan[11].

## Self-Help-Groups in India

Among the different types of self help groups, thrift and credit management groups are popular in rural areas, of India especially among women. It has long been assumed that poor women cannot save money. Rural women face double deprivation, i.e., not only by virtue of being poor but also because of being women. Since they have little of no collateral to offer they are considered as 'too high a risk group' by banks. Despite having a wide network of rural bank branches in the country and implementation of many credit linked poverty alleviation programmes, a large number of the very poor continue to remain outside the fold of the formal banking system. Various studies suggested that the existing policies, systems and procedures of formal banking system often did not meet the needs of the hardcore and assetless poor especially women. Particularly women's access to credit in rural areas is beset with a number of problems like insistence of collateral security, cultural distance between rural women and banks, high transaction cost, restricted and fixed banking hours, inflexibility in quantum and purpose of credit, inconvenient repayment schedule, cumbersome procedure, denial of credit to women due to default by male members of the family and exploitation by intermediaries. Therefore, women fall a victim in the hands of money lenders who inevitably charge exploitative rate of interest and very often women get locked into even greater poverty while trying to pay off debts. Credit is often tied and it selection for a share cropper, timing of market channel etc., Credit in such cases is often used for extracting a higher share of the surplus of farmer and needs to be distinguished from credit as an input for production. But these moneylenders operate in rural areas by providing timely credit and personal contacts enable simple and informal assessment with no procedural burden. The informal sector enables prompt repayment due to the knowledge of extensive information about the borrower and sometimes due to bending of credit input and product markets or due to the use of situation has left with wide gaps in the availability of credit for poor household wherein the NGOs have experimented with alternative methodology of credit through self help groups, combining the flexibility, sensitivity and responsiveness of the informal credit system with the strength of technical and administrative capabilities and financial resource of the formal financial institutions.

Self-Help-Group (SHG) also called as thrift and credit group is a homogeneous group of rural poor voluntarily formed to save whatever amount they can out of their earnings and mutually agree to contribute to a common fund of the group to be lent to the group members for meeting their production and emergent credit needs. The role that the NGOs (called as Self Help promoting Institutions) have played in formation of group can be broadly classified as mobilisation of rural poor, promotion of savings, provision of credit and linking group with banks.

**Group Organisation**

The NGOs focus on mobilisation, organisation and empowerment of the poor. Many NGOs have promoted SHGs to encourage decentralised problem analysis and collective action including periodic group based savings and credit. The promotion of savings and provision of credit from common fund are used as entry point for group from common fund are used as entry point for group organisation and empowerment. This can over time lead to new initiative including sharing of responsibilities and assets on community/group initiality started with. Periodic cash savings and credit at the group level provides a very simple but powerful mechanism to enable groups to initiate, manage control and finally own their institution unturned around local savings and credit[12].

The loans are available for consumption and small production schedule are decided by the group. Such group may be informal or registered and should not have a membership of more than 20. The credit is available virtually at the doorstep of the woman borrower minimising the transaction cost and time. As of now there are different models that have emerged in the rural credit both for farm and house purposes without rotates credit both for farm and house purposes without external link. In the second model NGOs play to role of a facilitator and provide matching grants. The NGOs are supported by foreign based donor agencies. In the third model, the SHGs receive loan either from commercial banks who get 100 per cent refinance from NABARD or from Rashtriya Mahila Kosh or from SIDBI (Small Industries Development Bank of India).

As on 31st March 1998, 14,317 SHGs have been linked to banks among which the share of women's groups was 77.33 per cent[13]. As many as 120 banks participated in it and distributed credit to the tune of Rs. 23.64 crores. In all 220 NGOs who involved in this programme. According to the target set by Budget 1999, during 1999-2000 NABARD and STDBI are expected to redouble this effort in this direction and ensure coverage of at least 5,000 SHGs[14].

**Strategies adopted by Self-Help-Groups**

Ultimately, the goal of the SHG-Bank Linkage programme is not just promotion of SHGs. The focus is on poverty eradication among rural women through cost effective methods of credit delivery system. The organisation of women in the form of SHGs has laid the seeds for economic improvement of women. SHGs has lied at the root of disempowerment. The basic strategies adopted to promote empowerment of women through SHGs comprise (a) organising women SHGs at the village level around savings and rational credit programmes using their own resources, (b) facilitating regular interaction, exchange of information and exposure within and across these groups to increase the mobility and awareness level of the members and to provide an opportunity to them for collective learning, (c) linkage of the SHGs at the hamlet level with external credit sources such as Banks, RMK, Tamil Nadu Women's Development Corporation and enabling women members to manage their credit and repay the loan promptly and linking the SHGs with government programmes like Swarna Jayanthi Gram Samridhi Rozgar Yojana enabling the members to expand generating to expand their investment capacity to carry on income generating activities.[15]

Group dynamics among women members empower them to fight against rural social evils in the community like female infanticide, dowry problem, evils of drinking and corruption. A well developed SHG implies a three structure namely groups at the village, cluster committees at the cluster level and federation at the district level. A cluster consists of 10-15 groups and cluster namely the Federation are drawn from the cluster committees. The functions of federation of groups which is registered as a trust are (a) to provide credit support for productive activities of members on a large scale, (b) to create linkage with formal financial and other research institutions, (c) to enable groups to liaise with government departments, (d) to facilitate group to take up economic enterprises, and (e) to develop a model for community based financial institution.

### Women's Federation — A Case Study

Covenant Centre for Development (CCD) an NGO in Madurai district has organised 96 groups called Kalasams with members spread over the villages in the districts of Madurai, Virudunagar, Ramanathapuram. The groups have accumulated a common fund of over 18 lakhs. All Kalasams are members of the Mahakalasam. However, only those groups that are three years old, pay Rs. 2,000 as subscription fee to the Mahakalasam and have corpus of Rs. 20,000 can avail of its credit facilities. The subscription fee is treated as deposit to the federation and groups receive interest at 12.5 per cent per annum. The Mahakalasam works through an advisory committee which consists of district official, Lead bank manager, and members of research institution an active research team and an apex body. Both the advisory committee and the action research team are informal bodies that work towards building the capacities of the Mahakalasam. Federation loans are given to group for livelihood activities only after scrutinizing the financial health of the group, and experience of the borrowers in the proposed activity. The federation undertakes evaluation of group along with cluster level committees. The evaluation includes assessment of savings, ability to repay loan, capacity to raise funds and the degrees of conflict within the group. The Federation has access to loans from SIDBI, Indian Bank, NEERA, and NGO network and FRLHT funding agency. The federation has accumulated a common fund of 10 lakhs from several sources for different livelihood strategies (See Table 10.1).

**Table 10.1** : Federation Funds

| Source of Fund | Activity | Amount |
|---|---|---|
| Capital raised from Kalasam | Trade or business loan, house maintenance or repair, agricultural loan | 3,64,500 |
| NEERA, and NGO network | Palm based activities | 35,000 |
| Foundation for Revitisation of local health traditions (FELHT) | Neem seed collection, processing & Marketing tamarind collection, Semi processing, marketing | 2,69,000 |
| SIDBI | Charcoal making | 3,41,500 |
| | Total | 10,10,000 |

## Strategies to Upgrade Existing Livelihood Activities

Strategies adopted by Mahakalasam to upgrade existing livelihood activities include

- Providing loan for productive activities through the Federation so that women are not compelled to sell at low rates to constructors and intermediaries who pay in advance,
- Ensuring that women have access to information on local demand, supply and pricing,

- Providing storage facilities to withhold and sell later so that a better price can be obtained,
- Semi processing to add value to products,
- Converting non-commercial activities into commercial activities,
- Pooling resources and collectively undertaking an activity to achieve economies of scale, and
- Directly linking women's groups with consumers or institutions thereby eliminating middleman.

The above strategy is used by Kalasam for utilising the locally available resources like groundnut, neem seeds and tamarind. For example when groundnut is harvested women who work as wage labour are often paid in kind. Women exchange groundnuts for other provisions at the local grocer. The grocer usually undervalues the product paying less than the actual worth of the groundnuts. Six months later the grocer would sell the groundnut back to women as seed for the next agricultural season. The Kalasam women decided to put an end to this kind of exploitation. They undertook a market price analysis, and found that immediately after the harvest, groundnut can be sold at the local markets for Rs. 2 per measure. The women found out that if they did not sell groundnut at Rs. 2 per kg and stored it for six months, dried and processed, it can fetch upto Rs.12 per kg. The Kalasam identified women with good business sense and advanced them money to procure groundnuts, pay wages to local women to semi process the groundnut and then sell them as seed. The advantage for women is that they get a fair price for their produce, build their capacities to do business while employment opportunities are also created.

## Involvement of SHGs in Village Development Schemes in different States

The assessment of the performance of women SHGs in various studies highlights the facts that (a) poor women in rural areas need credit, (b) they can save if motivated, (c) rural poor women are bankable, (d) SHGs are people's institutions and with their support member can march towards empowerment, (e) SHGs can promote individual/group ventures of income generating programmes under the guidance of NGOs, and (f) SHGs have, as their primary characteristics a common perception of the needs for and impulse towards collective action. In a village by name Saruthupatti in Theni District, Tamil Nadu, with 597 households and total population of 2,877, there are 8 women groups and 5 men groups with members constituting 296 and 152 respectively. The groups have been formed and promoted under the guidance of an NGO called SIRPI (Social Initiatives for Rural People Integration). The total savings of the group as on May 1998 amounted to Rs. 1,64,213 out of which savings by women groups was Rs. 1,60,088 (97.49%). The common fund of women Sanghams of Sarathupatti increased from Rs. 2,80,221 as on March 1998 to Rs. 5,21,628 in March 1999[16]. In addition to rotation of common fund, women's group have raised issues of social relevance at community level. Following were the benefits which the people of Sarathupatti received under various government schemes since 1995, due to the untiring efforts taken by women groups.

*Benefits received under Government Schemes through SHGs*

| S. No. | Particulars | No. of beneficiaries | Cost of Project in Rs. |
|---|---|---|---|
| 1. | Group housing scheme | 30 | 7.20.000 |
| 2. | HUDCO scheme | 5 | 2.60.000 |
| 3. | Free forestry connection | 112 | 1.12.000 |
| 4. | Social Forestry Scheme | 80 | 880 |
| 5. | Water tank | 1 village | 30.000 |
| 6. | Accident benefit | 1 | 10.000 |
| 7. | Gobar gas plant | 1 | 10.000 |
| 8. | Drainage scheme | 1 village | 30.000 |
| 9. | T.V. Set | 5 | 82.500 |
| 10. | Widow benefit scheme | 15 | 13.200 |
| 11. | Old age pension | 2 | 200 |
| 12. | IRDP dairy animals | 11 | 77.200 |
| 13. | Sheep rearing scheme | 6 | 90.000 |
| 14. | Petty shop | 3 | 18.000 |

*(Contd.)*

| S. No. | Particulars | No. of beneficiaries | Cost of Project in Rs. |
|---|---|---|---|
| 15. | Latrine construction under National Rural Sanitation Scheme | 2 | 18,000 |
| 16. | Street light | 50 | 10,000 |
| 17. | Crop loan | 2 | 2,000 |
| 18. | Free accident relief | 20 | 10,000 |
| 19. | Hand pumps | 2 | 30,000 |

*Source* : Group records.

The members of the women groups of Saruthupatti could achieve the benefits due to collective strength of the women, effective leadership and proper guidance by the SIRPI. In a village called Veerajakkammalpuram, Theni District, the members of women SHG constructed a school building at a cost of Rs. 42,000 contributed by member savings and other donations by the villagers. The members of the groups monitor the functioning of the school. The members of Meenakshipuram succeeded in getting 10 cents of land from the Panchayat for burial ground and arranged for approach road for one km distance. A relationship was opened at Sarathupatti and is being run by women group. The group members of community hall for conducting meetings and for running non-formal education entries. The union office was pressured by the group to install street light at Savadapatti, Vadapudupattu and Jallipati. In a village called Vadapudupatti under DWCRA scheme, revolving fund of Rs. 50,000 was sanctioned to two women groups for promotion of coir units and the units are run successfully by the members[17].

In Gossaigaon sub-division under Kokrajhar district of Assam the sub-divisional administration motivated women to form SHGs. The village headmen take efforts to form Mahila Samiti (thrift groups) in their villages. To everyone's surprise, in Gossaigaon sub-division, 516 thrift groups have been formed with total savings of Rs. 10,09,407-47 as on March 1999[18].

Further given the poor lifting of rice under Public Distribution System by the co-operative societies, the sub-divisional administration offered to the thrift and credit groups to lift the unlifted rice who started lifting this rice at government rates. In the process they learnt to deal with government officials and also to do business. They command respect from the weaker sections of the village by selling the rice at the rate of Rs. 8/kg against market price of Rs. 10. Similarly, they have started lifting of whole wheat and atta as government fair-price shops fall to lift the same. For the convenience of women groups and other administrative works, two days i.e Wednesday and Thursday are exclusively spared for women by the sub-division office (SDO civil), Gossaigaon. The most unique feature of this thrift activity is involvement of all communities– adivasi, Assamese, Bengali, Bihari, Muslims, Nepali, Rabha, Rajbanshi and others.

The sub-divisional administration has ordered all co-operative societies to issue a copy of village dealer-wise (agent-wise) the sub-allotment of PDS systems. Further they are given training in "Supervising PDs system at agent level". All dealers are directed to take endorsement of proper lifting and proper distribution from thrift groups every month before next allotment. Similarly thrift groups are being involved in mid-day meals programme.

The women thrift groups are also involved in over-seeing, execution and monitoring of rural development programmes under DRDA in the form of vigilance committees at every Gaon Panchayat level. In this regard, Gram Panchayat secretariats have started holding meetings with vigilance committee members on 7th of every month to review and monitor the progress of the works and to check malpractice. The involvement of women groups in the selection of beneficiaries and work under different schemes through Gaon Sabhas is also excellent. Already thrift groups are involved in construction committees. Similarly all other departments are requested to involve Mahila Samitis. Thus the involvement of women group not only empower them but also enable them to shape themselves as social activists by trying to check the malpractice and injustice in the implementation of different schemes and in the system. Administration has been availing their services in creating awareness about different schemes and activities of government viz Development works, Economic census and functioning of health sub-centres. To enable women groups function for around development of villages besides thrift and credit activity, administration helps them to get registered under Registration of Societies Act, 1986. Till now more than (March 1999) 400 numbers of Mahila Samitis have applied for registration.

Kuttanadu Vikasana Samithy (KVS) a reputed NGO in Kuttanadu, Kerala has rich and varied experience in organising SHGs. A total of Rs. 17 lakhs was raised by the SHGs and an equivalent amount has been given by the banks to the SHGs. The rate of interest at which the banks have lent to the SHGs is at 13 per cent. SHGs make the loan amount available at the group meeting and the repayment is also done at the group meetings. NABARD took special initiative to impart training to SHGs in vermi-composting and organic farming in Kuttanadu.

India Canada Environment facility has awarded a project on drinking water to Kuttanadu. This project envisaged to work only through SHGS. The SHG members have begun to show their organised strength and presence in the local Gram Sabhas. The members have become more vocal and active in articulating their problems. interactions with the Panchayat Raj Institutions (PRIs) have increased and people have become more responsive to the local self government and its institutions. There are indicators that new power centres are evolving in the local community. SHGs are gearing up to fight elections to the local bodies. Conventional type of politics and power centres are likely to give way to the rural micro level institutions such as SHGs in the near future.The Kerala State planning board has taken note of the development functioning of SHGs in the near future. The Kerala State planning board has taken note of the development and functioning of SHGs in Kuttanadu and has arranged for a series of lectures on SHG experience to Panchayat presidents and officials. This resource and faculty support sought by the planning board can only be considered a spin off from the strong impact SHGs are making in the local life in Kuttanadu. Block Development officers in Kuttanadu have recognised SHGs organised by KVS for fund support for DWCRA activities. Another important aspect of SHG functioning is the impact it makes on the village economy. SHGs are involved not only in parallel banking activities but also in initiatives such as production of vegetables, organic farming, cultivation of mushroom, cultivation and propagation of herbal medicines, orgnaisation of preventive and promotive health programmes and anti-pollution campaigns. Besides the direct economic impact, it also makes and enhanced local flow of capital, rather than letting the capital flow out of the local economy.

## Empowerment of Women

The SHGs have the potential to empower women through economic changes/material gain secured through access to credit and better bargaining power and social changes brought about through group dynamics on sustainable basis. Summarising the economic and non-economic benefits of the empowerment strategies of women's group in various countries Marilyn Carr *et.al.*[20] classified three broad types of economic changes — direct tangible results, indirect tangible results and less tangible outcomes. (See Table 10.2).

**Table 10.2** : Empowerment of women through group strategies

| Strategy | Tangible results | | Less tangible result |
|---|---|---|---|
| | Direct | Indirect | |
| Financial | -low interest rate - high savings rate<br>-ability to buy in bulk | asset-creation<br>-rise in flow of income<br>-safety net | -increased control over resources<br>-less reliance on money lenders<br>-becomes credit worthy |
| Micro-enterprises and marketing strategies | -Upgrading of skills<br>-improved knowledge<br>-access to quality<br>-inputs | -Improvement in quality of life due to rise in family income | -expanded awareness<br>- improved image<br>- become articulate<br>- Increased self-confidence<br>-overcome mobility restrictions |
| Organising and support services | -improved wages<br>-improved working conditions<br>-collaborative production and marketing<br>-released time<br>-reduced risk | -improved health and well-being | - saving women from exploitation<br>-develop decision making power |

*Source* : Marilyn Carr, Mautharthen, Renana Jhabvala, "Speaking out", Vistaar Publications, New Delhi, p. 204.

**Women in Panchyati Raj System**

When women achieve an equal share of political power, many things, besides politics will change profoundly...... Women's increasing political participation is both a source and a signal of social change. As a global trend, rising numbers of women on politics will indicate that human beings are making progress towards a more humane world — not because women are necessarily more humane than man, but because any society that categorically excludes half the members from the process by which it rules itself will be ruled in a way that is less than fully humane[21]. In India, the 73rd Amendment of the Constitution has made one-third reservation for women in local bodies mandatory. The Constitution (Seventy Third Amendment) Act 1992, Article 243 D(3) reads thus "Not less than one-third (including the number of seats reserved for women belonging to the SC/STs) of the total number of seats to be filled by direct election in every Panchayat shall be reserved for women and such may be allotted by rotation to different constitutions in a Panchayat".

And clause (4) of the act has the following provision: ".....not less than one-third of the total number of offices of chairpersons in the Panchayats at each level shall be reserved for women. Provided also that the number of offices reserved under this clause shall be allotted by rotation to different Panchayat at each level". The gender based reservation is certainly a mandatory measure to draw out women and enhance their participation. A new opportunity for the participation of women in local self government has come about and the participation of women in Panchayati Raj system has been considered as the most effective instrument to remove the inequality, invisibility and powerlessness of women. As on May 31, 1998, 8,18,194 women have been elected to local government at various levels throughout India (See Table 10.3). However the reservation itself or even the mobilization of women in effect does not constitute real empowerment. But certainly it provides a firm legal empowerment. But certainly it provides a firm legal foundation from which women's involvement in grass roots democracy can take off. Empowerment of women in the context of Panchayati Raj system implies that women in the context of Panchayati Raj system

**Table 10.3** : Number of Elected Women Members (as on May, 1998)

| S. No | States/UTs | GP | | | PS | | | ZP | | |
|---|---|---|---|---|---|---|---|---|---|---|
| | | Women | Total | % | Women | Total | % | Women | Total | % |
| 1 | 2 | 3 | 4 | 5 | 6 | 7 | 8 | 9 | 10 | 11 |
| 1. | Andhra Pradesh | 78000 | 230529 | 33.84 | 5420 | 14644 | 37.01 | 363 | 1093 | 33.21 |
| 2. | Arunachal Pradesh | — | — | — | — | — | — | — | — | — |
| 3. | Assam | 7458 | 24860 | 30.00 | 745 | 2486 | 29.07 | — | — | — |
| 4. | Bihar @ | — | — | — | — | — | — | — | — | — |
| 5. | Goa | 468 | 1281 | 36.53 | — | — | — | — | — | — |
| 6. | Gujarat | 41180 | 123470 | 33.35 | 1274 | 3814 | 33.40 | 254 | 761 | 33.38 |
| 7. | Haryana | 17928 | 54159 | 33.10 | 807 | 2418 | 33.37 | 101 | 303 | 33.33 |
| 8. | Himachal Pradesh | 6013 | 18258 | 32.93 | 558 | 1661 | 33.59 | 84 | 252 | 33.33 |
| 9. | Jammu & Kashmir @ | — | — | — | — | — | — | — | — | — |
| 10. | Karnataka | 35305 | 806279 | 43.79 | 1343 | 3340 | 40.21 | 335 | 919 | 36.45 |
| 11. | Kerala | 3883 | 10270 | 37.81 | 563 | 1547 | 36.39 | 104 | 300 | 34.67 |
| 12. | Mahdya Pradesh | 156181 | 474351 | 32.93 | 3169 | 9097 | 34.84 | 319 | 946 | 33.72 |
| 13. | Maharashtra | 100182 | 303545 | 33.00 | 1174 | 3524 | 33.31 | 587 | 1762 | 33.31 |
| 14. | Manipur | 576 | 1556 | 37.02 | — | — | — | 22 | 61 | 36.07 |
| 15. | Orissa | 28595 | 81077 | 35.27 | 1870 | 5260 | 35.55 | 294 | 854 | 34.43 |
| 16. | Punjab | 23892 | 78983 | 30.25 | 326 | 2441 | 13.36 | 89 | 274 | 32.48 |

*Contd......*

*Table 10.3 (Contd.)*

| 1 | 2 | 3 | 4 | 5 | 6 | 7 | 8 | 9 | 10 | 11 |
|---|---|---|---|---|---|---|---|---|---|---|
| 17. | Rajasthan | 38791 | 119419 | 32.48 | 1740 | 5257 | 33.10 | 331 | 997 | 33.20 |
| 18. | Sikkim | 27 | 1827 | 1.48 | — | — | — | 1 | 145 | 0.69 |
| 19. | Tamil Nadu | 31548 | 94304 | 33.45 | 2295 | 6499 | 35.31 | 225 | 648 | 34.72 |
| 20. | Tripura | 1809 | 5427 | 33.33 | 67 | 196 | 34.18 | 24 | 70 | 34.29 |
| 21. | Uttar Pradesh | 174410 | 682670 | 25.55 | 14002 | 58165 | 24.07 | 648 | 2551 | 25.40 |
| 22. | West Bengal | 22014 | 62172 | 35.41 | 3202 | 9516 | 33.65 | 227 | 664 | 34.19 |
| 23. | A & N Islands | 229 | 667 | 34.33 | 25 | — | — | 10 | 30 | 33.33 |
| 24. | Chandigarh | 22 | 109 | 20.18 | 2 | 6 | 33.33 | 3 | 10 | 30.00 |
| 25. | D & N Haveli | 46 | 135 | 34.07 | — | — | — | 4 | 16 | 25.00 |
| 26. | Daman & Diu | 25 | 63 | 39.68 | — | — | — | 5 | 15 | 33.33 |
| 27. | Lakshadweep @ | — | — | — | — | — | — | — | — | — |
| 28. | Pondicherry @ | — | — | — | — | — | — | — | — | — |
| | Total | 768582 | 2449759 | 31.37 | 38582 | 129871 | 20.71 | 4030 | 12671 | 31.80 |

*Note :* @ Elections have not been held.

implies that women should be well equipped to fulfil the functional responsibilities associated with the position which they represent. the process of challenging existing power relations and of gaining greater control over the sources of power is termed as empowerment[22]. It is not as much women's strength in terms of numbers but their effectiveness as local body leaders/functionaries that will determine to what extent the Act has succeeded in empowering them. Participation has two dimensions — quantiative and qualitative. Many a time only the quantitative aspects of participation is taken care of. Women's participation in terms of mere number alone will not a serve the purpose. Women often make up the majority of the rank and file but compromise a majority as for as decision making process is concerned[23]. As long as women are left behind in the process of decision making, it would be hard to fight the inequity in the development process. Active participation in social economic and political spheres would help in enhancing the process of empowerment and it would give women the self respect and social dignity which are prerequisites of empowerment. Viewed in this context the early trends of women's representation in the post-amendment period does not merit much euphoria[24]. It is their men folk who have often usurped the actual power. During the election campaign women were always projected as sombody's mother or wife or sister or widow as the case may be[25] and not as herself. The experience of Karnataka reveals that though the elected women attended meetings regularly, only a few women members participated effectively while participation of others was limited or extremely limited. But the women at the Zilla Parishad were more articulate than the Mandal Panchayat Women[26].

A number of constraints have tended to severely limit the capability of women and their participation in Panchayati Raj system in India. One of the major constraints stems from their depressed economic status. Poverty, economic dependence on men, exclusion from ownership of property, lack of access to resources like land, credit, technology and development assistance have rendered them helpless and powerless. For most of the women in rural areas, a struggle for livelihood assumes an overwhelming and the possibility of their taking an active part in local government seems to be remote. Secondly, the gender stereotyped activities and dominance of traditional value system over centuries have depressed their status socially and economically and thus they have been deprived of opportunities for participation in development process. They have become 'objects of oppression' or 'subjects of welfare' partly because of the invisibility of women's issues and partly because of the State's patriarchal attitude and priorities[27]. Consequently 'stree shakti' which has the potential to yield tremendous power is left dormant. As a result of the deep entrenched social attitude and practices, women by and large have not been independent decision makers. Their decision in most cases have been influenced by the wishes and dictates of the male family members. They are guided by a patriarchal social system and are, therefore, discriminated against in terms of access to opportunities. Thirdly, a vast majority of rural women are illiterate and are not aware of their rights and responsibilities which makes that ill-equipped to become active participants in the political sphere. Fourthly, lack of organisation among women adds to the process of polarisation in favour of men. Organisation can provide them with much needed strength to protect themselves against abuse and deprivation of rights. The all pervasive male hegemony as an insurmountable barrier to women's participation and tends to treat politics as an exclusive male domain.

The two major obstacles for making reservation a reality are illiteracy of women and discrimination exploitation and oppression they face in society[28]. Even those who are not proxy candidates are finding the new role reversal uncomfortable and even intimidating.

The Constitutional Amendment providing for one-third reservation for women has not only political connotation but also far reaching social impact which will go a long way in furthering the development of women. However the decision by itself cannot prove revolutionary unless accompanied by appropriate measures to equip the prospective candidates and also elected women representatives with necessary education, training and orientation about the roles they are supposed to play, functions they are required to perform and to instil confidence in their minds about their role performance. This approach is supported by "Identity Empowerment Theory" which is grounded on the assumption that empowered women make meaningful commitment and undertake effective goal-oriented activities that they choose for themselves[29]. Identity empowerment theory that has been built on documented patterns and predict abilities in interpersonal, family and group behaviour. The theory suggests that women's understanding of the strength and weakness of their personal and collective past and present will increase their sense of purpose and direction for their future.

Women should be able to act on the strength of being women and not merely despite being women. They must be visible politically as women and be empowered to act in that capacity because there is the continual possibility that they may have needs on vital issues which differ from those of men. This does not imply that women have no needs and preferences in common with men. Experts[30] have formulated three different lines of reasoning found in discussions concerning women's political participation. They are resource reasoning, interest reasoning, and justice reasoning. The essential point in justice reasoning is that women have the right to participate in politics. The resource reasoning claims that if women do not participate in politics, society is deprived of knowledge and skills that women possess. According to interest reasoning, women's interest are different from men's and often in conflict. Women need to act politically for their own interest.

## Empowerment of Women in Panchayati Raj System — SHG show the way

The objective of Amendment will become exclusive and its impact on women's right and development will be eroded of supportive and supplementary steps are not promoted to strengthen the hands of law. Empowerment — economic, social and political — implies redistribution of power in favour of deprived group. Women cannot be empowered unless they find their rightful place in the societal power structure. Therefore, structural and institutional reforms to neturalise the present power equation is an absolute must for women's empowerment. Such an institutional structure should enable them to help themselves to break the barriers — social, economic, cultural and psychological and convert them from passive recipient of programme to managers of their own affairs. It should enable the women realise their full identity and powers in all spheres of life. Such an institutional structure should empower women to have greater access to knowledge and resource, greater autonomy in decision-making, greater ability to plan their lives, greater control over the circumstances that influence their lives and free them from shackles imposed on them by custom, belief and practices. The institutional mechanism should also be instrumental in (a) equipping the candidates with necessary knowledge information, skill and instilling self confidence and leadership qualities, (b) identifying the potential women candidates, and (c) preparing the candidates, for the election.

The self-help groups in the rural areas will serve the purpose ideally. While reservation in itself can only provide a fair field for women's participation along the prescribed lines, women's effective participation can become a reality through women's instructions like SHGs. SHGs strive for counteracting the forces which lie at the root of disempowerment. In fact the experience gained in the group meetings has also empoldened some women members to assert their voices not only in the immediate context of their community but also in the larger democratic bodies. the opportunities given to women in Sangham meetings has also paved the way for further participation in the local Panchayat election. For example two members from SHGs promoted by Arogya Agam, the NGO in Madurai District have been elected to the Village Panchayat as Presidents.

## Involving Women SHGs in Panchayat Programmes

It is expected that gender issues in development process will be well looked after, nurtured and promoted with women sharing and chairing the Panchayat administration. There is need to place gender issues in the wider context of poverty, inequality, population growth and the economic development strategies. It is this perspective alone that can bring out the importance of gender issues in development process and enable policy makers and planners to understand as to why it is important to invest in education of women, health and what benefits would accrue to the society by bringing women into politics[31].

Local government should become a model in the incorporation or women's talents because of the special relationship between women's concerns and local issues[32].

Rural women know pretty well this problem's, priorities but do not know whom to contact, how to initiate action and how to mobilise resources. The 73rd Amendment Act apart from its potential to draw women with political authority to implement schemes in general and also schemes which affect their lives most. This would include agriculture, social forestry, fuel and fodder, drinking water, family welfare, sanitation and public distribution system. Through participation in Panchayat administration, women leaders can help womenfolk in the village in a more constructive way because men can never perceive or understand women's problems can be carried out involving women SHGs need assessment, implementation, monitoring and evaluation. Following are some of the activities which the SHGs can undertake and contribute for the successful implementation:

- the women groups can take up prohibition of illicit liquor in the villages;
- can take up the cause of women rights;
- can fight corruption in the implementation of government schemes in the villages;
- can undertake government contracts work;
- can be involved in efficient administration of village school by including the SHG members in the village education committee under DPEP programme;
- can liaise with social forestry department in the afforestation schemes of villages;
- can involve the maintaining existing infrastructural facilities like health sub-centre, safe water and assets created under developmental schemes;
- can participate in village peace brigades;
- can maintain village libraries and run public distribution system; and
- can run creches.

In short women groups can contact administration directly for establishing their rights and to redress the grievances boldly and disprove the myth that women can get work done only through middle men and thus become victims of social evils.

**Breaking the Barriers**

The women representatives should be well equipped with relevant information and planning skills for which they need orientation. It was orientation and capacity building training which created confidence in the minds of Fatima Bi, Sarpanch of the Kalvagra Panchayat in Kurnool district of Andhra Pradesh who received the United Nations Development Programme's Race Against Poverty Award for the Asia Pacific Region in 1998. She has also been the recipient of the Best Sarpanch Award from the State Government for her illustrious work. Initially she was the rubber stamp in the hands of her husband and the *de facto* Sarpanch was her husband. Three days of orientation and capacity building attended by the Sarpanch at the State capital transformed her as *de fecto* Sarpanch. She formed 'Proddu' (Village Organisation) for women. She inspired women to save one rupee a day under thrift scheme called 'Proddu Lakshmi'. UNDP granted Rs. 12 lakhs as interest free loan to the Proddu. At present Proddu has 430 women committees of SHGs with Rs. 20 lakhs[33] at their disposal. With the help of Proddu, women have started various gainful activities ranging from repairing borewells, to stitching and embroidery. The president has given pattas to landless, constructed metal roads and with the help of women members repaired and cleaned village ponds which is irrigating sugar fields and vegetable plantation around the village. Empowerment of women and over all development of the village is her agenda. *Ammavodi* (Mother's Lap) is being run by Proddu for the working women. This organisation picks up children from homes to school, child marriage is a thing of past. With the support of the Proddu members the women Panchayat president has unleashed the hitherto suppressed energy of women and is breaking the barriers. In fact Fatima Bi has exploded the myth of the gender based difference in respect of participation and efficiency.

## Beyond Credit

Going beyond credit is a prerequisite for SHGs for eradicating poverty. The ultimate aim of SHGs is lifting poor rural women from poverty and promotion of sustainable development with gender equity. Hence, it is essential to address the issues of development such as health, education and meeting other community needs. The profit earned by the groups and federation of groups should be deployed for providing these civic programmes augmenting the government resources and building the capacities of local communities to manage. The community should be built not to duplicate these services already provided by the government but to ensure that the government institutions work effectively[34].

Concerns such as health, child-care, water sanitation or schooling have been utterly neglected in development decisions because of their under representation and women are expected to accentuate and accelerate the pace of policy and implementation having a bearing on gender[35]. In order to extend the outreach of SHGs, influencing the policies of government and building alliance with the mainstream becomes imperative. Policy without the focus on action and mere action in the field without focussing on policy or advocacy would not lead to required dent on poverty.

The reservation of seats is a necessary but not sufficient condition for women to take part in the political process in an effective manner. The all pervading gender bias needs to be tackled through an integrated and multi-pronged attack. Women have to be capacited both economically and socially to enable them emerge as equal partners in the process of development. The SHGs adopt various strategies to organise women to promote awareness of their rights and duties and implement capacity building exercises through training to equip them with necessary knowledge, skill, leadership qualities and decision making power paving the way for economic, social and political transformation of women. As the groups mature in terms of size, outreach and administrative capacity and women's credit needs are met with, methodology has to be found for integration of community based issues with groups and for assumption of new responsibilities by women for solving the problems of community. Here the Panchayat Raj Institutions offer promising opportunities to women members of SHGs who can display their skill to utilise the newly acquired empowerment for the benefit of the society. The successful experiments of women SHGs have brought home the realization that no outside agency can ever contribute to development of people unless local people themselves have stake in the development. SHG provides a viable local forum. The spin off from this local experiment is likely to be much more deep and long standing in the years to come. Participation of women self help groups in Panchayat Raj activities will give women due recognition in society and lasting solution to the problems of village paving the way for sustainable development.

## NOTES

1. United Nations Development Programme, *Human Development Report – 1995*, Oxford University Press, Oxford, 1995. p. 4.
2. Kuhn, Johannes, 'The Role of Non-Governmental Organisation in Promoting Self Help Organisations' seminar paper, Druckerei Franz Pappenholz, Bomheins (FRG) 1992.
3. David C. Korten, "Rural Development Programmes – The Learning process approach" in David C. Korten and Rudi Klaus (eds), *People Centered Development Contributions Towards Theory and Planning*, Frameworks Hartford, CT, Kumaran Press, 1984.
4. Edgar S. Dunn, "The Nature of Social Learning" in David C. Korten and Rudi Klans (eds) *People Centered Deve'opment Contribution Towards Theory and Planning*, *op.cit*.
5. David C Korten, "People Centered Development Towards a Framework" in David C. korten and Rudi Klaus (eds), *op.cit*.
6. *Ibid*.
7. Peter L. Berger and Richard Neuhaus, "To empower people" in David C. Korten and Rudi Klaus (eds), *op.cit*.
8. Louse G. White "Creating opportunities for change", Boulder Co., Lynne Richer, 1987.

9. Kirsh Ottfried C; A. Renjacov and L. Schujmann, "The role of self-help groups in rural development", Research Centre for International Agarian Development, Verlag Brietenbach, 1980.

10. Combs P.H. (ed), *Meeting the Basic Needs of Rural Poor : The Integrated Community Based Approach*. Pergamon Press, London, 1980.

11. Pretty and Chambers, "Towards a learning paradigm : New Professionalism and institution for sustainable agriculture", Discussion Paper. IDS Brighton. 1989.

12. Action Aid India, Strategy paper for savings and credit, "Non-farm and savings & credit", Sector Strategy Paper 1996-98, p. 69.

13. NABARD, Annual Report, 1997-1998, p. 79.

14. Budget speech 1999, *Business Line*, February 28, 1999, p. 4.

15. Swayam Shikshan Prayog, "Visiting Alternatives — an inter-state study tour on savings and credit", November 1998, p. 27.

16. SIRPI, Annual Report, 1998, p. 20.

17. *Ibid.*

18. Ariz Ahmed, M. "Women Empowerment and Self Help Groups", *Kurukshetra*, April 1999, p.19.

19. Thomas Peelianickai, "Development experience in Kuttanadu through self help groups", Discussion Paper, 1999.

20. Marilyn Carr, Mardha Chen, Renana Jhabvala (eds), "*Speaking Out: Women's Economic in South Asia*", Vistaar Publications, New Delhi, 1996.

21. Kathteen Newland, "Women in Policies : A Global Review", World Watch Paper 3. Washington DC, December 1975, pp. 19

22. Batliwala, Srilatha, 'The Meaning of Empowerment', *Women World*, 1995, pp. 23-24.

23. Sushama Sahay, *Women and Empowerment*, Discovery Publishing House, New Delhi, 1998.

24. Neera Agnimitra, "Women in Panchayats : Empowerment or Illusion", *Gandhi Marg*, Vol.17(4), January-March, 1996, p. 32.

25. George Matthew, "Will Reservation Ensure Participation", *Social Welfare*, Vol. 42(56) August-September, 1995, p. 32.

26. Vidya, K.C., *Political Empowerment of Women at the Grassroot*, Kanishka Publishers, Distributors, New Delhi, 1997, p. 246.

27. Neera Agnimitra, *op.cit.*

28. Adiseshiah Malcom S., "Realising goals of 73rd Amendment through Literacy", *Kurukshetra*, June, 1994.

29. Hall, C.M., *Women and Empowerment : Strategies for increasing Autonomy*, Hemisphere Publishing Corporation, Washington, 1992.

30. Kraditor Aileen, *The Ideas of the Women Sufferage Movement, 1890-1920*, Anchor Book, New York, 1965, p. 49.

31. Ilabeen Jani, "Gender Issues in New Panchayati Raj System" in S.P. Jain and Thomus W. Hockgesang (Eds), *Emerging Trends in Panchayat Raj In India*, NIRD, 1995, pp. 127-129.

32. Bhargava.B.S. and Subha, "Women in Panchayat Raj : Some Reflections on Karnataka Experiences", *Kurukshetra,* June 1994.

33. Mahipal. "Fatima Bi Sarpanch : Saga of Struggle Against Poverty", *Kurukshetra*, March 1999, pp.12-13.

34. Nasendar, K., "Impacting Poverty", *Health Action*, Vol.12(7), July1999, pp. 6-8.

35. Amal Mandal, "Gender Bias in Panchayati Raj : Reservations from a District", *Kurukshetra*, June 1997, p. 54.

11

# PANCHAYATI RAJ AND EMPOWERMENT OF WOMEN
## A Case Study of Kanyakumari District in Tamil Nadu

K. Pazhani

Panchayati Raj Institutions (PRIs) have been recognized as the vehicles of socio-economic transformation of the rural India. They are the grass root unit of self-government playing a pivotal role in bringing changes in power, structure and functions of both male and female members in the rural communities. According to Heyzer (1985), social and economic conditions in the developing regions of the world are changing rapidly as a result of the worldwide multi-sectoral development process. Development impact on women and men are different, and the past few decades of development have been an alarming degree of feminisation of poverty. Development in many cases has had negative impacts on a large proportion of women in general and rural women in particular. This situation may be attributed to traditional attitude, socio-economic and psychological conditions of women, which prevent the entry of rural women into Panchayati Raj Institutions to contribute and to serve for the development of their locality.

### Role of Women in Development

In economic and political debates development refers to attempts aimed at improving the living conditions or material welfare of a given population often the inhabitants of a particular country. Development is defined as a process of expanding human choice, taking into account equity; sustainability and empowerment aspects (Opschoor: 1998) Women are the marginalized sections of the society whose activities are considered as "family-centred". The traditional attitude of the people in the Third World countries made women as passive recipients of development rather than participants in the development process. But their role in household management and child rearing cannot be simply discarded. The term "women in development" was initiated in the early 1970s by the Women's Committee of the Washington DC Chapter of the Society of International Development (Moser: 1993). But, this change has taken place only in the 1990s in India.

In 1958, National Committee on Women's Education under the chairmanship of Mrs. Durgabai Deshmukh recommended the two existing views on women — (i) a woman did not have much of a role to play outside the home, and even if she did, this was definitely secondary and subsequent to the demands and exigencies of her role within the home, and (ii) a woman should have open to her all avenues to life which are open to men. Also, the Committee on Status of Women (1964) stated, "In the progressive society of tomorrow, life should be a joint venture of men and women. Men should share the responsibilities of home and women in turn should share the social and economic responsibilities of men". These statements reveal the necessity of having time and space for women in the process of development and change in the society.

## The Problem

Women are the source and resource of the nation. Their contribution to development cannot be set aside without due consideration. Even after five decades of planned development in India, women are compelled to fight for their right. There is cross discrimination against women and they are deprived from enjoying many benefits, which their counterparts enjoy in the present social and political set up. There have been various shifts in the policy approaches of the central as well as the State governments from the concept of 'welfare' to 'development' and then to 'empowerment'. But, the fate of half of humanity (women) remains unaltered. Even now, procreation and maintenance of family are considered as the foremost duties of women. Larger family size compels them to do some external work to supplement the income earned by their husband to maintain their family. An overwhelming majority of women are engaged in the informal sector and mostly remain unorganized. They are compelled to work for long hours at a minimum wage under insanitary surroundings. But they have not been recongnised as producers of their own right.

Under this situation, the 73rd and 74th Amendments to the Constitution provide that women form one-third of all representation in local bodies. Now many questions emerge out of the prevailing conditions in the Panchayat Raj Institutions. Did they properly reserve the seats to women? Did they give due importance and equal rights in planning and implementing various welfare programmes? Do female members are given chances to participate in meetings without any hesitation? Do they actively participate in decision-making? The present study is an attempt to find answers to the above questions.

**Review of Literature**

In his book *Woman Unbound*, Justice Krishna Iyer (1984) has given a brief account of the role of women in development in different walks of life, especially their role during two World Wars. He has pointed out that women and children are the first change on development, a pregnant proposition ignored poignantly. According to him, India with all its boasts and all its hopes can never really be free until its womanhood is delivered from its suppressed status.

According to Anupama and Susan (1995), we cannot make democracy meaningful in a traditional society like ours without the full involvement of women. The constitutional amendment is only the necessary legal step, which must be followed by effective measures of women's uplift in the country. Reservation under Panchayati Raj for rural women is in a state of flux at present and the women are not adequately empowered to play an effective role because of social, economic and political factors.

According to Usha Mehta (1996) it is an irony of fate that despite the reservation of 33 per cent of seats for women in all legislative bodies from Panchayat onwards, it was found in a recent survey of women elected to the Panchayats in Maharashtra, that there are several of them, who do not even know that they have been elected let alone knowing something about the functions they are supported to perform.

Dr. Ujwala (1997) has conducted a study in Karnataka to study the role of women in PRIs. According to her, a basic factor affecting women's participation in politics is their role as citizens. Further, political participation of women is hampered by their lack of literacy and the social obligations they have to fulfil. Many Panchayat members are told what to do by their husbands or colleagues. Reservation acts as a stimulant and as an instrument to breakdown the stranglehold of vested interest which have prevented women from getting their due place in public life.

Bhagyalakshmi (1998) has pointed out that the 73rd Amendment to the Constitution empowers PRIs to function as institutions of self-government. They also endowed with devolution of powers and responsibilities at appropriate levels regarding preparation and implementation of schemes related to economic development and social justice. As a result of Panchayat election there are new entrants particularly from weaker sections and women. To impart training to them, a provision of Rs. 5 crores has been proposed for the year 1998-1999.

In his paper, Sekher (2001) has remarked that the policy of reservation has provided a unique opportunity to the weaker sections, particularly women, for political participation and decision-making in the local governance process. Given the relatively lower educational qualifications of members, lack of any kind of exposure outside, and their lack of political experience, their participation in the PRI system of local governance and their ability to discharge their responsibilities are not effective. He has also mentioned about the importance of empowerment of grass root level leaders through motivation and education and the need to train these local leaders in fulfilling their new roles and responsibilities.

Samarthan's study (1998) of Madhya Pradesh PRIs reveals the following as obstacles to gender mainstreaming in these institutions:

1. The women representatives of PRIs are not getting the co-operation from their Panchayat colleagues, government officials and Panchayat staff/secretary.

2. The women PRI members face considerable problem in commuting from one place to another.
3. The level of awareness of women PRI members regarding Panchayat laws/regulations/rights etc. and of the ongoing developmental schemes/projects is very low.
4. The decision for contesting as Panchayat member has been taken by their family members.
5. Participation in PRIs has led to increase in women's workload as they have to strike a balance between domestic / farm / official responsibilities.

All the above studies reveal that women are lacking in education, general awareness, and time to spend over and above their household activities. In this chapter, an attempt has been made to study the status and role of women in PRIs in a highly educated district (Kanyakumari) in Tamil Nadu.

**Objectives**

1. To know the socio-economic conditions of the women participating in the PRIs.
2. To study the factors inducing women to participate in the PRIs.
3. To know the extent of involvement of women in the activities of PRIs and the problems involved in it.
4. To make possible suggestions to the identified problems.

**Methodology**

The study requires both secondary and primary data. The secondary data related to number of Panchayat Unions (PUs), number of Village Panchayats, total number of presidents and number of women presidents are collected from the Rural Development Assistant Director (Panchayats) office. Primary data related to family size, education, employment status and family income are collected by interviewing the respondents personally by the author.

The simple percentages are used to measure the important variable in the study. For the present study, Kanyakumari District is purposively selected. The study has been undertaken during April 2001. Out of the 39 women presidents (WP) 10 are selected as samples. Similarly out of the 30 women ward members (WWM) in the selected Village Panchayats 10 are selected for the study. .

Table 11.1 indicates that 39.39 per cent of the Village Panchayat Presidents is women. It shows that women in this district are ready to serve the society than the reservations made and also the acceptance of women in PRIs by men.

**Table. 11.1** : Distribution of sample respondents

| Sl. No. | Name of the Panchayat Union | Number of village Panchayats | Number of WP | Number of WWM | Total No. of samples |
|---|---|---|---|---|---|
| 1. | Agasteeswaram | 13 | 6(1) | 3(1) | 2 |
| 2. | Thovalai | 16 | 6(2) | 6(2) | 4 |
| 3. | Rajakkamanglam | 15 | 5(1) | 3(1) | 2 |
| 4. | Kurunthancode | 9 | 3(1) | 3(1) | 2 |
| 5. | Thuckalay | 7 | 3(1) | 3(1) | 2 |
| 6. | Thiruvattar | 10 | 5(1) | 3(1) | 2 |
| 7. | Killiyoor | 8 | 3(1) | 3(1) | 2 |
| 8. | Munchirai | 11 | 4(1) | 3(1) | 2 |
| 9. | Melpuram | 10 | 4(1) | 3(1) | 2 |
| | Total | 99 | 39(10) | 33(10) | 20 |

*Source:* Assistant Director Panchayats. Nagercoil

*Note*: Figures in the parantheses indicate the number of samples.
WP — Women President
WWM — Women Ward Members

## Description of the Study Area

Kanayakumari district is the smallest district in Tamil Nadu, having a total area of 1,684 sq. km. It has a total population of 16 lakh people. Its density of population is 950 (as against 429 in TN and 273 at the national level). Next to Chennai, this district is having the highest literacy rate (82.06 %). Female literacy rate is 78.39 per cent, which is greater than the State average (51.33 %) and national average (39.29 %). Male literacy rate is 85.7 per cent. The literacy rate in the rural and urban areas of this district are 88.36 per cent and 80.76 per cent respectively and 83.36 per cent people are living in the rural areas. There are 9 Village Panchayat unions and

99 Village Panchayats. Out of the 99-village panchayat presidents 39 (39.39%) are women. Each Panchayat is having three women Ward members. This situation denotes the increased place of space for women in PRIs in Kanyakumari District.

**Women and Panchayat Raj**

Traditionally, motherhood is considered as the most important role, for women in society. According to Anupama and Susan (1995), in the traditional rural society politics is regarded as unwomanly and this traditional attitude prevents women from taking an active role in the body politics. Various policies framed because of the world bodies like the U.N.O, International Women Conferences and also the Central Government of our country have not been implemented properly. Women in the developing countries like India are not aware of the benefits conferred on them by these policies. In fact, women's presence in Panchayats is not encouraged by a larger section of the society. Though women's representation has become mandatory through the 73rd and 74th Amendments to the Constitution, women's presence and participation in the Panchayats remain negligible (Rainuka Dagar: 1998). The nuclear family and women's participation in work force has engendered stress in the family. Women are expected to play a dual role with equal efficiency in both home and office. The answer to the problem of social injustice lies in the enlightenment of the victims. They have to be liberated from themselves, from their age-old mental conditions. Women's presence and participation in PRIs will do well for the social emancipation of women and gain social acceptance.

**Socio-Economic Background**

It is essential to look into the socio-economic conditions of the women participants in the PRIs since they act as inducing / preventing factors in various social activities.

**Family Conditions**

Women are the managers of their family. The family size and its composition are influencing much the decision of women, whether to contest and participate in PRI elections or not. If their family size is larger and include babies and elder people (above 60 years)

**Table 11.2** : Sex-wise and family size-wise distribution

| Family Size | WP family | | | WWM family | | | Grand Total | | |
|---|---|---|---|---|---|---|---|---|---|
| | M | F | T | M | F | T | M | F | T |
| 4 | 12 | 8 | 20 (5) | 4 | 4 | 8 (2) | 16 | 12 | 28 (7) |
| 5 | 15 | 10 | 25 (5) | 13 | 17 | 30 (6) | 28 | 27 | 55 (11) |
| 6 | - | - | - | 3 | 3 | 6 (1) | 3 | 3 | 6 (1) |
| 7 | - | - | - | 3 | 4 | 7 (1) | 3 | 4 | 7 (1) |
| Total | 27 | 18 | 45 (10) | 23 | 28 | 51 (10) | 50 | 46 | 96 (20) |

*Source:* Survey data.
*Note:* Figures in parentheses indicate number of families
M—Male, F—Female, T—Total

no women will have enough time to manage the house and participate in social activities of PRIs.

Table 11.2 indicates that out of 20 families 7 (35%) are having four members in their family. 11 (55%) families are having 5 members and two (10%) families are having six and seven members each. The sex ratio remains at 3:2 and 6:7 in the two categories. It indicates that the rich people prefer male children more. Of the 10 women presidents only one is having a baby (6 months), all others are having school-going children. All the 20 selected women respondents are in the age group of 29-50 years.

**Educational Status**

Education empowers women. Only educated people can understand the rules and regulations, and the systems to be followed while planning and implementing various welfare programmes and projects. They can easily know the felt needs of the people and fight for more fund which are scarce in the Panchayats.

Table 11.3 indicates that 60 per cent of the respondents are having S.S.L.C. and above level of education and the remaining 40

**Table 11.3** : Educational status of sample respondents

| Sl.No. | Education | W.P. | WWM | Total |
|---|---|---|---|---|
| 1. | Primary | — | 1 | 1 (5) |
| 2. | Middle | 3 | 4 | 7 (35) |
| 3. | High School | 1 | 1 | 2 (10) |
| 4. | HSC | 2 | 3 | 5 (25) |
| 5. | TTC | 2 | 1 | 3 (15) |
| 6. | Degree | 2 | — | 2 (10) |
| | Total | 10 (50) | 10 (50) | 20 (100) |

*Source:* Survey data.

*Note:* TTC — Teacher Training Certificate

per cent are having lower level of education. Women representatives of Panchayats from Harayana have mentioned that their lack of education still "makes them to do what the elders say and put thumb impression wherever they are asked to" (*The Hindu*, 2001).

But the situation prevailing in Kanyakumari district in Tamil Nadu is different. The establishment of so many schools and few colleges by the Christian missionaries is a cause for it. Now-a-days women are members in one or many social organizations and enrich themselves about the country/world. Higher level of educational status of husband of every woman representative is also a contributing factor to this state of affair.

## Employment and Income

Employment and income status of family members are contributing much to the participation of women in PRIs. Education and the village in which they are living put the heads of the families in different employments.

**Table 11.4** : Employment and income status

| | Income (Rs.) | | | |
|---|---|---|---|---|
| Employment | Below 15000 | 15001-23000 | Above 25000 | Total families |
| Coolie | 6 | — | — | 6 (30) |
| Fishing | 2 | — | — | 2 (10) |
| Farming | — | 3 | 2 | 5 (25) |
| Social work | 1 | — | — | 1 (5) |
| Others | 1 | 2 | 3 | 6 (30) |
| Total | 10 (50) | 5 (25) | 5 (25) | 20 (100) |

*Source:* Survey data.

*Note* : Figures in parantheses indicate percentage to total.

Table 11.4 shows that 50 per cent of the sample households are receiving less than Rs. 15000 as income and 50 per cent are better placed. 30 per cent of the head of the families are employed in government services. This situation helped the women to participate in rural Panchayats.

It is a general trend that those who decorates high offices try to make their family members to push up after their retirement. It has also happened in the case of PRIs. Out of 10 women Panchayat presidents their husband being presidents during the earlier periods backs two. One president's father happened to be the Panchayat president earlier. An enquiry with some of the local people revealed that the name and services of their father and husband made them presidents. They too are performing well than their elders.

**Table 11.5** : Status-wise distribution of sample respondents

| Sl.No. | Category | WP | WWM | Total |
|---|---|---|---|---|
| 1. | Wife of former president | 2 | 1 | 3 (15) |
| 2. | Daughter of former president | 1 | — | 1 (5) |
| 3. | Party compulsion | 1 | — | 1 (5) |
| 4. | Social worker | 4 | 2 | 6 (30) |
| 5. | Economic soundness | 2 | — | 2 (10) |
| 6. | Others | — | 7 | 7 (35) |
| | Total | 10 (50) | 10 (50) | 20 (100) |

*Source:* Survey data.

## Empowerment of Women

Empowerment refers making people to understand their capabilities and responsibilities in the society. According to Dr. Palanithurai (*The Hindu*, 2001), the new Panchayat Raj system is an unique opportunity for transforming the rural areas by empowering the people to develop their own vision, design their own strategies and launch action on their own to improve the standard of health, education, nutrition and to augment family income. This would also help to change the status of women in the rural areas. A great deal of people's participation, especially women are essential for the sustainable development of the rural areas.

Women in India are victims of a multiple socio-economic and cultural factors. Though women need to be empowered in all the areas, it is economic independence, which is the most prominent means of empowerment. Therefore, enhancing income-earning opportunities is increasingly viewed as an effective means for empowering and improving their status (Suman, 2000). According to him, empowerment can be measured by the ability of the collective to alter conditions (social, economic, political or cultural). In the present study, an attempt has been made to analyse the empowerment of women through the participation and implementation of various programmes and projects for the socio-economic uplift of the rural masses.

Women participation also tends to increase their empowerment level. Empowerment of women is a long-term objective and it can be achieved only by increasing the educational status of women, creating several chances for their participation and also provision of social justices by providing equal opportunities on par with men. Increasing women's participation, access and improving share of the development were seen as necessary and sufficient conditions to bring about dramatic changes in women's economic and social positions.

The participation of women in PRIs and the welfare and developmental activities undertaken shows the empowerment of women in the study area. All the 10 women Panchayat presidents have taken steps and completed many felt needs of the people. They are (1) providing drinking water supply, (2) street lights, (3) concrete roads, (4) drainages, (5) construction of public libraries, (6) construction of small bridges, (7) construction of free houses and (8) implementing various welfare schemes for the rural poor funded by the State government.

All the respondents revealed that there is inadequacy of funds for the completion of some other projects. Two presidents from the coastal villages revealed that funds are not available to provide and maintain even streetlights. They have also felt that shortage of funds is the cause for the insufficient supply of drinking water in their villages. Three respondents reported that the funds provided by MLAs are inadequate even to undertake a small work in their Panchayats. But, the actual utilisation of the Rural Infrastructure Development Fund (RIDF) by the States has been coming down over the years. The share of loans disbursed under the RIDF scheme has come down from 84.6 per cent in 1995-96 to 13.5 per cent in 1999-2000 (*The Hindu*, 2000). All these things reveal that participation of women in PRIs has empowered them to plan well, implement the plans properly with the available resources and also to fight for common welfare.

**Problems Encountered**

Nothing can be achieved without making any sacrifice in any form. Women have to play a dual role—one in their house and another in the Panchayats. 50 per cent of the respondents revealed that their family life is affected to a greater extent. They have no time to look after their children properly. There is no return for the services rendered than negative comments passed by opposite groups in the Panchayats. The only satisfaction is that we have a chance to do something for the welfare of the people in cooperation with Ward members and higher-level officials in Panchayat administration.

**Summary of Findings**

1. Reservation of seats in Village Panchayats exceeded the provisions made in the Constitution. There is 39.39 per cent reservation for women in PRIs.

2. All the 20 selected respondents are in the age group of 29-50 years.

3. 60 per cent of the respondents are having S.S.L.C. and above level of education and the remaining 40 per cent are having lower level of education.

4. All the heads of the respondent's family are employed and 50 per cent of them receive less than Rs.15,000 as income per annum.

5. The study also reveals that members of influential families always seem to have an edge over the other people.

6. There is active participation by women representatives in planning and implementation of various schemes and projects.

7. All the respondents reported their difficulties in mobilising funds locally and also the insufficient allocation of funds for the development of rural areas.

8. There is full cooperation from male Panchayat Ward members while taking policy decisions and implementation.

9. Most of the respondents revealed their difficulties in allocating more time for Panchayat development activities ignoring their duties as mothers.

10. All the respondents are of the opinion that the reservation policy should be continued for a long period; say 20 to 25 years to stimulate women to be active participants in PRIs.

**Suggestions**

1. To impart education regarding PRIs, the rules and regulations and also duties of Panchayat presidents and Ward members should be included in the school and college syllabi.

2. Though female literacy rate is 78.39 per cent, most of them are having only school level education. So steps should be taken to empower rural women by providing college level free education. It will be helpful to reduce the growth of population also.

3. Most of the people in the rural areas are of the opinion that the administration of Panchayats by women representatives is better than the previous periods. Therefore, women should be allowed to contest and participate in PRIs more than one-third seats if time and situation permit them.

4. Since more than 80 per cent of the total population is living in the rural areas, due consideration should be given to rural development than urban development while allotting funds.

5. The Central government should take steps to motivate the State governments to utilise the funds allotted for rural infrastructure development to ease the financial problems of the Panchayats.

6. Non-Government Organisations may be better used to create social awareness among the rural population, especially rural women regarding PRIs and also other things related to their empowerment.
7. Periodical surveys and researches may be conducted to find whether the PRIs are performing properly or not and to set everything in the right direction to achieve rural development as the base for the development of our country.

## Conclusion

The present study clearly shows that education empowers women to participate in the PRIs to do well for the socio-economic emancipation of the rural population. All the elected representatives, especially small Panchayats and coastal Panchayat presidents and Ward members, do feel the pinch of the resource crunch. While addressing the NIRD Foundation Day Seminar on 'Emerging Institutions for Decentralised Rural Development' (January 7-8, 2001) in Hyderabad, Shri Mohandariaji has given a solution to this problem. According to him, allocation of funds to MPs and MLAs are not a healthy sign of democracy. They discriminate and do favour to their party people. Therefore, no more special programmes for funding MPs and MLAs. Funds should be directly given to the 'Grama Sabha' or Panchayats, where planning is made to fulfil the felt needs of the people by utilizing the scarce resources for the most urgent ones. May the Central and the State governments take appropriate steps to make the flow of available funds for rural development through PRIs without any leakage of funds here and there in order to achieve growth with equity and social justice.

## REFERENCES

Bhagyalakshmi, J. (1998), 'Panchayat Raj Empowering the People', *Yojana*, Vol. 42, No. 7, pp. 21-24.

Dagar, Rainuka (Ed.) '*Manual on Women's Development and Gender Justice*', Institute for Development and Communication, Chandigarh, 1998, p.135.

Heyzer, N. (1985), '*Missing Women: Development Planning in Asia and the Pacific*', Asia and Pacific Development Centre, Kuala Lumpur.

Hiremath, Ujwala (1997), 'Women in Grassroots Politics', *Social Welfare*, Vol. 44, No. 2, pp. 7-14.

Jain, Suman, 'Empowerment of women through NGOs: The Sewa Bank Experience', in Kamta Prasad (Ed.), *NGOs and Socio-Economic Development Opportunities*, Deep & Deep Publications Pvt. Ltd., New Delhi, 2000, p. 114.

Justice Krishna Iyer, V. R. (1984), "Woman Unbound: A Plea for Gender Justice", Society for Community Organisation Trust, Madurai.

Mehta, Usha (1996), 'Status of Women', *University News*, Vol. xxxiv, No.12, March 18, p. 14.

Opschoor, J.B. (1998), 'Sustainability, Economic Growth and Development Theory', *Journal of Social and Economic Development*, Institute for Social and Economic Change, Vol.1, No.1., p. 17.

Shah, Anupama and Susan Jacob (1995), 'Attitude Towards Reservation for Women', *Social Welfare*, Vol. 2, No. 8, Nov. 1995, pp 3-9.

Sekar, T.V. (2001), 'Empowerment of Grassroots level leaders in Health and Population: A Training Experiment in Karnataka'. Paper presented in the NIRD Foundation Day Seminar on 'Emerging Institutions for Decentralised Rural Development' held during January 7-8, 2001, Hyderabad.

*The Hindu*, May 13, 2001.

*The Hindu*, May 21, 2001.

12

# ADDRESSING GENDER NEEDS THROUGH PANCHAYATS
## A Study in Tamil Nadu

S. NAGABHUSHANA RAO

### NEED

Water is a basic necessity of human life. In many Indian villages safe drinking water is a serious problem. In rural areas the women bear the burden of drawing the water for household. Traditionally the women plays an important role in collecting, storing of water and in deciding which water source to use for what purpose, how to draw and transport it.

According to a study by the UNICEF (NDWM, 1990), collectors of water in an Indian household are women between the ages of 15 and 35 years fetching 192 litres of water a day for an average of household of seven. Due to environmental degradation and depletion of water resources the women have to walk longer distance to fetch water.

Thus, supply of safe drinking water to a large rural population scattered over a vast area including isolated and inaccessible habitations assumes prime concern of administrators. As the water resources are limited and the uses are quite diverse, a judicious use of this resource necessary, particularly in the desert and drought prone areas. For this, the conservation of water resources and management practices assume importance. (Ghosh *et al.*, 1995).

There is a direct relationship between water, sanitation and health. Inadequate provision of safe drinking water, improper disposal of the human excreta and unscientific disposable of sewer and solid wastes leads to unhealthy environmental conditions. This coupled with the lack of personal hygiene, often breeds many water borne diseases, particularly diarrhoea and tetanus. Malaria, the killer disease in rural areas, is caused by negligent environment and sanitation habits.

About 2.5 lakhs people die due to tetanus in India. Every year 1.5 million children under five years of age die due to dehydration caused by diarrhoea and other water borne diseases (NDWM, 1993). This alarmingly high rate of infant mortality is attributed mainly to improper sanitation facilities.

Sanitation is a composite and comprehensive expression covering personal hygiene, domestic cleanliness, favourable environmental condition, disposal of human excreta, solid waste and wastewater disposal (Bakshi & Menon, 1996). Contaminated water and poor sanitation are the main causes of high mortality in our country, i. e., 53 per thousand population (UNDP, 2000).

It is recognised that lack of supply of safe drinking water and sanitation facilities are the main factors adversely affecting the life of people. According to the available information, 0.1 per cent of our rural population had access to sanitation facilities in 1970, 0.5 per cent in 1980, and 2.45 per cent in 1990. A mere 5.58 per cent out of 623 million rural population (as per the 1991 census) has been covered by both safe drinking water and toilet facilities (Bakshi & Menon, 1996).

There is no perceived priority attached to this programme as far as individual is concerned. It has become a part of urban, semi-urban and pro-urban habits of living and to some extent of the affluent rural elite. The problem arises with the people who cannot afford to invest in this account. Because of their limited purchasing power, the government has formulated Central Rural Sanitation Programme (CRSP).

Due to lack of awareness, sanitation has not been perceived as a priority need by the people and development administration. The progress under drinking water and sanitation programme has been slow due to: (i) Lack of initiative at all levels particularly at the implementation; (ii) Inadequate support available for this sub-sector; (iii) Lack of perceptions as a matter of importance on the part of the people, and (iv) lack of people's participation in the whole programme (NDWM, 1993).

In the course of implementation of water supply programmes the category of under assets, piped water supply and installations of hand pumps are taken by the agency and the operation and maintenance has been entrusted to the users, without any instruction. This arrangement of water supply and sanitation has led to several problems.

**Problem**

To solve the drinking water problem the government has come with various programmes of supply of drinking water. But these schemes were implemented some 20 years back. These village schemes were handed over to the Panchayat Union (Block Development Office) for maintenance in Tamil Nadu. But the proper maintenance was not taken up because the non-availability of adequate maintenance staff and the limited staff have to visit many villages. The other problems are lack spare parts, breakdown of hand pumps or power pumps, electrical fixtures and dried up bore wells etc. It is because of this, most of the water supply schemes became defunct in the villages and the situation in villages is one of despair. 'The main lacuna in villages is lack of an organised Water Management System'. The DANIDA water supply and sanitation project addresses some of these problems.

## THE STUDY

This chapter is based on an empirical study and it discusses about the drinking water and sanitation project assisted by Danish International Development Agency (DANIDA) in Tamil Nadu State. The main objective of this chapter is to analyse the gender needs addressed through the Panchayats and participation of women in planning, implementation and maintenance of drinking water supply and sanitation projects.

The study was conducted in two Village Panchayats, i.e., Vela Kollai (Water Supply) and Keerapalyam (Sanitation) Gram Panchayats in Cuddalore district of Tamil Nadu State. For the study the Panchayat representatives, Sarpanchs, women user group members were interviewed informally, individually and in group. The PRA techniques were used to elicit the required information.

During the past three decades the DANIDA has been providing assistance to rural water supply projects in the States of Orissa, Kerala, Madhya Pradesh, Karnataka and Tamil Nadu. DANIDA, a Danish organisation with the agreement of Government of Tamil Nadu is funding the water supply and sanitation schemes through a project implemented in Cuddalore district of Tamil Nadu.

**Objective**

The objective of the water supply scheme is to provide a water supply of 40 litres per capita per day (lpcd) to the Village Panchayats. Priority was given to defunct water supply schemes in the Village Panchayats, implemented by the Tamil Nadu Water Supply and Drainage Board (TWAD). The objective of the sanitation project is to create awareness about sanitation and provide hygiene environment in the village.

**Approach**

The uniqueness of the project is 'Demand Driven Approach'. The project has been implemented in the villages, on the demand of Village Panchayats. By October 1999 in 56 villages of Cuddalore district, the water supply projects were completed and in 122 villages the scheme is at various stages of implementation. The DANIDA is having the sentimental attachment to the Cuddalore district, as it was their colonial district (South Arcot) and thus initiated this scheme in the district. The sanitation project is implemented in the villages, on the demand of Village Panchayats who came forward with contribution of fifty per cent of the cost from the villagers.

**Strategy**

The precondition for funding the project is the mandatory involvement of Village Panchayats. In the village, PLA, known as participatory learning exercise, has been conducted to equal distribution of water to all villagers. The participation of women in PLA exercises was made mandatory. The Village Panchayat also must select women mechanics to be trained by the DANIDA at district headquarters for a week. This is to ensure immediate repairs of taps and hand pumps.

To implement the sanitation project the beneficiary has to contribute the fifty per cent of the total cost. After collecting the contribution from the beneficiary DANIDA normally releases their share of project and distributes to the women in Village Panchayat meeting. The Village Panchayat selects the women masons from the village to be trained by the DANIDA at district headquarters for a week. The trained woman masons construct the toilets. The main focus of the scheme is on (i) Strengthening of local bodies (ii) Gender Equality, and (iii) Women Empowerment.

**Methodology**

The project is implemented through the Panchayats. To initiate the project the DANIDA volunteers conducted a meeting to all Gram Panchayats at Block level for two days. In the meeting the concept, strategy, contribution, utility of the scheme and contribution towards the project cost of the village people was emphasised. To commence the water supply scheme, Rs. five per capita is collected from the villagers. After that, DANIDA gives approval to implement the scheme in the village level. After approval by the DANIDA the Village Panchayat and people prepares a comprehensive plan of water supply, which includes overhead tank, public taps, hand pumps according the village needs the estimates are prepared for village. After the plan preparation, the villagers collect one-seventh of the cost of the project as a contribution. After collecting the amount the DANIDA sanctions the rest of the amount. From the year 2000 onwards, the contribution of the villagers increased to one-third of the project cost.

For sanitation the DANIDA is funding two types of projects in the district:

1. Institutional latrines, and
2. Household latrines.

The institutional latrines are mainly for the schools particularly the preference was given to the girls sanitation. Household latrines were given to individual houses in the Village Panchayats. In sanitation project the fifty per cent of the project cost to be borne by the villagers. But the beneficiary was given flexibility of construction of size of toilets and bathroom - cum - toilet. The participation of women must be ensured in sanitation meetings conducted in Village Panchayats. The ideas of women would be given prominence in the meetings.

## WATER SUPPLY

### Experience from Vela Kollai Gram Panchayat

VELA KOLLAI, Gram Panchayat is one of the Gram Panchayats benefited by the water supply scheme of DANIDA. Vela Kollai Gram Panchayat President Shri P. Sundaram, attended the meeting at Block level conducted by the DANIDA. Drinking water is a dire need of Vela Kollai village. The Tamil Nadu Water Supply and Drainage Board (TWAD) provided arranged water supply about 10 year's back. But at present the scheme was defunct due to bad maintenance or the repairs were never attended by the mechanics from Block. The villagers were not empowered to technically to repair the pumps. Thus, the Vela Kollai Gram Panchayat President decided and came forward to implement the scheme.

For commencing of the project Rs. five per capita was collected by the Village Panchayat. After DANIDA had given approval to implement the water supply project, one-seventh of the project cost contribution was collected from the villagers to sanction the entire cost of the project.

After approval by the DANIDA the villagers prepared a comprehensive plan, for village which included overhead tank, public taps and hand pumps. The Participatory Learning Exercise was conducted to place the taps and hand pumps to give the equal distribution of water to the villagers. The participation of women was made mandatory in preparing the plan and during the PLA exercise.

After approval of the village water supply plan, the work was awarded to contractor following public tender. But the President and Vice President was having the full control of the funds and thus have the full control of the contractors involved in execution of works. This was to check the any sub-standard material used in the scheme and to maintain good quality.

In Vela Kollai village 14 public taps were put up at different places. With precaution the project includes eight water pumps in case of power failure. The water taps and pumps were placed in different places, with the help of PLA exercises by the villagers. The villagers contributed to the scheme without any hesitation, as water supply is their dire need. The rich people contributed more and the poor people and the people belonged to Scheduled Caste and Scheduled Tribe contributed less. The people's contribution and DANIDA assistance are given below.

Cost of Water Supply in Vela Kollai Village

| Source of funding | Amount (Rs.) |
|---|---|
| People's Contribution | 44,205 |
| DANIDA sanctioned amount | 2,65,280 |
| Total Project Cost | 3,09,485 |

*Source:* Field Survey (Vela Kollai Village Panchayat).

*Impact*

The scheme satisfied all the people. At present regular water supply was provided to the villagers for four hours. In the morning the water was supplied from 6 a.m to 8 a.m. and in the evening 4 p.m. to 6 p.m. In case of power failure the bore wells which were set up at different points were provided the water to the villagers. For proper maintenance the women user groups were formed. The mechanics were readily available in the village. The minor repairs are done by mechanics and the major repairs are done by the Panchayats. The villagers informed that even the problems arise, it is not of technical but social in nature.

Vela Kollai Gram Panchayat President, Shri P. Sundaram, says, during elections they promised many things, mainly regular water supply to the village. They thought that the government would provide the money, and thus they promised to the people. Only few villages will get an opportunity. Having elected they were astonished that the money was not available for the schemes and thereby, they were worried about their political future. So DANIDA water supply scheme was a golden opportunity for them to ensure their future in political arena.

## SANITATION

### Experience from Keerapalyam Gram Panchayat

The awareness building is a gigantic task concerning sanitation, as the villagers in many places were not having the culture of using toilets. The Keerapalyam Gram Panchayat is one of the Gram Panchayats in Chidambaram Taluk in Cuddalore district was benefited by the sanitation scheme. The motivation efforts put by the DANIDA volunteers and Gram Panchayat president yielded the desired results of total sanitation in the Keerapalyam Village Panchayat.

The success of total sanitation in the village is a credit to Gram Panchayat President Shri K Paneer Selvam. He is an educated (postgraduate), young and self-motivated person. Most of the youths of the village rallied behind him in creating awareness and motivation. The President says, 'In highly competitive atmosphere I was elected as the President. The faith of the people in me should not be evaporated. I will develop this Gram Panchayat as an urban area with all the facilities'. He has collected Rs. 28 lakh of rupees as a contribution from the public to construct drains, roads, community hall and school building, kalyana mandapam, shops for educated unemployed youth and for construction of institutional latrines for schools.

Keerapalyam Gram Panchayat President attended the meeting conducted by DANIDA volunteers at the Block level. The President decided to have good sanitation facilities in his village because in the village the pigs and rodents roam freely in the streets and this created an unhygienic environment in the village.

The Panchayat President felt that he was impressed with flexibility of the sanitation project. The CRSP scheme allows the latrines can be constructed with the approved size whereas the DANIDA scheme provided flexibility and people have the opportunity to construct the latrines and bathroom according to their wishes.

He went and conducted a meeting of Gram Panchayat regarding the sanitation scheme of DANIDA. For the meeting, he invited the youths and women to participate in the meeting. In the meeting on sanitation a large number of women were attended. The women in meeting unanimously decided that the sanitation programme should be implemented in the village. The women took a decision because they face a lot of hardship while attending the nature call. The real fact is that, the women can attend nature call only in the darkness. In darkness scorpions and snake bites affected many women and they slipped into the ponds while they go for nature call in nights. Hence, women unanimously decided to construct the latrines to overcome the hardship. In implementing the sanitation scheme the students and youth in the village helped him.

*Impact*

The Keerapalyam Gram Panchayat completed 100 houshold latrines covering almost the entire village with DANIDA assisted sanitation programme. After completing the sanitation in the village, district level officials, the press, radio, DD, and Minister for Local Administration visited the Gram Panchayat. Finally the Hon'ble Chief Minister of Tamil Nadu visited the Gram Panchayat and issued a certificate on "Total Sanitation Award and Best Gram Panchayat Award" to Keerapalyam Gram Panchayat.

*Weakness*

The only lacuna of the project seems to be the elite people who can contribute the fifty per cent of the project cost had taken advantage of the project. The poor and weaker sections that cannot pay the contribution (fifty per cent) are left out of the project. From the weaker sections and poor people 25 per cent of contribution should be collected to provide the facilities of sanitation to them. The importance of sanitation should be explained to the poor so that they can realise it.

In the words of the DANIDA Project Coordinator, 'the sanitation awareness is main problem in rural areas and in future the sanitation project will cover every house of the village without any economic barriers'.

**Innovative Elements that made the Success of the Project**

(i) *Strengthening of Local Bodies:* The pre-condition for commencement of the water supply and sanitation projects in 1996 was elections to the local bodies. After the elections were over, the scheme was sanctioned on 'Demand Base' to the Village Panchayats. Both the schemes were made mandate to implement through local bodies.

(ii) *People's participation:* The community participation was vital element from the beginning to the end of the scheme. People's participation was stressed in every stage. To commence the water supply scheme at village level, the PLA (Participatory Learning and Action) exercises were conducted in the village to prepare a plan and the placement of power pumps, public taps and hand pumps in the village. This provided equal access of the water for all villagers. The Participatory Learning and Action (PLA) provided an equal opportunity for men and women, poor and rich to participate and thus empowering the villagers in planning.

(iii) *Gender Equality:* Woman bears the brunt of water scarcity in the village and, therefore, women were aware of the problems in the village. Involving of women in water supply projects requires recognition of their traditional roles and cultural status (Churchil, 2000).

Women have long been neglected in the process of development and secondary role is assigned to them whether in taking part in crucial issues related to development or as beneficiaries of the process itself (Neelima & Swaroop, 2000).

In many societies instead of women in water supply schemes men are more likely to be represented in political and social institutions. This is because to speak publicly to the community, particularly in front of outsiders. In some societies, women before introduction of these projects were not allowed by customs to take part in public affairs (Churchil, 2000).

The women's participation in development is a positive concept, related to their ambitions and aspirations that symbolizes their conviction about their personalities in relation to society (Neelima & Swaroop, 2000).

The scheme envisaged that women must participate in planning and implementation of the project and Participatory Learning and Action (PLA) exercises to decide the equal distribution of water to all the villagers. The decisions taken by women were given prominence in the PLA exercise.

(iv) *Maintenance by Women User Groups:* The unique feature that distinguishes the DANIDA Water Supply Project was maintenance by the women user groups. These groups were established at all water points, public taps and hand pumps. Each Group contains 5 to 10 women as members. The members of women user group collected Rs. 5 to 10 from the user families/ stakeholders in the village. The women user groups maintain the accounts and the amount was deposited in the bank. This amount was utilised for minor repairs without the help of the Panchayat. However, Panchayats assisted in major repairs of water pumps.

(v) *Women Empowerment:* Another special feature of the scheme is the women from the Village Panchayat were selected for the training as mechanics to repair the pumps. The Gram Panchayat selected the women for training with willingness of the women. The selected women was trained as pump mechanics by the DANIDA for one week at district headquarters and was sent to the Village Panchayat to take up the repairs in Village Panchayat.

**Sudha — The Pump Mechanic**

Sudha, a pump mechanic of Vela Kollai Gram Panchayat says, 'I will earn Rs. 500 - 600 per month'. Sudha is an illiterate woman, trained as a pump mechanic by the DANIDA. She was selected by the Gram Panchayat President and members of Gram Panchayat as she showed interest and her husband also encouraged her to be trained as pump mechanic.

This will serve the two purposes. Availability of the mechanic in the village and amount earned from the repairs is a supplementary income to the family. The women mechanics stay in the villages and are easy to approach in time of need. The women mechanic attends repairs immediately. Women in the village expressed that they are more comfortable in approaching a woman mechanic for assistance.

**Kamalamma — Lady Mason**

For sanitation scheme to construct the toilets in the Village Panchayat the women from the Village Panchayat was selected as masons. The Gram Panchayat selects the women for training with the willingness of the women. The selected women were given training as masons for one week at the district headquarters by DANIDA. After the training they are engaged in construction of toilets in their villages. These women are paid the wages on par with men.

From Keerapalyam Gram Panchayat, Kamalamma was selected as a lady mason. She was trained for a week by DANIDA. Before undergoing training, she was a casual labourer. The Gram Panchayat President selected her in the Gram Sabha meeting due to her poor economic condition. Her husband left with another women. After that, she became the head of the family and responsible for its maintenance. Due to depressing economic condition in her house she was selected as a lady mason. As a casual labourer she was earning Rs. 40 per day and the availability of work was irregular. After training as mason she was earning Rs. 110 per day. Kamalamma asserted that, 'except two or three days throughout the month I get the work'.

The villagers particularly women felt happy to construct toilets because of availability of lady masons. In some houses the lady masons do the technical work and the members of the family will provide labour assistance to minimise the cost of construction of toilet.

## FINDINGS

The study reveals that, the people are receptive to new concepts, if the awareness created and they are motivated. In DANIDA projects, the maintenance was done by the stakeholders and the repairs were immediately attended by the mechanics as they are available in villages. The participation of women and Panchayats in planning and learning exercise, implementation and maintenance by the women user groups makes the sustainability of the scheme. The women were the mechanics and in problem areas the women was found it easy to approach the women mechanics without any hesitation for attending immediate repairs. The women user groups were also found easy to collect the money from the stakeholders. The Panchayats are locally based institutions and helped the women user groups in selecting the mechanics and masons for water supply and sanitation schemes and thus addressing the gender needs. The involvement of Panchayats makes the scheme sustainable.

Panchayats represent the need of the people at grass root level, so involving Panchayats means making the people involved in the process of planning and implementation. This becomes easy for maintenance as the local bodies are directly involved in the development of village infrastructure. Thus, the replicability of these elements in the scheme across the country will pave the way for sustainability.

## REFERENCES

Bakshi, D.S. and Menon, P.S.K., (1996), *Environmental Sanitation, Health and Panchayati Raj*, Institute of Social Sciences, Concept Publishing Company, New Delhi.

Churchill, A.A. (1987). *Rural Water Supply and Sanitation (Time for Change)*, The World Bank, Washington D.C.

Ghosh, G.; Mazumdar, K.; Dubey, A.K.; and Chander J., (1995). *Water Supply and Sanitation in Rural India : Policy and Programme*, Ashish Publishing House, New Delhi.

GOI, (1993). *Rural Water Supply and Sanitation Programmes in India*, Rajiv Gandhi National Drinking Water Mission, New Delhi.

Neelima, B.N. and Swaroop, T.S., (2000), "Gender Perceptions of Ecological. Development", *Social Welfare* 47 (3).

UNDP, 2000, *Human Development Report*, Oxford University Press, New Delhi.

13

# EMPOWERMENT PROCESS
## Experience of the Elected Women Representatives in Grass Roots Institutions in Tamil Nadu

G. PALANITHURAI

### Introduction

Ever since the enactment of the 73rd and 74th Amendments to the Constitution of India, "empowerment of women at the grass roots" has become a popular concept that is used by many, (Kumud Sharma, 1992; Srilatha Batliwala, 1996; Srilatha Batliwala, B.K. Anitha, Anita Gurumurthy, Chandana S.Wali; 1998) with varied meanings and explanations. One-third of the seats at three levels of the grass roots institutions[1] have been reserved for women of all categories. This has raised expectations among the different sections of the community that this group of women will become a critical mass, which, in turn, will make an indelible difference to the management of these institutions at the grass roots level. Such an expectation has grown to the extent that the existing development paradigm will undergo a drastic change in the system of benefits (Nirmala Buch, 1998).

Women elected to grass roots institutions have been performing their roles and functions for the past five years. The impact and the implications of the management of these institutions by women leaders have been felt in many spheres. While the critical mass of women formed via the reservation system has not performed its crucial role on the scale that was expected, yet, changes have been brought into the system. The problems faced by women are expected to be addressed by these women leaders since these leaders are assumed to be sensitive about issues affecting women. Women's issues are expected to become central and receive the attention of all, especially policy makers.

From a cursory analysis, it is seen that the representation provided to women at the grass roots level has not been fully utilized. Instead of tackling the problems of women, the elected representatives have started facing a plethora of problems because of their gender. The women representatives face many problems. As a result, more failures, rather than success stories have been projected in the media. However, such representations are largely based on assumptions, not facts. As per government statistics, failures comprise no more than five per cent of the cases (P. Krishnaswamy, 2001).

An in-depth analysis will show the systematic effort on the part of the mainstream system to project the failures of women leaders rather than their problems in handling power and institutions. It is also observed that in the name of training and capacity building, the women leaders have been encouraged and oriented to give up their identity and become coopted by the administrative system. The women leaders' vision and their sense of self have been eroded. This has been evident over the past five years, during which women grass roots leaders have been silently suppressed and coopted by the system.

A conscientious move has been made to equip the women leaders to stand on their own legs, initiated by the Gandhigram Rural Institute, founded as an institution for empowering women by the disciples of Mahatma Gandhi at the dawn of independence. This new initiative has also highlighted scores of problems faced by the women representatives on various fronts. In order to overcome these, associations for Elected Women Representatives have been formed and they are federated with other associations of Elected Women Representatives in South India.

The problems, issues and encounters faced by the women leaders and dealt with herein are location specific and they are only confined to Tamil Nadu. These observations, analyses and explanations cannot be generalized. All these problems are to be seen within the backdrop of the environment of the State of Tamil Nadu. This chapter, therefore, seeks to illuminate the problems faced by the women representatives of the grass roots institutions of Tamil Nadu. Further, it highlights some of their experiences while trying to achieve their avowed goals. It also indicates some suggestions on the support needed to sustain their position of power in this space created for them.

The problems of the women representatives were collected from two sources. First, while conducting training programmes for the women representatives, a specific sharing session was arranged in which all the problems faced by the women representatives were discussed and documented in detail (G. Palanithurai, 2001). Second, when the women representatives formed an association and federated themselves with the support of Gandhigram Rural Institute, they organized regional meetings in several places in order to consolidate the demands of the women representatives in the local bodies. The above exercise was carried out in four zones and the exchanges and interactions with the women leaders have been documented (G. Palanithurai, 2000, 2001).

## The Reservation Debate and Process

While looking at the issues of the women leaders, one has to bear in mind the environment in which the institutions have been created through 33.3 per cent reservation of seats for women and how they have carried out the duties and responsibilities assigned to them. Right from 1941, report of the Sub-Committee of the National Planning Committee[2] to the recent report of the Committee on Status of Women in India every report (Government of India, 1975) has emphasised that the condition of women is unacceptable and that they have been denied their rights and opportunities. While commenting on women's predicament, Justice V.R. Krishna Iyer observed : "Rethinking on the separate terms from the perspective of women who, despite the constitutional guarantees, had not achieved real justice or liberty or equality or dignity produced the holistic concept of gender justice which united all the principles into one to challenge the persistent denial of these promised objectives to the overwhelming majority of the women of India within a quarter of a century after the birth of the Republic" (Leela Kasturi and V. Mazumdar, 1994, p. 8).

It is true that Indian history (A.S. Altekar, 1978) provides ample proof that the rights and freedoms enjoyed by women change in inverse proportion to the status of their families, especially the men in their families, within the social hierarchy. Further, it is horrifying to note from the observation of an IAS officer, based on the latest two censuses, (Satish Agnihotri, 1996) that the only section of India's multiple people who neither destroy their baby daughters before or immediately after birth, nor allow them to die in infancy through discrimination in nutrition and health care are the *adivasis* whom the rest of us have been taught to regard as the most backward and least developed/civilised members of our nation. There have been a series of reviews and observations (Caroline Moser, 1989; Gita Sen, 1994) about the condition of women based on which new schemes and programmes have been chalked out for the welfare of women. Yet one cannot see any significant impact on the society. In fact, women had been increasingly viewed by the planners as not being in need of an independent livelihood to the point where women's decreasing work participation rate and share of employment, increasing poverty and insecurity in certain sectors of the economy in which they used to dominate earlier were not even viewed as unfortunate problems of change. This kind of marginalisation of the majority of women in the economy and the consequent neglect and demonstration of gender, class and urban bias led to a complicated situation in the general political framework of the society.

It is also true that even the opportunities that have been provided to the women have not been properly used by them for their upliftment as they are trained to be insensitive towards their own issues (Sakuntala Narasimhan, 1999). In a democratic country, power is always with the people and they should have the strategy to handle power. It is not the government that gives power to the people. The government derives power from the people.

To liberate the oppressed women, steps have to be initiated from the side of the oppressed and not from the oppressor's. The government in a patriarchical society will look at issues only in a patriarchical way. To overcome these problems, feminists have fixed two long term goals—freedom and empowerment (Asia Pacific Centre for Women and Development, 1979). Freedom from oppression for women involves not only equity but also the right of women to freedom of choice and the power to control their own lives within and outside their homes. Control over their lives and bodies is essential to ensure a sense of dignity and autonomy for women. 'Power' refers to the sense of internal strength and confidence to face life, the right to determine choices in life, the ability to influence the social process that affects their lives as well as the direction of social change (Sushama Sahay, 1998).

Empowerment of women is prominent everywhere and has gained currency among academics and policy makers now. Empowerment has been defined differently by different scholars contextually (Srilatha Batliwala, 1995). But, at present, most scholars (Gita Sen and Caren Grown, 1987) have come to give a broad meaning to the concept. It is a method of tackling powerlessness in encountering and combating personal and social problems. It is distinguished by its focus on developing critical awareness, increasing the feeling of collective and self efficacy and developing skills for personal, interpersonal or social change. In other words, empowerment can be defined as control over material assets, intellectual resources and ideology. Thus empowerment is a process of awareness, capacity building, leading to greater participation, to greater decision making power and control and to transformative action.

This process takes shape in two forms, internal and external. Women should realise their inner worth and they should be made to realise their worth. In order to perform the above tasks, the problems faced by the powerless should be first eliminated from the social environment. In the 1970s and 1980s, systematic steps were taken through the Five Year Plan proposals (Government of

India, 1976; Government of India, 1980). Consequent to the pressure brought on the government by the women's movement at the national and international levels commissions were constituted.[3] Yet, the struggle is still going on to acquire a legitimate space in all spheres of life for women. Thus, the position of women has not changed drastically or dramatically as dreamt of. The problems of women representatives at the grass roots have to be looked at against this background.

## Problems faced by Elected Women

To empower women, the elected women representatives have to be first empowered through the available means. In this process, it is essential to understand the problems faced by the women representatives while performing their roles and functions and to solve these problems as far as possible.

Elected women representatives to the grass roots level institutions have been facing numerous problems, apart from within their families, in their social, political and administrative setting. This has led to ineffective administration of the bodies by the women leaders. They don't have a common platform to express their grievances and get them redressed. Experiences from capacity building exercises conducted in various parts of the State have propelled us to prepare an action programme for empowerment of women leaders at the grass roots level. This can be done by forming an association of women representatives and federating it with similar associations of women representatives in local government in different parts of the country and making them articulate their issues on their own.

In the Indian context empowering women is a herculian task as social and cultural moorings have established strong roots in the belief system of the people. As a result, there has always been an uncommon disparity in the upbringing of women and men. All social reconstructions take place only through political activities, that too through political systems. Democracy provides enough scope for such reconstructions through polity. Hence every social segment is moving towards power. Yet, women hesitate to take part in politics as if the space is for men alone. In order to break this barrier at the micro level, a new device has been worked out through the 73rd Constitutional Amendment Act. This act provides women with one-third reservation of seats at all levels in all positions of the Panchayat institutions. But this provision has not yielded the expected results as this space is not perceived properly by the women leaders, because the elected women representatives of these grass roots institutions are facing a variety of problems in their social, political, administrative settings. They have been made ineffective in administration since they have come to these institutions as freshers. Yet, laudable achievements have been scored by women leaders in Panchayats.

In order to achieve success in Panchayats, the women leaders have to face numerous problems. They are engaged in constant struggle. The leaders have been made insensitive to their own and women's issues. They have been oriented to lose their identity. They have been made instruments to operationalise certain processes for others. This process has made them sink in localism and voicelessness. As a result, their space is still severely limited. In order to overcome all these hurdles, an attempt has been made to associate the women leaders into a federation in order to address all issues which they are facing in administration and to focus on the issues of the women.

**Need for this Programme**

The finding of the capacity building programme is that women leaders are in need of an alternative arrangement for the continuous flow of information and consultancy to stabilise their activities for development. The existing grass root leaders' organisations do not provide space for grievance redressal of the women leaders. Moreover, the requirements of the women leaders are not adequately fulfilled by these organisations. Hence, the demand for a full-fledged professional organisation to assist the women local body leaders. Against this background, a series of programmes covering the entire

State of Tamil Nadu was organised in four zones. The details of the programmes are in Table 13.1.

**Table 13.1** : Network Meetings of the Elected Women Representatives

| Sl. No. | Category of Participants | Programme | No. of Leaders attended | Venue |
|---|---|---|---|---|
| 1. | Panchayat Union Chairmen, Village Panchayat Presidents, Ward Members and Self-Help Groups | South Zone Network Meet on Associating Women Representatives in Local Bodies | 25 | Madurai |
| 2. | Village Panchayat Presidents, Ward Members and SHG Leaders | North Zone Network Meet on Associating Women Representatives in Local Bodies | 32 | Chengulpet |
| 3. | Village Panchayat Presidents, and Ward Members | East Zone Network Meet on Associating Women Representaitves in Local Bodies | 23 | Tiruvaram |
| 4. | Panchayat Union Chairmen, Village Panchayat Presidents, Ward Members and | Central Zone Network Meet on Associating Women Representatives in Local Bodies | 48 | Karur |
| | Total | | 128 | |

*Source* : Computed

A facilitating centre for grass root women leaders is being considered at the Gandhigram Rural Institute.[4] Before proceeding further, it is necessary to take a glance at the problems of the women leaders.

The problems are drawn from the elected women representatives who have attended training programmes organised by Rajiv Gandhi Chair for Panchayati Raj Studies funded by various agencies. The details of these programmes are given in Table 13.2.

**Table 13.2 :** Details of the Training Programme Conducted for Elected Women Representatives

| Sl. No. | Training Programme | Funding Agency | No. of Participants |
|---|---|---|---|
| 1 | 2 | 3 | 4 |
| 1. | Empowering Panchayati Raj Institutions on the issues of Population, Health and Social Development | Population Foundation of India | 6834 |
| 2. | Capacity Building for Gram Panchayat Presidents | CAPART Hyderabad | 681 |
| 3. | Training of Presidents and Vice-Presidents on Panchayat Administration with Special Reference to Water and Sanitation | DANIDA Villupuram | 815 |
| 4. | Training of Presidents and Vice-Presidents on Panchayat Administration with Special Reference to Water and Sanitation | DANIDA Cuddalore | 416 |
| 5. | Training of Women Presidents of Gram Panchayats | Social Welfare Board | 825 |
| 6. | Training of Elected Women Representatives of Urban Local Bodies | Tamil Nadu Institute of Urban Studies | 2150 |
| 7. | Training of Trainers in Multi Level Planning | State Planning Commission | 71 |
| 8. | Capacity Building for Weaker Sections in New Panchayati Raj System | CAPART Hyderabad | 425 |

*Contd......*

*Table 13.2 (Contd.)*

| 1 | 2 | 3 | 4 |
|---|---|---|---|
| 9. | Capacity Building for Gram Panchayat Presidents | CAPART Hyderabad | 317 |
| 10. | Training Programme for Panchayat Leaders in Nilgiris District on Ecological Empowerment of Panchayats | Rural Development Organisation The Nilgiris | 102 |
| 11. | Training for Village | DRDA | 682 |

*Source:* Computed

| | | |
|---|---|---|
| Total Number of elected local body leaders trained | = | 13,318 |
| Total Number of Panchayats covered | = | 2,354 |
| Total Number of urban local bodies covered | = | 294 |
| Districts covered | = | 17 |

The problems of the women representatives of local bodies are classified under two categories, based on their perception as women and as women Panchayat representatives respectively.

**Increasing Workload**

The moment the women filed their nomination, their workload increased doubly and so did constraints. No woman representative from the rural areas reported that her workload in the home front decreased due to her work in the public space. In a joint family system, attention to the routine work cannot be reduced. At every stage, the elected women representative has to tackle the problems carefully in the family, otherwise, she will court trouble. The family burden, coupled with the workload in the Panchayat, made the elected women representatives tired of the activities in the public space. Their efficiency could neither be exhibited nor improved as they had no time. On most occasions, the elected women representatives opted for a joint workshop with the males of their families. Instead of discussing the problems faced by them among themselves, a workshop could be organised to which the elected women representatives and their husbands or any family males assisting them could be invited. All the issues of the women representatives could be discussed and that could bring about change in their attitude.

### Varied Concerns of Women Leaders

Politics has its own ramifications and dimensions—whether it is State politics or national politics. Till they entered grass roots institutions, women had confined themselves to voting. After the reservation of seats for them in the grass roots institutions, they have also been made players in the political game. So far, they had not been dragged into this game and hence they are novices in this art. In order to acquaint them with politics, they need the support of men. But, while drawing upon the support of men for their work, they run the risk of the men trying to coopt the women representatives in their work. Now they are gradually learning the art of politics.

### Illiteracy

Illiteracy is a basic problem among the newly elected women representatives. They are not able to write and read, but they are allowed to file nomination. After they are elected to positions, they feel very much annoyed about their inability to read and write. They have the aspiration to read and write and are prepared to undergo training but their husbands prohibit this since they are operating the Panchayat at present on behalf of their spouses. Wherever the elected women representatives establish contact with NGOs, they are properly oriented and trained to manage the institutions on their own by the intervention of the NGOs. To maintain thirty-one records, every one requires adequate skill. The training programme is intended to impart skill in the art of management of Panchayat institutions, for which literacy is a prerequisite. Near about 9 per cent of the participants are lacking this skill. Hence they have to rely on others for managing the Panchayats.

### Usual Shyness

Having traditionally secluded themselves from society, especially the menfolk, women face difficulties in interacting with men in office and in public life, after being elected to Panchayati institutions. They have had no previous experience of working with men but when they become leaders they have to interact with both men and women of the community. The women leaders are, therefore, inhibited in their interaction with men in public contexts. When Gram Sabha meetings were convened, the women representatives had to conduct the proceedings as chairpersons of the Gram Sabha by sitting along with men in a crowd, which is unusual in the remote villages. In the first-three to four Gram Sabha meetings she was not comfortable sitting with men, observed Ponnikailasam, the president of the women Panchayat leaders' federation.

**Domination of Males**

It is clear from the experience of the elected women representatives that their capacity had not been recognised by the males of their families. After their election, they have been attending meetings and training programmes. They learn many things from the training. Initially the men in the family, under the guise of helping them, accompanied the elected women representatives to offices and public places. Over a period of time, the women learnt the art of administration through interaction and training. But the males will not accept that their family women, who have been elected to Panchayats, have equipped themselves to manage the institutions. It is an irony that though the elected women representatives feel that they can manage the affairs of the Panchayat on their own without the help of any male from their families, this cannot be communicated to the males of their families. Further, the elected women representatives are facing problems in Panchayats when the males of their family interfere in the administration. In the absence of interference in administration by the males of the families of the elected women representatives, trouble from male representatives would be minimal and negligible. This is partly so because the men feel that the women are not elected on their own merit but because of their men's support. This sort of attitude is very difficult to change since the women leaders too are of the belief that they have been elected to Panchayat institutions only because of the influence of their husbands or the other men of their families. While narrating her experience, Mrs. Minnalkodi of

Adhanur Panchayat reported that the men in her family take decisions and impose them on her. She said that she did not have adequate courage to change this.

The women representatives pointed to yet another problem: the restriction placed on their movement. The people of the village have been used to approaching their Panchayat representatives with their problems at any time they wished. Although the women representatives indicated their willingness to attend to such work any time, they were not permitted to do so by their husbands or other family members. They need the permission of their husbands or in-laws if they want to go to the police station or the hospital at night. On such critical occasions, people want the support of the leaders. If the leaders are not coming out to help the people, the public criticise the Panchayat leaders.

## Forced not to Raise Issues of Women

Although women in the rural areas are facing a multitude of problems, men ensure that such problems are never raised openly in public fora. The women representatives feel suppressed by this. Alternatively, the women representatives feel that those problems could be raised by the affected women in the fora. However, the affected women feel that those problems should be raised by the women representatives. The family members of the elected women representatives, however, prevent the elected women representatives from articulating women's problems in public.

Environmental degradation and depletion of natural resources are affecting the life of women in rural areas, especially the poor women. Even though the elected women representatives are aware of the gravity of the problem, they are unable to raise the issue in public fora as some mafia gangs are involved in such despicable activities. Only NGOs are creating awareness about this problem among the *dalit* women and the poor in the rural areas.

The menace of alcoholism breeds all sorts of troubles for the family, especially women. Women are facing innumerable problems in the family and in society because of alcohol. Every woman and every child is affected and yet nobody has the will to oppose this practice, since everybody knows that this illicit trade takes place with the active support of the government and politicians and with the connivance of the police. No one need create awareness about this menace among the people as they are all aware of it. But they are all afraid of the police who are behind it.

The health of womenfolk is not seriously viewed in rural areas by men. Even women themselves do not realise the importance of their health. In every respect, women are discriminated against in the family. No one dares to create awareness among the women. Even in carrying out activities in the Panchayat, men are not sensitive to the issues confronting women. Worse, the women are not sensitive to their own issues, be it guiding the pregnant women to avail themselves of ANC or motivating girls to go to schools. In such circumstances, the elected women representatives taking up these issues are not appreciated and, instead, they are being criticised.

### Negative Attitude of Officials

Elected women representatives find it very difficult to convince the officials in the government offices as they have a poor opinion about the women representatives. The officials feel that the elected women representatives are in position simply because of the reservation policy and that they do not have any opinion or vision of their own. The officials assume that the women representatives will accept whatever the officials advise. Consequently, women representatives who go to offices with aspirations and expectations from the officials feel frustrated. Ms. Ponnikailasam, the chairperson of the federation of the women Panchayat leaders, while presenting the report about the plight of he women leaders in her presidential address in 2001, indicated how the officials were indifferent towards the demands of the women representatives of local bodies.[5]

### Illtreatment

It is a sorry state of affairs in government offices that the elected women representatives with high social and economic background get respect while the poor elected women representatives, especially the *dalits*, face only illtreatment. To illustrate the tragedy of *dalit* leadership, a case is narrated here. A poor *dalit* woman who served as a construction worker assisting the mason got elected as Gram Panchayat President. She went to the Panchayat Union office to clear a file for her Panchayat. The moment she met the concerned clerk, she was asked to bring a cup of tea from the nearby tea stall by the clerk. She readily agreed to do so and picked up a glass tumbler and got a cup of tea for the clerk without a murmur. Later she was asked to meet him at his residence. She went to his residence and she was asked to do some work in his garden. She did that work also. Later, she got the cheque from him and went home happily. When she narrated the incident in a training programme she was asked why she did not resist. She said that previously it was her routine to bring tea to the mason at the construction site. Now she was asked to do so by an official and so she obliged. Illtreatments continue unabated, despite the *dalit* movement. Likewise, a Gram Panchayat President, Mrs. Reeta, narrated her experience with officials and police in her experience sharing session in the annual convention of the elected women representatives of rural local bodies in Tamil Nadu. She explained how she responded to challenges.[6]

**Information Blockade**

There are several blocks and barriers to the process of women empowerment. Information blockade is the most powerful weapon used by the officials to disempower the women. Generally, women do not have access to newspapers. Moreover, all government information is transmitted from one department to another only among officials. The officials circulate the information booklets and details only among the men and not among the women. Even the elected men representatives are not willing to share their knowledge with the women representatives. Mrs. Susila, Karungulam Gram Panchayat President, narrated in her presentation in the group discussion while she was undergoing a training programme sponsored by the Social Welfare Board that she was discriminated against by the officials and the male Gram Panchayat leaders in giving copies of the Government Orders on Rural Development and Panchayat Raj.[7]

When women representatives are invited for training programmes permission is not accorded by many of the families. When the elected women representatives insist, they are allowed to attend the training programme along with their husbands or other males of the family. Now, the government insists that the elected women representatives should not be accompanied by their husbands or others while attending training programmes.

**Domination of Caste Panchayats**

Traditional caste Panchayat leaders are yet another barrier to the elected women representatives as they impose conditions and restrictions on the women leaders. If the elected woman representative belongs to the caste of the traditional Panchayat leader, he extends all support to her to be in power but not in attending to the works on her agenda. The traditional Panchayat leader expects that elected women representative should adhere to the advice of the traditional Panchayat. She is expected to carry out the works from the agenda of the traditional Panchayat. If the elected woman representative belongs to other castes, particularly *dalit*, she cannot do any work at all. Invariably, she has to be under the control of the traditional Panchayat leader. Otherwise, she has to spend sleepless nights.

Party men also expect the same. Normally, women in the Panchayat do not have any political identity and hence they look at issues on the basis of the reality. On the contrary party men want the elected women representatives to look at the issues from the party angle, failing which the women representatives will face problems from the party high command. Why do party men take such a stand? Because, it is a normal practice that when a seat is reserved for women, a male of the party gets permission from the party to field his wife or sister in that place. Hence, the party men feel that it is the responsibility and duty of the elected woman representative to adhere to the dictum of the party men at the local level. Issues such as domination of caste Panchayat leaders over the formal Panchayats headed by women and the control of political party leaders at district level over the women Gram Panchayat leaders, repeatedly figured in the training programme while the women gram Panchayat presidents narrated their experience in Panchayat administration.[8]

**Lack of Communication Skills**

Communication skills are most important for the success of any leader in the modern era. The elected women representatives never had a public space experience and hence they lack communication skills. The elected women representatives have to manage the councils and the public. Since they feel that they lack skills, they cannot achieve what they want to. Even the federation chairperson Ms.Ponnikailasam stated in the training programme that she felt very much about her poor communication skill.[9] But now she speaks for an hour in meetings along with ministers and higher level officials.

When the elected women leaders are presiding over the council of local bodies, some men use unparliamentary words with the intention of making the elected women leaders nervous. The men councillors or Ward members even threaten the women leaders. This is common in many places.

**Poverty Prevents**

There are elected women representatives from the working class who have to rely on their daily wages. Though the elected women representatives have been entrusted with so much of responsibilities and duties there is no means of reimbursing their loss of wages. This deprives them of their livelihood and hence some are forced to use proxies in their office. Ms. V.R. Kalaiyarasi of Veppangulam Panchayat argued that this provision in the Constitution has created a space even for a poor scheduled caste woman to occupy a position in Panchayat but it has not created a conducive climate for them to work as leaders. She explained her plight in managing her family without economic compensation.[10]

**Oriented to Lose Self**

Commonly, we expect that women would be very sensitive to women's issues. However, it is not true in the case of the elected women representatives as they have been continuously oriented formally and informally not to be sensitive to women's issues. In the same way, *dalit* women representatives are insensitive *dalit* issues. One argument put forward is that they are the representatives of not only women or *dalits* but the whole village community. Therefore, they address neither all the women's issues nor the issues of *dalit* women effectively. Most of the training programmes concentrate on procedural matters and not on developmental issues.

So there was further training in team building and vision building (G. Palanithurai, 2001).

### Interference of MPs and MLAs

They face yet another botheration in their administration i.e., the interference of MPs and MLAs. The elected women representatives feel that everyone has his or her own domain for action. Roles are different for all the representative institutions. MPs and MLAs feel that the Panchayats are under their control and that the local body leaders have to accept whatever they say regarding rural development. This has been raised in many fora (G. Palanithurai, 2000).

### Lack of Managerial Skills

In order to achieve success, one should possess managerial skills. Managerial and administrative skills are essential for any successful administrator. The elected women representatives are lacking in accounting and managerial skills. Since they have this deficiency they are misguided by the officials and the males of their families. Sometimes women are trapped on this count and thereby they are coopted in all the underhand dealings of the officials. They say that they need managerial and accounting skills to overcome the problems which they have been facing. To overcome this problem, the Hunger Project in India is offering leadership training to the women leaders in which accounting and auditing procedures have been given a major thrust.[11]

### Women Leaders Coopted

When the elected women representatives meet the officials with the males of their family, the officials talk to the males and not to the representatives. Even the reserved seats are offered to their husbands and the other males of their family and not to them. Initially, they felt this very much and later they developed a practice of ignoring such things. Only after attending training programmes have they realised the mistake. Most of the matters transacted between their husbands and the officials were not known to them. The training programmes which they attended made them understand the issues in administration. At every level the ignorance of the women representatives is exploited.

However minor the politics at the local level, muscle and money power have their due role and hence, all activities are planned in the context of managing the muscle and the money. In order to overcome this problem, the women have to rely on either the family or caste leader or party heads. At a later stage, whoever comes to the rescue of the woman representative comes to the Panchayat for personal favours and obligations. When such obligations are denied, the women representatives are criticised and castigated. This was reported by the federation leader Ms. Ponnikailasam in the network meeting organised at Thiruvarur.

**Social Cleavage**

The caste division in the villages has been another kind of hindrance to the elected women representatives. While forming Self-Help-Groups (SHGs) all women are united and do not entertain any cleavage. But, after forming the same and functioning for a period of time, the women are compelled by their menfolk to look at issues from the perspective of caste. As a result, many groups have collapsed. In the same way, while distributing the benefits to the poor, women leaders are compelled to distribute the benefits on the basis of caste considerations. Caste has entrenched itself everywhere and become a barrier to the smooth functioning of Panchayats. Elected women representatives are often put into trouble because they look at issues beyond the perspective of castes.[12]

**Lack of Motivation**

To perform any job motivation is important. The elected women representatives are new to this job. All of them have not taken up this assignment willingly or voluntarily. Further, they have been facing problems without any support. There is no motivation for them. As a result, many elected women representatives are in a state of mental depression. How to solve this problem? Nobody knows the solution. The problem has reached such a stage that they are searching for a counselling centre for the mentally depressed elected women leaders.

They are asked to carry out a variety of programmes and schemes. Before one starts his or her work, one should know what role one has to perform. They filed their nominations without knowing what for! They are not aware of the 73rd Amendment to the Constitution of India and the State Conformity Act of 1994. Without knowing the basis of decentralization of powers, they have been assigned the task of realising it in practice. Normally one would expect that the women organizations would start the exercise of pepping up the elected women representatives. In the absence of such initiative, the elected women representatives have taken steps to form their own association through which they have decided to articulate their grievances and the problems they have been facing in Panchayat administration. Gandhigram Rural Institute has decided to support such kind of activities since women empowerment is one of the basic objectives of Gandhigram. Periodical meetings of the women leaders have been arranged for which the institute has generously extended its support.

**Caste Discrimination**

Untouchability is in practice in the rural areas. For the *dalit* leaders, it becomes a problem. Whenever a *dalit* heads the Panchayat Council and Gram Sabha, we may witness pandemonium. *dalit* leaders are not respected and, in many villages, the traditional leaders conduct the proceedings. In the meeting the elected women representatives merely serve as spectators. Further, the two tumbler system prevails in the rural areas where the *dalit* leaders are the presidents. They are not able to speak on those issues as they have developed mortal fear. It is the duty of the Panchayats to administer social justice but, in reality, they are not able to do so. Only a few political parties highlight the issues and plight of the *dalits* and submit critical reports to the government periodically.

**Dalit Women Leaders Marginalised**

*Dalit* women representatives, unless oriented by some political party, are powerless and voiceless. *Dalit* leaders are not allowed to speak and that too about the problems of *dalit*. Even if some *dalit* oriented decisions are taken in the Panchayat, they are not allowed to be executed. Genuine and basic facilities to *dalit* are not allowed to be provided. In certain areas, the traditional Panchayat leaders ask the *dalit* women representatives to hand over the office to them. In many places, the Gram Sabha is being organised and conducted by the traditional Panchayat leader and the elected women representative remains one among the spectators. She has no voice and she has to sit along with other *dalit* women in the audience section. Ms. Kalaiyarasi of Veppangulam Panchayat explained that in Sivagangai District wherever the *dalit* leaders are able to adjust with caste Hindu traditional Panchayat leaders, there is no problem in Panchayat administration and where there is no cooperation between the traditional and formal Panchayats the *dalit* Panchayat leaders are in trouble.[13]

## Husbands Coopted

When the husbands of the *dalit* women representatives are working on the farms of the traditional or caste Hindu leaders, it is all the more easy to take over the Panchayat office. Her husband insists that she has to obey the dictum of the caste leaders in order to avoid conflict and to lead a peaceful life. Officials, for their part, terrorise the *dalit* women leaders to execute whatever programme, they want to be executed in the rural areas, irrespective of the needs of the Panchayats. *Dalit* women representatives are easily coopted in the corrupt administrative system without any resistance. Whenever the misdeeds are found out, the poor *dalit* women are penalised and not the officials.

## Non-Cooperation of Police

It is a well known fact that police officials are always in the hands of the upper class or upper caste people. Despite the repeated steps taken by the *dalit* women representatives, nothing favourable comes to the *dalits* from the police. Police officials are not taking cognizance of the genuine grievances of the *dalit* representatives. *dalit* representatives complain to the police about the encroachment of the common properties by the caste Hindus and influential party men in the rural areas. As per the government order, the police have to take action and eviction has to be carried out. But, contrary to expectation, no action is taken against the encroachers despite repeated complaints. Common property resources are the lifeline of the poor. But now several hundred acres of common properties have been encroached upon by party men. When they are identified, action is being initiated by the Panchayat president. But there is no action from the police. But police act in accordance with the government order in the Panchayats headed by caste Hindu women leaders. The basic question here is why do we have such discrimination?

## Design of Caste Hindus

Since the *dalit* women are poor, they hand over the Panchayat responsibility to someone, mostly caste Hindu traditional leaders with a view to earning their livelihood. No one can refute this. But one has to look at the reality. Why is the poor *dalit* woman preferred by the caste Hindu leaders, when a *dalit* woman with sufficient economic background contests in the election? It is the design of the caste Hindus to elect a poor *dalit* woman so that the woman could be easily coopted in their design, whereas the economically sound *dalit* woman cannot be easily coopted in their design, as she has needed economic background to manage her livelihood.

Paucity of funds is a general problem for all the Panchayats in Tamil Nadu. For the *dalit* women, it is a serious problem because the women of the *dalit* community expect that a woman representing their community would do many things in favour of the *dalits*. But, contrary to expectations, the elected women *dalit* representatives could not do anything for *dalits* due to paucity of funds. The caste Hindus are not allowing the elected women *dalit* presidents to carry out programmes earmarked for *dalit* as they also need such programmes, for which there is no sanction from the government. Even the allotted works for *dalit* could not be carried out in the rural areas. Hence, the *dalit* presidents have got a poor name among the people of their own caste. They get neither the support of *dalit* nor the support of non *dalit*.

## Dalit Problems Not Focused

*Dalit* representatives face another constraint in all public fora. They realise that there are a large number of problems unattended to so far but could be attended to now through the reservation system. But it is deliberately ensured that the elected women *dalit* representatives do not take up *dalit* issues either in Gram Sabha or in Panchayat council meet or in any meeting. This kind of prevention keeps *dalit* representatives alienated from the *dalit* community and they continue to be in the hands of others. Even if they are ready to take up such issues, their family members are not ready to support them as they are in the fold of the caste Hindu families. Thus, their expectations are belied and the *dalit* youths are in an agitative mood, paving the way for social and communal conflict in the villages.

**Non-Cooperation of Caste Hindus**

Another silent attempt is made by the caste Hindu leaders in their Panchayats through non-cooperation, which makes the elected women *dalit* leaders non-functional and unsuccessful. Thereby they declare that *dalit*, especially women of that caste, are totally incompetent to manage the public institutions. In many places they have successfully done this. Wherever the elected women *dalit* representatives agree to coopt with the caste Hindus, they are allowed to carry out certain works which are not favourable to the marginalised.

The elected women representatives face yet another problem in Panchayats. The caste Hindus have cleverly created a design of usurping the power of *dalit*. Even during the time of election, in many Gram Panchayats, the caste Hindus resort to a ploy by which they get an assurance from the candidate that the Vice-President would be elected from the caste Hindus, especially a male. After the election, the president is asked to agree to the proposal that the Vice-President could be elected from the caste Hindus, particularly a male, so that they can get cooperation from the caste Hindus. As a result the *dalits* are victimised as the Panchayat administration is virtually under the control of the Vice-President. The elected woman *dalit* President has to accede to the proposals of the Vice-President. In many places, Vice-Presidents are making the Presidents commit mistakes and become victims of Clause 205 of the Tamil Nadu Panchayat Act. Further, in these Panchayats infrastructure facilities are created in the settlements of the caste Hindus and not in the *dalit* settlements. This has been raised many times in the Gram Sabha by the *dalit* youth to which the Vice-President gives a vague reply whereby the President is made to face the problem in the *dalit* community.

## Neglect of Vital Issues in Training

Training and orientation is given to the elected women representatives by the government but these programmes do not touch upon the vital issues of the marginalised people. In the training programme, orientation is given to the leaders to take up the schemes and programmes of the government. There is no scope for discussion on gender issues, issues of the *dalit* and participation of the people in the planning process. Proper orientation is not given to women leaders in the training programme conducted by the government and some of the non-governmental agencies. So, Gandhigram Rural Institute has designed a training module to train elected women Panchayat Presidents. This initiative was supported and approved by the Rajiv Gandhi Foundation.

## No Support Base

Another pertinent question discussed by the women is the support base of the women leaders. Discussions have been held on all the aspects based on which the women leaders have taken the initiative to carry out certain schemes and programmes. They have faced a variety of problems in the field. To overcome these problems they are in need of some supportive organisations. But, in reality, there is no support base for women leaders. In the absence of such support mechanism, one cannot expect exemplary achievements from the women leaders at the grass root level.

## Encroachment Encounters

As per the New Panchayat Act, the President of Gram Panchayat can take action against encroachments. To evict an encroacher, Panchayat Presidents have to get the village map from the village administrative offices. In many of the villages, the administrative officers do not give the village map to the Presidents of the Gram Panchayats. With great difficulty the Gram Panchayat Presidents take the initiative to retrieve the common property from the encroachers. This act has incited the encroachers to fight against the women leaders. This is yet another challenge to the elected women representatives. Ms.Menaka of Urapakkam Panchayat has paid with her life for taking steps to remove encroachments. This issue was discussed in many meetings of the women leaders' association. The women leaders have exerted pressure on the government to support the move of the Panchayats to remove encroachments.

## Crowd Management

Another problem they face is the problem of crowd management. Gram Panchayat Presidents have to convene Gram Sabha meetings four times every year. Our rural masses have not been oriented in the orderly presentation of issues in public fora. In a crowd they normally tend to shout. Even the speaker of the Lok Sabha is not able to manage enlightened representatives and the Legislative Assemblies do not fare any better. But in a Gram Panchayat, even if it is four hundred in an open place, it is always a free for all. When women representatives are presiding, anti-social elements deliberately use unparliamentary words in order to drive away the womenfolk. Nobody regulates the meeting except the family members of the elected women representatives. When family members come to the rescue of the elected women representatives other members of the Gram Sabha oppose it. But the same Gram Sabha members do not help the elected women representatives while they are facing problems in the Gram Sabha due to anti-social elements. People under the influence of alcohol participate in and disturb the proceedings. But no one is ready to control them. What is the way out of this?

Local body leaders are invited for public functions and they are asked to address the public. The elected women representatives are not in a position to speak like others in the public meeting as they don't have the required communication skills. It is the felt need of every elected women representative. This deficiency is responsible for poor management of crowds also.

## Accounting Procedure

Another hardship they undergo is the accounting procedure. In the computer era, Gram Panchayat Presidents have to maintain a total of 31 records. All the 31 records are to be regularly maintained. Even postgraduates with a Commerce background find it difficult to manage the thirty-one records. How can a poor uneducated *dalit* woman representative maintain so many records? They are not properly oriented in account-keeping but they are taken to task when they commit mistakes in accounting. Most of the elected women representatives are victims of this procedure. Either the procedures have to be simplified or the women's capacity has to be enhanced.

**Representatives' Perception of Women's Issues**

The above posited issues are the problems faced by the women leaders in the Panchayat administration. They have perceived the problems faced by the women in the rural areas. The issues are classified and presented hereunder. Primarily, the aspirations and feelings of the women are not respected and are not taken into consideration for decision making. It is common at the family level and at the community level. There is not much difference between the rich and the poor. Gender discrimination prevails in the family, community, office, parties, cultural organisations, and religious organisations. Women are discriminated against in providing facility, service and benefits. From the family level to the Central Government level one can find discrimination on the basis of gender. Girl children are poorly fed and malnourished. They are not given fair treatment on par with the male children. Women are harassed in the family and sexually exploited in the workplace.

Girls are generally not permitted to go in for higher studies or even beyond primary school. Women are discharging dual responsibilities with great difficulty, yet, their burden is not appreciated properly. When women move beyond the routine, their workload increases with nobody to share the workload. For the poor women, there are no proper amenities in the workplace. Health facilities are not provided to the women as extended to the men. Women are also not sensitive to their health problems. Female infanticide and foeticide are the problems that women face in many villages. Due to non-availability of water, fuel wood, medical facilities, proper public distribution system, women are the worst victims. Women are denied property rights even though the Equal Property Rights Act has been passed in the Tamil Nadu Legislative Assembly. Women workers are paid poor wages compared to men. Women are made to be dependent. Assertive women are subjected to character assassination. Panchayats have no perspective plan for gender development.

## What They Need

These are some of the vital issues they have perceived as problems of the elected women representatives. Solutions could be found to all these problems. The women representatives have identified some solutions. They are listed hereunder. Proper orientation has to be given to the elected women representatives by way of periodical training. The women representatives are to be sensitised on the issues of the women. They have to be organised at a larger level and enabled to address their issues on their own by creating a suitable support base. Institution based legal support has to be provided to the women who take up the struggle to administer social justice. Periodic interface between successful women and women leaders who lead struggles has to be organised. Managerial skills, leadership qualities, accounting skills and communication skills have to be developed through periodic capacity building exercises.

Comprehensive awareness programmes have to be conducted in rural areas on the problems of the women. Information has to be provided to the women representatives on all vital matters pertaining to improvement in the quality of their life. Women's participation has to be ensured in Gram Sabha meetings. Women component plan has to be initiated at every level. Stringent laws are to be enacted to deal with individuals committing atrocities against women. The women segmented on the lines of political party, caste, religion and class have to be united and they should be helped to stand as a single entity. As a prelude to this, the elected women representatives have to be organised at State level and further federated with other State level organisations so that they will gain added strength. They can espouse the cause of women and legitimately claim political space in order to address the women's issues effectively.

## Where They Are

Though the elected women representatives face innumerable problems while discharging their duties, they continue their struggle to succeed in their mission. But their perception of their self and their desire vary from individual to individual and from group to group. There are six kinds of leaders, namely aggressive leaders, sober capacitated leaders, ambitious capacitated leaders, leaders with aspiration, leaders in a mood of withdrawal and leaders without an idea. A few cadre parties and a few committed NGOs have been continuously orienting a set of leaders and extending all their support to the women leaders having links with the parties and the NGOs. They always exhibit an aggressive character which enables them to discharge their duties more effectively than the other leaders. Twelve per cent of the representatives belong to this group.

There is yet another category of leaders, who have been oriented and trained but are not committed to any ideology or organisation. But they are committed to their work. They have participated in the programmes organised by the NGOs but they do not have continuous linkage with the NGOs. They are capacitated leaders concentrating much on their responsibilities and they have performed very well as they have enhanced their capacity. They have aspiration to continue in public service but no specific position. Whether they win the next election or not they will remain in the public sphere. This group constitutes 22 per cent.

There is another category which is slightly different from the previous one. The capacitated leaders have concentrated much on enhancing their capacity continuously and performing their duties. While performing their duties, they see the response of the people, based on which they have a desire to continue in office. But this category has an ambition to continue in the same position, for which they have developed an art of managing the people in the local bodies. All their deficiencies are compensated by their public relations. Their linkages with the people are strong as they are always with the people. Nearly 24 per cent of the leaders belong to this category.

The fourth category of leaders have a different aspiration. Though they have a number of deficiencies, by keeping themselves very active in discharging their duties, they want to demonstrate to their party leaders that they are the apt candidates for membership in the Legislative Assembly. They are always busy meeting the people and familiarizing themselves with the people. They consider the Panchayat institution as a launching pad for their political career. Though their number is very small they are certainly the models for emulation. Eighteen per cent of the leaders have this type of aspiration.

Another category of leaders are unable to meet the challenges of their role and unable to bear the pressures of the society and the family. They have expressed their desire to withdraw from public life. These leaders were brought to the public life by force by their husbands. In most of the cases the relationship between the husband and wife has undergone a change in the whole process of administering development through Panchayat Raj Institutions. Many husbands realized the fact that their wives have acquired needed capacity and, hence, they have to withdraw from the support space. But there is another segment of men who have determined not to allow their wives to attend to their duties on their own. Most of the women leaders have stated that they have been facing problems in the local body institutions because of the interference of their husbands. This factor cannot be explained to their husbands by the women leaders of Panchayats on their own. This group constitutes 20 per cent of the leaders.

There is yet another category which has no idea. They are in the hands of the males of the family, despite the pronouncements of the government. The women leaders do not move out of their houses for public work. They do not meet the people. Virtually their husbands are operating the machinery. They are not bothered about it. It is a money spinning device which is ably tackled by their husbands by their muscle and money power. Officials are also cooperating with such leaders. They have no idea about the Panchayats and they have no aspiration to contest in the next election. If their husbands ask them to contest they will contest; otherwise, they will not bother about it. They are only four per cent; yet their cases have been repeatedly quoted in public places. It is true that a withdrawal symptom is visible among the women leaders in local bodies. They face a volley of problems from the officials, caste groups, own family members and even their own political party leaders.

Yet the majority of the leaders have exhibited their determination to occupy the public space. Having entered and tasted power, the women leaders have come to the stage of enlisting themselves as members of various organisations to fight for their rights and legitimate spaces. In their struggle, they have identified the organisations and institutions which are supporting empowerment of women and, through them, they have determined to continue their struggle. Further, they have started forming their own organisations and federating their organisations with other organisations. Another interesting development is that a large number of women are being trained in the self help group (SHG) to move over to this power domain. Women leaders have come to the public sphere and they will continue to keep their hold over the institutions and try to expand their space.

## Observation and Conclusion

Women have come to positions in the local bodies as provision has been made in the Constitution. The attitude of society towards women has started changing. But, in the process of empowering women, the hurdles are continuing. Steps are being taken by the women on their own to overcome the hurdles. It is a long drawn process. A structure which has been created over centuries to work against the interests of women cannot be dismantled within a short span of four or five years. It can be changed only by creating a movement by the masses for which this provision of one-third reservation of seats for women will help. To fight against the designs of the structure, an organised movement of the masses is an imperative. In order to make the women achieve results in their positions an array of interventions are necessary.

They need orientation, sensitization, capacity building, information and counselling continuously through organisations. The ongoing experiments and experiences suggest that periodical training, orientation and sensitization make the women leaders perform the assigned role in a better way than the novices. When the women leaders are responding to the socio-political challenges in society, they are to be supported by the organisations and institutions which are working for empowerment of women. Wherever such interventions are available the achievements of the women leaders are substantial and impressive. The government will respond to the needs of these women leaders only when they are supported by organisations well known for their credentials and are to be reckoned with as a force.

## NOTES

1. Gram Panchayat, Block Panchayat and District Panchayats.

2. This report was published in 1941 but it was missing and later it as decided to republish the document by the Centre for Women Development Studies in New Delhi.

3. The details of these activities are recorded in the article entitled "Women : From Equality Empowerment" by Vina Mazumdar in *Independent India: The First Fifty Years* (ed) Hiranmay Karlekar, New Delhi: Oxford University Press, 1988 pp. 262-263.

4. A State Resource Centre would be created in Gandhigram Rural Institute. This centre would provide needed information to the Panchayat leaders through regional resource centres which would be created in different regions through NGOs.

5. For more details see Rajiv Gandhi Chair, *The Annual Convention of the Elected Women Representatives of Rural Local Bodies in Tamil Nadu*, Gandhigram: Rajiv Gandhi Chair for Panchayati Raj Studies, 2001.

6. *Ibid.*

7. Rajiv Gandhi Chair, *Report of the Training Programme Conducted for Women Presidents of Gram Panchayats in Five Districts of Tamil Nadu*, Gandhigram: Rajiv Gandhi Chair for Panchayati Raj Studies, 1998.

8. Rajiv Gandhi Chair, *Report of the Training Programme Conducted for Gram Panchayati Women Presidents of Madurai, Ramanathapuram and Pudukkottai Districts*, Gandhigram: Rajiv Gandhi Chair for Panchayati Raj Studies, 2000.

9. Rajiv Gandhi Chair, *Report of the Training Programme Conducted for Women Presidents of Gram Panchayats in Five Districts of Tamil Nadu*, Gandhigram: Rajiv Gandhi Chair for Panchayati Raj Studies, 1998.

10. Rajiv Gandhi Chair, *Report of the Training Programme Conducted for Gram Panchayat Presidents*, Gandhigram: Rajiv Gandhi Chair for Panchayati Raj Studies, 1998.

11. Rajiv Gandhi Chair, *A Report on Elected Women Representatives Network Meeting, Gandhigram*: Singamma Sreenivasan Foundation, 2002.

12. G. Palanithurai, "*Role of Case Groups in New Panchayati Raj System: A Case Analysis of Tamil Nadu*" presented in the UGC National Seminar organised in the University of Madras from 4th to 5th January, 2001.

13. Rajiv Gandhi Chair, *Report of the Second Annual Convention of the Elected Women Representatives of Rural Local Bodies in Tamil Nadu*, Gandhigram: Rajiv Gandhi Chair for Panchayati Raj Studies, 2002.

## REFERENCES

Agnihotri, Satish (1996), "Juvenile Sex Ratios in India: A Disaggregated Analysis" *Economic and Political Weekly* (special number), 28, December.

Altekar, A.S. (1978), *The Position of Women: Hindu Civilization*, Motilal Banarasidass.

Asia-Pacific Centre for Women and Development (1979), *Feminist Ideology and Structures: Report of an International Seminar*, Bangkok, UNESCAP.

Batliwala, Srilatha (1996), Empowerment of Women's Autonomy, *Proceedings of* a consultation on women's Health and Rights: Rethinking Population, HIVDS Technical Report Series, 1:4.

Batliwala Srilatha (1995), "The Meaning of Women's Empowerment", *Women's World*, pp. 23-34.

Batliwala, Srilatha; Anitha B.K.; Gurumurthy Anita; and Wali Chandana.S. (1998), *Status of Rural Women in Karnataka*, Bangalore: National Institute of Advanced Studies.

Buch, Nirmala (1998), "Decentralized Governance, Women's Participation and Poverty Eradication, *Women and Political Empowerment* (eds), B. Mohanty and S. Haider, New Delhi: Institute of Social Sciences, p. 82.

Government of India (1975), *Towards Equality: Report of the Committee on the Status of Women in India.*

Government of India, *The Fifth Five Year Plan*, New Delhi: Planning Commission, 1976.

Government of India, *The Sixth Five Year Plan*, New Delhi: Planning Commission, 1980.

Kasthuri, Leela and Mazumdar Vina (1994), *Women and Indian Nationalism*, Delhi: Vikas.

Krishnaswamy, P. (2001), "Women Panchayati Leaders more sinned against than sinning", *The New Indian Express*, 22 Aug, p.3.

Mazumdar, Vina (1998) "Women: From Equality to Empowerment" in *Independent India: The First Fifty Years* (ed), Hiranmay Karlekar, New Delhi: Oxford University Press.

Moser Caroline (1989), "Gender Planning in Third World: Meeting Practical and Strategic gender needs" *World Development*, Vol. 17: No. 11.

Narasimhan, Sakuntala (1999), *Empowering Women : An Alternative Strategy from Rural India*, New Delhi: Sage Publications, pp. 44-45.

Palanithurai. G (2000), Report on Capacity Building for Gram Panchayati Presidents. Gandhigram: Rajiv Gandhi Chair for Panchayati Raj Studies.

Palanithurai, G. (2001), Report of the Workshop on Networking of Associations of Elected Women Representatives in Local Bodies, Gandhigram: Rajiv Gandhi Chair for Panchayati Raj Studies

Palanithurai, G. (2001), Report on the Capacity Building for Weaker Sections in New Panchayati Raj System, Gandhigram: Rajiv Gandhi Chair for Panchayati Raj Studies.

Palanithurai, G. (2001) *Capacity Building for Local Body Leaders*, New Delhi: Concept Publishing Company.

Sahay, Sushama (1998), *Women Empowerment: Approaches and Strategies*, New Delhi: Discovery Publishing House, pp. 8-9.

Sharma, Kumud (1992), "Grassroots Organizations and Women's Empowerment: Some Issues in the Contemporary Debate", *Samya Shakti*, Vol. 6, Delhi, CWDS.

Sen, Gita (1994), "Poverty, Economic Growth and Gender Equity : The Asian and Pacific Experience" in *Gender Economic Growth and Poverty*, Heyzer Nocleen and Sen Gita, New Delhi: Kali for Women.

Sen, Gita and Grown Caren (1987), *Development Crises and Alternative Visions: Third World Perspectives*, New York: Monthly Review Press.

14

# BUILDING ALLIANCES AND CAPABILITIES AMONG THE ELECTED WOMEN REPRESENTATIVES OF GRASS ROOTS INSTITUTIONS

G. Palanithurai and V. Ragupathy

## Introduction

It is beyond doubt that steps have been taken systematically from the enactment of the Constitution to empower women and that the condition of the Indian women has also improved since Independence in terms of literacy, life expectancy and maternal mortality. Yet their position has not improved on par with that of men and, till date, they occupy only a subordinate position in political, economic and social life. Even the improvements achieved are not uniform among different categories of women[1]. In some cases the condition has worsened among a few categories of women.

In a positive move, women have now started organizing themselves to create awareness among women and to work for the development of women through different strategies, organizations, associations and institutions. Yet the process is not quite smooth or free from barriers and hurdles.

In the meanwhile, the globalization of the economy has exerted different types of impact on the Indian women at different levels with differences of intensity and nature. Likewise the localization of the political process is going to make an impact on the life of the women[2]. The negative impact of the globalization of the economy could be overcome through the localization of the political process if the women are properly oriented, trained, capacitated, conscientized and associated. The localization of the political process has brought one million women with varying social economic backgrounds to different levels of political institutions. This was facilitated constitutionally by amending the Constitution of India. The 73rd Amendment to the Constitution of India is a milestone in the history of women empowerment in India. How the constitutional provision of reserving seats for women in the grass roots institutions is going to be used will surely determine the process of empowering women in Indian society.

The globalization process has driven a variety of social groups into the poverty basket and poverty alleviation task has become quite complicated. Further, all the routes to access to resources for women, particularly poor women, have been closed as the market driven approach has taken away all the common resources. In the competitive market process the rights of women and the marginalized sections are the casualties. How to protect their rights enshrined in the Constitution and secure their livelihood are the major issues being faced by the women who are in the thick of the women's movement.

The decentralization process has opened up opportunities for women and other marginalized groups to influence the allocation of government and community resources in their favour and protect and promote their human rights[3]. However, there are a variety of barriers to women hailing from marginalized sections exercising their powers[4]. Really it is a challenge to work for the social, economic and political empowerment of women, particularly those from marginalized sections. No doubt it is necessary to work for the goal of empowering women for which the oppressive power of the existing gender relations is to be exposed and challenged. Further the gender relations have to be reshaped[5]. This exercise could be started at the level of the elected women representatives of rural local bodies as they constitute a critical mass since one-third of seats have been reserved for women. The critical mass will be able to perform the critical function only if they are oriented, conscientized and trained in the methodology of deconstruction and reconstruction of gender relations.

## Institutional Intervention

The Rajiv Gandhi Chair for Panchayati Raj Studies in Gandhigram Rural Institute has fixed the major objective of building the elected women leaders' capabilities to make use of the reservation made available to them for better delivery of services by conducting continuous capacity building exercises and performing the facilitating role in removing the barriers in their way to wielding power. A series of training programmes have been organized exclusively for Gram Panchayat women leaders with the support of the Ministry of Rural Development, Government of India. Capacity and capabilities cannot be built into an individual overnight. It is a slow and continuous process by which the leaders can enhance their capacity while practising what they have learnt in the training programme. While managing the institutions and tackling the issues women leaders face a lot of problems and they are also to be tackled.

It is to be taken note of that the barriers and obstacles for the women to take up power in the political process are formidable and that they require a powerful support structure beyond the training programmes to build up their skills to manage the institutions effectively and efficiently.

## New Initiative

An action project was undertaken with the following objectives: to build an alliance of women leaders; to conscientise them on the issues which affect the life of women; and, to orient them in the methods and nuances of tackling the problems. This initiative was a demand driven one. It was taken up by the Rajiv Gandhi Chair because of the repeated requests made by the elected women representatives who came to Gandhigram to attend the training programmes[6]. The question was whether Gandhigram Rural Institute would serve as a supportive resource centre for the elected women representatives facing problems in the Panchayats while managing the affairs of the Panchayats and the people. The capacity building programmes were organized mostly in class rooms and the leaders were taken to the field for brief exposure visits. Certainly this helped them to build up their skill and capacity. However, the rural socio-political scenario varies from region to region and hence the women have to face a volley of problems. While facing problems on the ground who will extend support to the women leaders is the major question. Gandhigram being a nodal centre for women empowerment from the beginning, the Rajiv Gandhi Chair accepted the challenge and took the initiative.

Sensitized and conscientised women leaders were keen on certain issues in the Panchayats after attending the training programmes, namely, ensuring entitlements to the poor and the needy, evicting the encroachers from the encroached common properties and creating awareness among the women about their problems and the remedies for the same. But the prevailing conditions were not conducive for the elected women representatives to tackle all those issues and they had to face a lot of problems in the Panchayat administration[7].

At this juncture, the idea of creating a network among the institutions working in different South Indian States with the same commitment to the issues of women struck the minds of development workers. The Singamma Sreenivasan Foundation, Bangalore, under the leadership of Devaki Jain, a well known woman activist and development economist, agreed to be a coordinating agency. Partners were found in Kerala and Andhra Pradesh. Thus this activity was initiated simultaneously in four States, namely, Kerala, Karnataka, Tamil Nadu and Andhra Pradesh. The Ford Foundation agreed to help these agencies in their work for women empowerment.

**Environment**

Tamil Nadu politics has its own significance in Indian politics from the perspective of social transformation due to the impact of the Dravidian Movement. In the Dravidian Movement, under the leadership of E.V. Ramasamy Naicker (Periyar), women emancipation was an important area of political action which trained the leaders to internalize the concept of women liberation and empowerment of women[8]. After the emergence of the Dravidian political parties in the electoral politics of Tamil Nadu, the issues of women captured the central stage. A series of legislations were enacted to liberate and empower women after these political parties assumed power in the State. Along with the left movement, the Dravidian Movement created an impact in the process of social transformation in Tamil Nadu. It does not mean that Tamil Nadu has come out of the clutches of patriarchy. It just means that the position of women in Tamil Nadu, compared with that in North Indian States, may be better. Despite all these progressive legislations, a variety of problems affecting the life of women, namely, female infanticide, foeticide, denial of access to common properties, atrocities against women, dowry deaths continue to haunt the womenfolk in Tamil Nadu. Even though women are elected to State Legislative Assembly and national Parliament from the Dravidian parties, their powers are severely restricted and they are being used by their husbands and the official machinery of the party as proxies. This is being extended to local bodies too. But in local bodies a large number of the women are from the sections below middle class and they will, by nature, assert themselves provided they are given the needed wherewithal.

In Tamil Nadu, women leaders in local bodies at the level of Gram Panchayats, from their experience with men leaders, thought that it was necessary to form an association of elected women representatives to sort out their issues. They formed associations locally at Block or district levels but these associations did not have any structure and standing. The women leaders used them as platforms to meet the officials collectively and individually to represent their problems and get them redressed. In this new exercise the women leaders obtained some positive response from the officials. On seeing the response of the officials the elected women representatives wanted to continue this kind of practice in the management of institutions. Upon seeing this development it was perceived that the elected women representatives' need was only facilitation. Since the Rajiv Gandhi Chair for Panchayati Raj Studies has the same objective of facilitation, the Chair perceived the women leaders' need as an appropriate opportunity for intervention.

The primary objective of the Chair is to activate grass roots democracy by conducting action research and extension programmes. It has to work with the Panchayat leaders for the regeneration of the rustic folk and to create awareness among the people about the new system of governance through the new institutional arrangement, namely, Panchayat Raj System. The Chair will work at different levels. It will also act as a nodal centre to offer training to the elected local body leaders in governance, particularly in administering development. Further it will act as a coordinating agency for NGOs for people oriented participative action for sustainable development and good governance. This approach emanates from the basic premise that people are capable, honest, sincere and committed in deciding their destiny and hence all the issues will be visualized from the perspective of the people.

Against this background it was planned to adopt the following as objectives and activities of this project: to enable the elected women representatives to be courageous and self confident and not to be intimidated by attrocities or yield to pressure in carrying out their role and responsibilities; to empower the elected women representatives to assert their rights; to facilitate the sharing of experience among the elected women representatives not only within districts and states but also across states; to build a movement of women political leaders to address issues on their own; to make the government listen to the collective voice of the elected women representatives; and, to institutionalize a gender perspective in decision making.

**Developing an Approach**

With these objectives, reputed action oriented feminists, gender specialists, lawyers, representatives from NGOs and academics were invited to deliberate upon the strategies and the approaches to be adopted for a transformation process through the women's organizations. The elected women representatives were invited to share their experiences with the feminists and gender specialists. On 26th August 2000, they deliberated upon the prevailing environment in the rural society for the functioning of the local bodies under the leadership of the women drawn from different socio-economic conditions.

In this consultation exercise, the following actions and approaches were evolved[9]. As a first step, the loosely organized associations have to be federated into a cohesive movement to address the issues of the women and the marginalized. To do this, regional meetings have to be organized and zonal or regional units have to be created for furthering the activities of the federation. While organizing such regional meetings, the problems faced by the women leaders have to be properly documented for policy advocacy and they have to be published through the media. Leaders from different regions are to be gathered for periodical meetings and they have to be sensitized on the basic issues of development like food security, livelihood security and more specifically on the issues of women. While sensitizing the women these issues are to be discussed contextually and futuristically. To gain confidence, they need hands on experience for which meaningful interface programmes could be organized on demand by taking these leaders from Tamil Nadu to Kerala and even from one region to another region within Tamil Nadu where success cases are reported.

An annual Elected Women Leaders Convention has to be organized where the documented problems of different regions have to be discussed in front of dignitaries and the media for popular dissemination and corrective action. The discussed issues have to be taken to the policy making level for lobbying for which Gandhigram Rural Institute should take up the responsibility. Through the regional outfits, needed information has to be provided periodically to the Panchayat leaders. The elected women representatives who are struggling in the Panchayat administration to deliver services should be given a helping hand by which it can be demonstrated to the other leaders that they are not alone and that there are thousands of leaders behind them and very many civil society organizations. To develop this movement the elected women representatives have to be trained in Panchayat management. They should be provided with needed skills and capability. Further the leaders of the Association in different regions are to be oriented in providing leadership to other elected women representatives. To adduce visibility to the issues of women and the organization, a proper media tie up has to be established. The media has to be sensitized on women in governance and the issues of women. The media's role in the movement is felt to be imperative. There are certain issues which are to be fought only through legal means for which the leaders are to be oriented for such an eventuality. To push forward the movement the strong support of the NGO network is required. It is to be underlined that the NGOs' activities should always be at the back of the Women Leaders Association and not vice versa. After finalizing the strategy, approach and action programme, another meeting was organized to create an NGO network to support the women's organization. It was held on 23rd October 2000[10]. The NGOs who have been working on the issues of women development were invited to participate in the meeting. The NGO representatives participated and deliberated upon the strategies and approaches evolved in the previous meeting. It was almost a workshop for women's solidarity activities and expressed their commitment to this work. They agreed upon the objectives and offered to extend their support in carrying out the activities as partners. It was decided to divide Tamil Nadu into five zones. The activities had to be carried out in all the five zones through the NGOs and the NGOs had to act as nodal agencies and resource centres for the activities of the elected women representatives.

Following this commitment of the NGOs, regional meetings were organized at Madurai on 21st December 2000, at Thiruvarur on 2nd February 2001, at Chengalpattu on 16th February 2001, and at Karur on 21st March 2001. In all the regional or zonal meetings, the problems faced by the elected women representatives in administering development were discussed and they were documented[11]. The documents were published and circulated among the representatives of the media for wider dissemination. The problems had to be taken to different levels for redressal. So they were classified and they were taken to the Block Development Office and to the State Legislative Assembly for redressal. On 5th August 2001 an annual convention of the women leaders was organized at Gandhigram and it discussed the basic issues of the women, strategies to overcome the problems and the problems faced by the Panchayats[12]. As they discussed the issues thoroughly all the issues were fully covered in the media which brought visibility to the women's federation.

**Interface Meetings**

After the zonal or regional meetings and the annual convention, it was decided to undertake the interface programme under which the federation leaders were to be taken to Kerala to visit some of the Panchayats and hold discussion with the leaders and functionaries on the issues of development. They concentrated more on the issues of social and economic development. Almost all the federation leaders got an opportunity to visit Kerala to have a glimpse of the social and economic development activities of the Gram Panchayats[13].

The elected women representatives tried to bring the Minister for Rural Development, Government of India, to their programme and succeeded in their attempt. On 20th February 2002, Mr.Venkaiah Naidu participated in their programme wherein the elected representatives discussed their issues with him and appealed to him to intervene at the appropriate level to redress their grievance. Along with the Minister, State level officials also participated and they were all asked by the Rural Development Minister to give replies to the questions raised by the representatives[14].

They organized the Second Annual Meet in Gandhigram on 3rd May 2002. In the second annual meeting, they discussed the 15-point programme of the Government of Tamil Nadu. In the course of the discussion they pointed out that, out of the 15-points, about 13 come under the purview of the Panchayati institutions. They went on to clarify at what level they can work and to what extent officials have to work to achieve the target. They compiled guidelines by which the details of the earmarked responsibilities could be identified[15]. For the annual meet they invited the Director of Rural Development, Government of Tamil Nadu, Mr. S. Ayyar, I.A.S. They made a powerful plea that in each and every district the District Collector has to convene a meeting of Gram Panchayat women leaders and redress their problems in the management of the Panchayats. He agreed to do so and promised to issue an order in this regard[16]. They further decided to form an advisory council consisting of retired officials, representatives from NGOs, academics and representatives from the media to facilitate the functioning of the federation. Subsequently, based on the deliberations of the Second Annual Convention, a regional leaders' meet was organized on 9th May 2002 to make an in-depth study of the 15-point programme and the problems faced by the women leaders[17] and consolidate their demands to be presented to the Government of Tamil Nadu.

## Implications

So far the sequence of events has been presented. But the implications of the activities have to be explained. One should not assume that the federation met once a year and deliberated only in Gandhigram. They organized several meetings in several places with the help of other NGOs also. They met political party leaders and officials for presenting their charter of demands. They used to meet the press periodically and express their opinions on vital issues which affect the life of the people, particularly women, children and *dalits*[18]. Based on the training programme, we have collected the problems faced by the Panchayati leaders generally, and women and *dalit* leaders specifically, and those problems have been documented by our centre. These documents have been used by this Federation for policy advocacy. It was very difficult for them to get information regarding government orders, rules and schemes. But now they are being received from Gandhigram Rural Institute and so they regard it as a resource centre. Contacting Ministers, higher officials, MPs and MLAs is no more a problem for them. Women leaders who are in this federating arrangement are highly sensitized on the issues of social development and more specifically on the issues of women and children. When the State government's proposal to introduce cheap liquor came as the most unkindest cut of all for the women heading Village Panchayats, the women Presidents reacted sharply that they were let down by a woman Chief Minister. They unequivocally argued and made it clear that they would launch an agitation if the government refused to drop the proposal. When the regional leaders of the Federation met at Gandhigram, they discussed this issue at length and spoke to Special Reporter of the *Hindu* Mr. S. Annamalai that they have been fighting at the village level for the past five years to eradicate illicit liquor, but now the government itself seeks to introduce liquor to make money. Subsequently the move was withdrawn in the rural areas. It was considered a victory for the women Panchayat leaders' Federation.

Subsequently, in 2002, in the month of December, when they met at Gandhigram, they made a plea to the Government of Tamil Nadu to increase the revenue of the Panchayats. The women Panchayat leaders' Federation suggested that the State government can hand over the common properties to the Panchayats. They indicated that quarries, tanks and trees which were now under the control of the Government's agencies and individuals would fetch adequate revenue to make the local bodies self reliant. They projected an alternative model of resource mobilization for Panchayats.

As they attend periodical meetings of the Federation, the restrictions imposed on them have been gradually removed. Without the assistance of the males of their family they travel to Chennai, Madurai and Trichy to attend the meetings of the Federation. Further their communicative ability has improved to a surprising level as the grass roots women leaders have developed their own style of communication which has been accepted as a formal mode of communication. Their bargaining capability has been enhanced to strike a deal with officials, MLAs, and MPs for the benefit of the people. The feeling of isolation that prevailed among the elected women representatives has gone as they meet frequently and share their joys and difficulties. When the elected women representatives face problems in administration, the Federation leaders take the issue to the District Collector and to the level of the Director for Rural Development. They get their problems redressed, failing which they go to court and get suitable legal remedy which has raised the morale of the women leaders. Frequent sharing has built up the idea that this kind of exercise is necessary for their success. Their media contact is frequent and its implications are also positive.

Though Tamil Nadu has a District Panchayat Presidents Association, a Block Panchayat Association, and a Gram Panchyat Association, only the Federation of Women Panchayat Leaders Associations is visible and reacts sharply on many of the vital issues. Even though the elected women representatives have a charter of demands, they are more keen on getting reservation of seats for women for ten years, retrieving common properties from encroachment, and, ensuring the entitlements of the poor through the public distribution system. Active leaders in the Federation are very much sensitized on these social development issues after visiting the Kerala Panchayats. During the first period the women leaders were harping on transfer of power, finance and functionaries. Now they speak about issues and problems. They have gained voice and bargaining power.

One major achievement that they have scored through their work is getting the reservation of seats for women in local bodies extended for one more term. It is unique in the whole of the country. Another important achievement is that the Federation has made the State government withdraw the plan for cheap liquor. They pleaded with the government that every month higher level officials at the district level should convene a meeting of the women Panchayat leaders and solve their problems. The Director, Rural Development, Government of Tamil Nadu, issued an order immediately to District Collectors to convene such meetings and solve the problems of the women leaders.

Because of their repeated pleas and activities, the Federation of Women Leaders Associations is visible to the policy makers and 33.3 per cent of seats have been reserved for women even in cooperative societies also. Likewise an order has been issued that in all statutory committees one-third reservation should be provided for women. Some of the women Panchayat leaders were in deep trouble. It was only the Federation which saved them. Menaka, the President of Oorappakkam, was murdered in the Panchayat office due to her stern action against encroachment. No FIR was filed till the Federation leaders went to the Panchayat. It was only because of this Federation that the culprits were booked. Another interesting noteworthy feature is that more number of office bearers in the Federation are now from the *dalit* community and the Federation has focused its attention on *dalit* issues.

## Learnings

Elected women leaders are of different categories. They are educated, uneducated, highly sophisticated, rich, poor, wage earners, *dalits* and others. There are leaders with political orientation and party background. They look at issues only from their party perspective. There are leaders without any political background but under the clutches of their husbands or the males of their families. There are leaders who have commitments and values but no awareness and information. There are leaders with high political aspirations. It is to be noted that the leaders who are deeply committed to the issues of the people without political background continue to be active members of the Federation. The Federation attracts more number of Gram Panchayat women leaders as the Gram Panchayat is freed from the party fold and the problems focused on in the Federation are mostly the problems faced by the Gram Panchayat women leaders. One layer of elected women representatives is alert and they are oriented and conscientized but the other segments are not so well oriented. When oriented and motivated leaders take up the development issues, they face a volley of problems. To tackle all these problems they require a support structure. They demand periodical sensitization on vital issues affecting women and other marginalized groups. They require periodical update on government orders and new schemes of the government. They are in need of periodical interface programmes. The Federation of elected women representatives does not include all the women leaders of rural and urban local bodies. Those who have come out despite obstacles and barriers and those who are struggling with determination have joined together. A large number of elected representatives have not come out of their houses and have not even visited their offices. The Federation is slowly moving towards them. Even now some women leaders are asked to remain inside their houses and the males of their families operate their offices. One positive aspect is that when the successful women leaders are being appreciated and covered in the media, the males of the families of the elected women representatives develop an aspiration that their women leaders should also get such appreciation. The Federation has created such a mindset. There is a potential danger in that potential leaders who can mobilize the masses at the grass roots level are lured by the political leaders. There are women leaders who look at issues from the perspective of the people and want to serve the people at the cost of their own prospects and hence they tend to toe the line of the ruling party in the State government purely with the intention of getting things done for the people.

## Summing Up

Women have started realizing the potential of the Associations and the Federation. Political parties have started identifying the potential leaders from Gram Panchayats and enlisting them as their party members and proclaiming their achievements as the achievements of the party. The media has been sensitized on the women issues and as a result the media has given wide coverage to the activities of the Women's Federation. Elected women representatives have learnt the art of managing bureaucracy. They have picked up communication skills. They have developed bargaining power. Moving with higher officials has become a routine affair and the fear to meet the District Collector and other higher officials has gone. A large number of new leaders are drawn from self help groups towards the Panchayats. Sharing the struggles and achievements in the regional and annual conventions has motivated other women leaders to emulate them. The fear syndrome and the dependency syndrome have gone. The group activities have developed a positive attitude among the women leaders to strive for achievements.

## NOTES

1. S. Raju, P.J. Aakkins, N. Kumar and J.G. Jownsend, *Atlas of Women and Mass in India*. New Delhi: Kali for Women, 1999.
2. Ranjani K. Murthy (ed), *Building Women's Capacities*, New Delhi: Sage Publications, 2001, p.18.
3. G. Palanithurai, *New Panchayat Raj System as Prosperity Movement*, New Delhi: Kanishka Publishers and Distributors, 2001.
4. G. Palanithurai, *Empowerment of Women: Problems Faced by the Elected Women Representatives in Tamil Nadu*, Gandhigram: Rajiv Gandhi Chair for Panchayati Raj Studies, 2001.
5. S. Wieringa, "Women's Interests and Empowerment: Gender Planning Reconsidered", *Development and Change*, 25(1994), pp. 829-848.
6. Rajiv Gandhi Chair for Panchayati Raj Studies has been recognised by the Government of Tamil Nadu as a nodal centre for training and hence series of training programmes had been organised with the financial support of CAPART, Government of India, Social Welfare Board, Government of India, Population Foundation of India, DANIDA and DRDA, District Administration. For more details about the training programme see the following reports.

List of Reports on Activities brought out by the Rajiv Gandhi Chair

| Sl.No | Year | Title of the Report | Sponsoring Agency |
|---|---|---|---|
| 1 | 2 | 3 | 4 |
| 1. | 1997 | Report of the training programme conducted for District Panchayat Council Members on Social Development | Population Foundation of India |
| 2. | 1998 | Report of the training programme conducted for Women Presidents of Gram Panchayats in Five Districts of Tamil Nadu | Social Welfare Board, Govt. of Tamil Nadu, Chennai |
| 3. | 1999 | Report of the training programme conducted for Gram Panchayati Presidents and Vice-Presidents on Panchayati Raj Administration with special reference to Water Supply and Sanitation in Villupuram District – Phase I | DANIDA Villupuram |
| 4. | 1999 | Training for Gram Panchayati Presidents and Vice-Presidents on Panchayati Raj Administration with special reference to Water Supply and Sanitation in Villupuram District – Phase II | DANIDA Villupuram |
| 5. | 1999 | A report on training on Improvement of Panchayat Administration and total Rural Sanitation Programme in Cuddalore District – Phase I | DRDA Cuddalore |

*Contd......*

*Contd......List of Reports*

| 1 | 2 | 3 | 4 |
|---|---|---|---|
| 6. | 2000 | A report on training on Improvement of Panchayat Administration and total Rural Sanitation Programme in Cuddalore District – Phase II | DRDA Cuddalore |
| 7. | 2000 | Report of the training programme conducted for Gram Panchayati Women Presidents of Madurai, Ramanathapuram and Pudukottai Districts | CAPART Hyderabad |
| 8. | 2000 | Report of the training programme conducted for Gram Panchayati Presidents | CAPART Hyderabad |
| 9. | 2000 | Report on the Training of Trainers on Multi Level Planning | State Planning Commission, Govt. of Tamil Nadu |
| 10. | 2001 | A report of the training programme on Testing of Training Module for Training of Panchayati Raj Functionaries | Rajiv Gandhi Foundation, New Delhi |

7. The problems faced by the women Panchayati Presidents have been documented. For more details refer to Rajiv Gandhi Chair, Empowerment of Women: Problems faced by the Elected Women Representatives in Local Bodies in Tamil Nadu, Gandhigram: Rajiv Gandhi Chair for Panchayati Raj Studies, 2001.

8. K.Veeramani, *Periyar on Women's Rights*, Madras: Emerald Publishers, 1994

9. Detailed proceedings are reported in the document. For more details, see Rajiv Gandhi Chair, State Level Consultation on Feminist perspective in Associating Women Representatives in Local Bodies: A Report, Gandhigram: Rajiv Gandhi Chair for Panchayati Raj Studies, 2000.

10. For more details about the discussion, see Rajiv Gandhi Chair, A Report on State Level NGO's Network meet on Associating Women Representatives in

Local Bodies, Gandhigram: Rajiv Gandhi Chair for Panchayati Raj Studies, 2000.

11. The entire discussions and deliberations have been documented. For details refer to the following documents: Rajiv Gandhi Chair, A Report on Regional Level Meet on Associating Women Representatives in Local Bodies - I, Gandhigram: Rajiv Gandhi Chair for Panchayati Raj Studies, 2000.

    Rajiv Gandhi Chair, A Report on Regional Level Meet on Associating Women Representatives in Local Bodies - II, Gandhigram: Rajiv Gandhi Chair for Panchayati Raj Studies, 2001.

    Rajiv Gandhi Chair, A Report on Regional Level Meet on Associating Women Representatives in Local Bodies - III, Gandhigram: Rajiv Gandhi Chair for Panchayati Raj Studies, 2001.

    Rajiv Gandhi Chair, A Report on Regional Level Meet on Associating Women Representatives in Local Bodies - IV, Gandhigram: Rajiv Gandhi Chair for Panchayati Raj Studies, 2001.

12. Rajiv Gandhi Chair, The Annual Convention of the Elected Women Representatives in Tamil Nadu: A Report, Gandhigram: Rajiv Gandhi Chair for Panchayati Raj Studies, 2001.

13. Rajiv Gandhi Chair, A Report on First Networking Meeting and Interface Programme, Gandhigram: Rajiv Gandhi Chair for Panchayati Raj Studies, 2002.

    Rajiv Gandhi Chair, A Report on Second Networking Meeting and Interface Programme, Gandhigram: Rajiv Gandhi Chair for Panchayati Raj Studies, 2002.

14. Rajiv Gandhi Chair, A Report on Women Panchayat Leaders Meet on 20.02.02, Gandhigram: Rajiv Gandhi Chair for Panchayati Raj Studies, 2002.

    The following constitute the 15-point programme of the Government of Tamil Nadu.

    Rajiv Gandhi Chair, Role of Local Bodies in the Process of Implication of 15-Point Programme Gandhigram: Rajiv Gandhi Chair, 2002.

    The Honourable Chief Minister, Selvi. J. Jayalalitha, has announced her commitment to make Tamil Nadu the best State in the country in every sphere. "To provide opportunities for a healthy and productive life for all" will be the goal of this Government. This vision will be realized through the implementation of the Chief Minister's 15-point programme which will encompass the following:

    (i) Evergreen revolution: Raising farm productivity in perpetuity; Saving every drop of rain; More crop per drop.

    (ii) Food Security: Physical, economic and social access to balanced diets to every child, woman and man.

(iii) Livestock Security: Upgradation of livestock, better veterinary care; Supplementing farm income; Improving fish diversity and increasing fish density.

(iv) Water Security: Safe drinking water and adequate water for agriculture, industry and ecosystem maintenance.

(v) Health Security: Control of all preventable diseases including leprosy, tuberculosis, preventable blindness, and eradication of diseases for which effective vaccines are available; reduction in birth and death rates and increase in average life span; Reduction of Infant Mortality Rate (IMR), Maternal Mortality Rate (MMR) and incidence of low birth weight children; Adoption of a maternal and child care code; Fight against HIV/AIDS; Special attention to physically and mentally handicapped children, women and men.

(vi) Livelihood Security: "Work for all" and transition from unskilled to skilled work; Integrated attention to rural on-farm and non-farm employment as well as to micro-enterprises supported by micro-credit; A New Deal to the self-employed through technology, training, techno-infrastructure and domestic and external trade.

(vii) Shelter Security: Promotion of housing activities designed to harvest sun and rain so that solar energy capture and rainwater harvesting become everybody's business.

(viii) Ecological Security: Conservation and enhancement of life support system like land, water, forests, bio-diversity, ocean and the atmosphere; Recycling of solid and liquid wastes and composting of all organic wastes; Safe disposal of hospital wastes; Bio-environmental control of malaria.

(ix) Energy Security: Building sustainable energy systems with concurrent attention to thermal, hydro, nuclear and renewable forms of energy like wind, solar, biogas and biomass; Energy self-sufficiency for the farm, industrial and domestic sectors.

(x) Infrastructure for Development: Provision of basic amenities in rural and urban areas; Connectivity to all habitation with population above 500; Bridging the rural-urban divide.

(xi) Literacy and Technocracy: Attention to quality improvement in education ranging from the pre-school to University; Special attention to the technological and skill empowerment of illiterate or semi-literate women and men; Eradication of child labour.

(xii) Folk, classical and modern arts, culture and drama: Generation of awareness and appreciation of the cultural heritage of Tamil Nadu and revitalization of cultural traditions, including the street theatre.

(xiii) Gender Equity: Removal of gender bias, elimination of adverse sex ratio, and support services to working women, taking into account the multiple burden on a woman's day-to-day life.

(xiv) New deal for the Oppressed Classes: Educational and economic empowerment of the Adi-Dravidas, Scheduled Tribes, Backward Classes, Most Backward Classes Denotified Tribes.

(xv) Technological Leapfrogging: Promotion of research and development in frontier areas of science and technology like biotechnology and information technology, coordination of efforts between academic know-how and field level do how. Launching a movement for fostering greater public understanding of science and promoting a new social contact between scientists and society; providing equal attention to connectivity and content in efforts to bridge the digital divide; including access to appropriate technologies in the basic minimum needs programme.

The Chief Minister's 15-point programme outlined here will be the road map for this government in the next four years. It will be the endeavour of this government to realize this vision by March 2006.

15. Rajiv Gandhi Chair, Report of the Second Annual Meet of Elected Women Representatives, Gandhigram: Rajiv Gandhi Chair for Panchayati Raj Studies, 2002.

16. Letter received from the Director Rural Development, Government of Tamil Nadu dated 20.05.02.

17. Rajiv Gandhi Chair, Report of the Special Meet of the Elected Women Representatives of Local Bodies at Gandhigram, Gandhigram: Rajiv Gandhi Chair for Panchayati Raj Studies, 2002.

18. Their activities are covered in the press. The details are:

| | |
|---|---|
| *New Indian Express* 06.05.2002 | Panchayat Chiefs favour Govt. programmes.<br>Women leaders keen on development activities of panchayats |
| *Dinamalar* 12.01.2002 | Nanillam Union-Panchayat Leaders meet |
| *Dinamani* 13.01.2002 | Network meeting of SSF-Thiruvarur<br>Cheap Liquor Scheme / Hitting below the belt. |
| *Dinamalar* 10.05.2002 | Second Annual Meet of SSF<br>Director of Rural Development – Suggest |
| *Dinamani* 29.04.2002 | Annual Conference of Women Leaders at State Level |
| *Dina Thanthi* 01.05.2002 | Annual Conference of Women Leaders at State Level |

| | |
|---|---|
| *The Hindu* 02.05.2002 | Elected Women Representatives Meet |
| *Dina Thanthi* 04.05.2002 | Elected Women Representatives Meet |
| *The Hindu* 04.05.2002 | Information kiosks coming up for SHGs in 10 districts |
| *The Hindu* 08.12.2001 | Cheap Liquor Scheme / Hitting below the belt. Women feel let down by a woman |
| *Theekkathir* 21.12.2001 | Funds to Local Bodies plan to file PIL |
| *Dinamalar* 05.03.2002 | A modified Family Card – Leader did – Minister encouraged |
| *Dina Thanthi* 04.12.2001 | Satisfying the basic needs – Funds to Local Bodies – A request |
| *The Financial Express* 19.12.2001 | Tamil Nadu panchayats plan to file PIL for release of statutory grants. |
| *News Today* 20.12.2001 | Funds to Local Bodies 'Relent or face a stir' Women Panchayat chiefs on warpath |
| *Dinamani* 20.12.2001 | Funds to Local Bodies 'Relent or face a stir' Women Panchayat chiefs on warpath |
| *Dina Thanthi* 20.12.2001 | Funds to Local Bodies 'Relent or face a stir' Women Panchayat chiefs on warpath |
| *Dinamalar* 20.12.2001 | Allot 20% of MLA and MP fund to panchayats – leaders wish |
| *Dinakaran* 20.12.2001 | EWRs meet at Chennai – a crisis on implementing activities – struggle on cheap liquor scheme |
| *The Hindu* 03.04.2002 | No nomination for wards, polls went empower *dalits* |
| *The Hindu* 19.03.2002 | Spell out stand on devolution: Tamil Nadu Panchayat |
| *Dinamani* 06.11.2001 | Fulfil the responsibilities and Commit your needy Dr. Pankajam, Vice-Chancellor, GRI – suggest |
| *The Hindu* 08.11.2001 | Village Panchayats told to concentrate on tax collection |
| *New Indian Express* 22.02.2002 | Centre fixes target of 14 lakh SHG – M. Venkaiah Naidu, Rural Development Minister, Govt. of India at GRI. |
| *The Hindu* 16.02.2002 | Participatory development key to Panchayat Raj |

| | |
|---|---|
| *Dinamalar*<br>16.02.2002 | From Education to Family Planning –<br>need for a change in training the leaders |
| *Dinamani*<br>15.02.2002 | New method of training to the president – suggest |
| *The Hindu*<br>13.01.2002 | Panchayat chiefs play key role in Primary Education |
| *Dinamani*<br>12.01.2002 | Panchayat chiefs play key role in Primary Education |
| *The Hindu*<br>20.12.2001 | Women Panchayat chiefs threaten stir |
| *New Indian Express*<br>18.12.2001 | Bureaucrats treat women Panchayat president as servants |
| *Dina Thanthi*<br>07.10.2001 | Women Panchayat chiefs threaten stir.<br>Say 'No' to corruption in Panchayat |
| *The Hindu*<br>06.10.2001 | Women Panchayat chiefs threaten stir.<br>Say 'No' to corruption in Panchayat |
| *Dinakaran*<br>06.10.2001 | Women Panchayat chiefs threaten stir.<br>Say 'No' to corruption in Panchayat |

# BIBLIOGRAPHY


Agnihotri, Satish, "Juvenile Sex Ratios in India: A Disaggregated Analysis", *Economic and Political Weekly*, (28 December, 1996).

Ahmed, Ariz, "Women Empowerment and Self Help Groups", *Kurukshetra*, (April, 1999).

Asia-Pacific Centre for Women and Development, *Feminist Ideology and Structures: Report on an International Seminar*, Bangkok: UNESCAP, 1979.

Bakshi, D.S., and Menon, P.S.K, *Environmental Sanitation, Health and Panchayati Raj*, New Delhi: Concept Publishing Company, 1996.

Batliwala Srilatha; Anitha, B.K.; Gurumurthy Anita; and Walichandana, S., *Status of Rural Women in Karnataka*, Bangalore: National Institute of Advanced Studies, 2000.

Batliwala, Srilatha, *Empowerment of Women's Autonomy, Proceedings of a Consultation on Women's Health and Rights: Rethinking Population*, HIVDS Technical Report Series, 1:4, 1996.

Batliwala, Srilatha, The meaning of empowerment, *Women World*, 1995.

Bella, Abzug and Devaki Jain, *Women Leadership and Ethics of Development, Gender in Development,* Monograph Series #4, UNDP, August, 1996.

Benerjee, N.K., *Grassroots Empowerment – A Discussion Paper*, Occasional Paper No. 22, 1995.

Bhaft, G.O., *Emerging Leadership in Rural India – An Empirical Study*, New Delhi: MO Publications Pvt. Ltd., 1994.

Bhagyalakshmi, J., "Panchayati Raj Empowering the People", *Yojana*, Vol. 42, No. 7, (1998).

Bhargava B.S. and Subha, K., "Developing Women at Grassroots", *Kurukshetra*, (February 1991).

Bhargava, B.S. and Rama Rao, S., *Indian Local Government: A Study*, Calcutta: Minerva Associates, 1978

Bhargava, B.S., and Subha, K., "Women in Panchayati Raj: Some Reflections on Karnataka's Experience", *Kurukshetra*, Vol. XLII, No. 9, June, 1994.

Buch, Nirmala, "Decentralized Governance, Women's Participation and Poverty Eradication", *Women and Political Empowerment* (eds), B. Mohanty and S. Haider, New Delhi: Institute of Social Sciences, 1998.

Charles P. Loonis, *Social Systems: Essays on the Persistence and Change*, New Jersey: Princeton, 1963.

Chris, Beasley, *What is Feminism*, New Delhi: Sage Publications, 1999.

Chrissie, D'Costa, "Women's Political Participation and Empowerment, Panchayati Raj Interactive System", *The Foundation for Research in Community Health*, Bombay, Vol. 2, No. 3, March 1996.

Churchill, A.A., *Rural Water Supply and Sanitation: Time for Change*, Washington - DC: The World Bank, 1987.

Combs, P.H. (ed), *Meeting the Basic Needs of Rural Poor: The Integrated Community Based Approach*, London: Pergamon Press, 1980.

David, Krech and Richard S.Crutchfield, *Theory and Problem of Social Psychology*, New York: McGraw Hill Book Co., 1948.

Dube, Leela, *Emerging Patterns of Rural Leadership in South Asia*, Hyderabad: National Institute of Community Development, 1965.

Freed, E. Fielder, *A Theory of Leadership Effectiveness*, New York: McGraw Hill, 1967.

Gayatri, A. Menon and Suranjana Gupta, "From Margin to Mainstream – Building Stakes in the SHG-Bank linkage Programme", *Swayam Shikshan Prayog,* (October 1999).

Ghosh, G.; Mazumdar, K.; Dubly A.K.; and Chander, J., *Water Supply and Sanitation in Rural India Policy and Programme*, New Delhi: Ashish Publishing House, 1995.

Government of Karnataka, *The Karnataka Zilla Parishads, Taluk Panchayat Samitis, Mandal Panchayats and Nyaya Panchayats Act 1985*, Bangalore: Government Press, 1985.

Government of India, *Rural Water Supply & Sanitation Programmes in India*, New Delhi: Rajiv Gandhi National Drinking Water Mission, 1993.

Government of India, *Sixth Five Year Plan,* New Delhi: Planning Commission, 1980.

Government of India, *The Fifth Five Year Plan*, New Delhi: Planning Commission, 1976.

Government of India, *The Karnataka Panchayati Raj Act*, 1993, Bangalore: Government Press, 1993.

Government of India, *Towards Equality: Report of the Committee on the Status of Women in India*, New Delhi: Government of India, 1975.

*Grassroots* - Vol. 1, No. 1 (9) - (January 2000).

*Grassroots* - Vol. 1, No. 2 (10) - (February 2000).

*Grassroots* - Vol. 1, No. 3 (11) - (March 2000).

*Grassroots* - Vol. 1, No. 4 (12) - (April 2000).

Hall, C.M., *Women and Empowerment: Strategies for Increasing Autonomy*, Washington: Hemisphere Publishing Corporation, 1992.

Heyzer, N., *Missing Women: Development Planning in Asia and the Pacific*, Kuala Lumpur: Asia and Pacific Development Centre, 1985.

Hiremath, Ujawala "Women in Grassroots Politics", *Social Welfare*, Vol. 44, No. 2, (1997).

Inamdar, N.R., "Panchayati Raj Leadership: Emerging Dimensions", *Journal of Rural Development*", Vol.10, No. 5, (September-October, 1991).

Institute of Social Sciences, *Panchayati Raj Update*, (July 1999).

Institute of Social Sciences, *Panchayati Raj Update*, (June 1994).

Institute of Social Sciences, *Panchayati Raj Update*, (September 1995).

Institute of Social Sciences, *Social Background of Zilla Parishad Members in Karnataka*, 1989, ISS Occasional Paper Series 6, New Delhi, 1989.

Iyer, Krishna V.R., *Women Unsound: A Plea for Gender Justice*, Madurai: Society for Community Organisation Trust, 1984.

Jain, Devaki, Panchayati Raj – Women Challenging Governance, *Gender in Development*, Monograph series No. 4, UNDP, September 1996.

Jain, S.P. and Thomus W. Hockguang (eds), *Emerging Trends in Panchayati Raj in India*, Hyderabad: NIRD, 1995.

Kannabiran, Vasanth "Censorship and Silence", *Economic and Political Weekly*, Vol. XXXV, (29th April, 2000).

Kasthuri, Leela and Vina Mazumdar, *Women and Indian Nationalism*, Delhi: Vikas, 1994.

Mahipal, Fatima B., "Sarpanch: Saga of Struggle Against Poverty", *Kurukshetra*, (March, 1999).

Mandal, Amal, "Gender Bias in Panchayati Raj: Deservations from a District", *Kurukshetra*, (June, 1997).

Marilyn, Carr, Marcha Chen, Renana Jhabvala (eds), *Speaking Out: Women's Economy in South Asia*, New Delhi: Vistaar Publications, 1996.

Mathew, George (ed), *Panchayati Raj in Karnataka Today: In National Dimensions*, New Delhi: Concept Publishing Company, 1986.

Mathew, George, "Will reservation ensure participation", *Social Welfare*, Vol. 42 (56), (August - September, 1995).

Max Weber, "Type of Authority", in *Essays in Sociology* (ed), H.H. Gerth and C.W. Mills, Oxford: Oxford University Press, 1946.

Mazumdar, Vina, "Women from Equality to Empowerment" in *Independent India: The First Fifty Years* (ed), Hiranmay Karlekar, New Delhi: Oxford University Press, 1978.

Mehta, S.R., *Emerging Pattern of Rural Leadership*, New Delhi: Wiley Eastern Private Limited, 1972.

Mehta, Usha "Status of Women", *University News*, Vol. XXXIV, No.12, (March 18, 1996).

Menon, Ritu, "Structured Silences of Women", *Economic and Political Weekly,* Vol.XXXV, (29th April, 2000).

Moser Caroline, "Gender Planning in Third World: Meeting Practical and Strategic Gender Needs," *World Development,* Vol.17:No. 11, (1989).

Mukhopadhyaya, Amal Kumar, *Political Sociology: An Introductory Analysis*, Calcutta: K.P. Sahchi and Company, 1980.

Murray, G. Ross and Charles, E. Hendry, *New Understanding of Leadership: A Survey and Application of Research*, New York: Association Press, 1957.

NABARD, Annual Report, 1997-1998.

Narain, Iqbal, *The Rural Elite in An Indian State – A Case Study of Rajasthan*, New Delhi: Manohar Book Depot, 1976.

Narain, Iqpal, Pande, K.C., and Lal, Mohan, *Rural Elite and Elections in an Indian State: A Study of Panchayati Raj Leadership in the Context of Rajasthan Electorsal Politics*, Jaipur: National Publishing House, 1976.

Narasimhan, Sakuntala, *Empowering Women: An Alternative Strategy from Rural India,* New Delhi: Sage Publications, 1999.

Nasendar, K., "Imparting Poverty", *Health Section,* Vol. 12 (7), July, 1999.

Neelima, B.N., and Swaroop, T.S., "Gender Perceptions of Ecological Development", *Social Welfare,* Vol. 47, No. 3, 2000.

Neera, Agrimitra, "Women in Panchayats: Empowerment or Illusion," *Gandhi Marg,* Vol.17(4), (January-March, 1996).

*Newsletter*, UMA PRACHAR, March-May, 1995.

*Newsletter*, UMA PRACHAR, September, 1995.

Opschoor, J.B., "Sustainability, Economic Growth and Development Theory", *Journal of Social and Economic Development*, Vol.1, No.1, (1998).

Ordway, Tead, *The Art of Leadership*, New York: McGraw Hill Book Co., 1963.

Palanithurai, G., *Capacity Building for Local Body Leaders*, New Delhi: Concept Publishing Company, 2001.

Palanithurai, G., *Empowerment of Women: Problems faced by the Elected Women Representatives in Tamil Nadu*, Gandhigram: Rajiv Gandhi Chair for Panchayati Raj Studies, 2001.

Palanithurai, G., *New Panchayati Raj System as Prosperity Movement*, New Delhi: Kanishka Publishers and Distributors, 2001.

Palanithurai, G., *Report on Capacity Building for Gram Panchayati Presidents*, Gandhigram: Rajiv Gandhi Chair for Panchayati Raj Studies, 2000.

Palanithurai, G., *Report on the Capacity Building for Weaker Sections in New Panchayati Raj System*, Gandhigram: Rajiv Gandhi Chair for Panchayati Raj Studies, 2001.

Palanithurai, G., *Report on Workshop on Networking of Associations of Elected Women Representatives in Local Bodies,* Gandhigram: Rajiv Gandhi Chair for Panchayati Raj Studies, 2001.

Pareek, Udai, *Studies on Rural Leadership,* Delhi: Behavioural Science Centre, 1966.

Rainuka, Dagar (ed), *Manual on Women's Development and Gender Justice,* Chandigarh: Institute for Development and Communication, 1998.

Raju, S.; Aakkins, P.J.; Kumar, N.; and Jownsend, J.S., *Atlas of Women and Mass in India,* New Delhi: Kali for Women, 1999.

Ranjani K. Murthy (ed), *Building Women's Capacities*, New Delhi: Sage Publications, 2001.

Sahay, Sushma, *Women Empowerment: Approaches and Strategies*, New Delhi: Discovery Publishing House, 1998.

Search, Impact of Reservation: The Status and Power of Women Representatives in Gram Panchayats, *Search Bulletin,* Vol. XIV, No. 2, (April-June, 1999).

Sen, Gita, "Poverty, Economic Growth and Gender Equity: The Asian and Pacific Experience" in Heizer Nocleen and Sen Gita, *Gender Economic Growth and Poverty,* New Delhi: Kali for Women, 1994.

Shah, Anupama and Susan Jacob, "Attitude Towards Reservation for Women", *Social Welfare*, Vol. 2, No. 8, (November 1995).

Sharma, Kumud, "Grassroots organization and women's empowerment: some issues in the contemporary debate". *Samyashakti*, Vol. 6, (1992).

Sharma, Kumud, Transformative Politics: Dimensions of Women's Participation in Panchayati Raj, *Indian Journal of Gender Studies,* 5:1, New Delhi: Sage Publications, 1998.

Sivanna, N., "Process and Performance of Panchayats," in *Decentralized Governance and Planning: A Comparative Study in Three South India States* (Mimeo) (eds), Abdul Aziz *et al*., Bangalore: ISEC, 1998.

Srinivastave, Vinayak N. "Decentralization without Devolution is Meaningless", *The Hindu*, 23rd February, 1999.

Subha, K. "Training: An aid to empower rural women leaders", *Kurukshetra*, (April 1995).

Subha, K., *Karnataka Panchayat Elections* 1995, New Delhi, Concept Publishing Company, 1997.

Sahay, Sushama, *Women and Empowerment,* New Delhi, Discovery Publishing House, 1998.

UNDP, Towards Just Development Identifying Meaningful indicators, South Africa, 1999.

United Nations Development Programme, *Human Development Report,* 1985, Oxford: Oxford University Press, 1985.

Vidya, K.C., *Political Empowerment of Women at the Grassroots*, New Delhi: Kanishka Publishers, 1997.

Vijayakumar, B. *et al. Training Programme for Grama Panchayat Members: A Process Evaluation* (Mimeo), Bangalore: ISEC, June 1997.

# INDEX